K. Ogle

working with

A P P L E **W** O R K S ™

working with

APPLEWORKS™

John Campbell

Sam R. Redden

Hayden Book Company
A DIVISION OF HAYDEN PUBLISHING COMPANY, INC.
HASBROUCK HEIGHTS, NEW JERSEY / BERKELEY, CALIFORNIA

Acquisitions Editor: RONALD POWERS
Production Editor: ALBERTA BODDY
Text Design: JOHN M-RÖBLIN
Cover Design: JIM BERNARD
Cover Computer Art: RON MORECRAFT/BOB NICOLL
Compositor: AMERICAN-STRATFORD GRAPHIC SERVICES, INC.
Printer: MALLOY LITHOGRAPHING, INC.

Library of Congress Cataloging-in-Publication Data

Campbell, J. L. (John L.)
    Working with AppleWorks.

    Includes index.
        1. AppleWorks (Computer program) 2. Apple IIc (Computer)—Programming.
3. Apple IIe (Computer)—Programming. 4. Business—Data processing.
I. Redden, Sam R. II. Title.
HF5548.2.A68C36   1985   005.36′9   85-22038
ISBN 0-8104-6759-3

1	2	3	4	5	6	7	8	9	PRINTING
85	86	87	88	89	90	91	92	93	YEAR

Preface

Great is the art of beginning,
but greater is the art of ending.
LONGFELLOW, 1881

For the first time, there is an integrated software package, AppleWorks, from Apple Computer Inc., for the Apple IIe and Apple IIc computers. This software package combines three of the most popular personal computer applications: the word processor, the spreadsheet, and the data base. AppleWorks offers three separate programs and the ability to easily move data from one application to another, allowing greater productivity when using a personal computer.

This book discusses and explores the capabilities and flexibilities of AppleWorks. It gives tips, shortcuts, and cautions on using this powerful software and getting the most from it. The book is separated into five parts, which allows you to use it as a teaching manual and a quick guide to AppleWorks. Part 1 offers a general introduction to the software package. Part 2 discusses in detail the word processor portion of AppleWorks and its capabilities. This section shows you how to easily create, enter, and edit text material, from interoffice memos to business letters to financial reports to large manuscripts.

Part 3 examines the spreadsheet. It illustrates how to create detailed financial statements, project management reports, and mathematical manipulation sheets.

Part 4 analyzes the data base capability of AppleWorks, and discusses how to create and edit lists of all kinds.

Finally, Part 5 shows you how to cut and paste data and text from one document to another. In this section the power and flexibility of AppleWorks is unleashed. It is hoped you will find this book useful and enjoyable.

Contents

*The more the pleasures of the body fade away,
the greater to me is the pleasure and charm
of conversation.*
PLATO, 4th century B.C.

working with

APPLE**W**ORKS™

P A R T   O N E

Nothing can be loved or hated unless it is known.
LEONARDO DA VINCI, 1500

Part 1 introduces you to AppleWorks. It includes basic operating information, a review of keystroke skills, and a listing of equipment needed to effectively use this software.

C H A P T E R   O N E

Introduction

It is better to begin in the evening than not at all.
ENGLISH PROVERB

1.0 OVERVIEW

Over the past few years, three types of programs have dominated the software-buying marketplace: word processing, spreadsheet, and data base or file management programs. Each of these was useful and relatively easy to understand. Unfortunately, users had to learn to manipulate three separate functions.

Now integrated software packages, like AppleWorks, combine these three areas with additional capabilities, allowing users to fully incorporate these functions in their work. These integrated software packages usually include:

- Writing correspondence and documents of all kinds using a word processing program.
- Performing financial and mathematical calculations using a spreadsheet program.
- Maintaining lists of things using either a data base or a file management program.

The remainder of this chapter will acquaint you with the operation of AppleWorks, the equipment required to take advantage of the program, how to get started, the main menu video screen presentations, and the many other activities available.

The next section of this chapter discusses the AppleWorks integrated software package, and briefly describes each of the major components of the package.

Section 1.2 describes the type of hardware you will need to effectively use AppleWorks.

Section 1.3 discusses how to get started using AppleWorks. This section will be your first real exposure to this software.

3

The remainder of the chapter discusses a number of very basic building blocks of information you will need in order to fully appreciate the scope of AppleWorks.

Finally, a brief summary of the chapter reviews what has been covered.

1.1 WHAT IS APPLEWORKS?

AppleWorks is an *integrated applications program.* Integrated means that you are able to move information from one part of the program package to another with a minimum of effort. Applications means that you are able to perform a number of different activities with the software. Program means that the software is a set of instructions that tells the computer exactly what to accomplish.

A *word processor* allows you to create, edit, and print any document easily, to your own particular specifications, on a computer video screen. The document can then be further modified or printed, either now or later. It is discussed in Chapters 2 and 3.

A *spreadsheet* program allows you to work with numerical information of all kinds, as long as it is expressed in either rows or columns. These programs have been known by various names, such as Financial Calculator, Visual Calculator, Financial Modeler, etc. As it turns out, more and more numerical information is being expressed in row and/or column form, ranging from corporate financial statements to project estimates to home checkbook balancing. Using mathematical formulas, data can be created, edited, manipulated, and printed. The spreadsheet is discussed in Chapters 4 and 5.

A *data base* program allows the user to easily organize lists of information into logical groups. For some reason, we always seem to be writing down lists of things and grouping items together. Everything from shopping lists to club membership lists to coin collection lists to inventories of equipment and goods are placed in lists. Data Base programs, as the term is used today in the microcomputer industry, may range from simple list managers to programs with their own built-in languages. The data base is discussed in Chapters 6 and 7.

Finally, there are those programs or program segments which allow you to move information from one part of an integrated software package to another. This capability is what becomes the distinguishing feature between single stand-alone programs and an integrated set of software programs. This has become known as *cut and paste* and is one of the main reasons for the power and flexibility of such a set of programs. The cut-and-paste capability embedded in AppleWorks allows you to move information from one portion of AppleWorks to another. For example, you can move information from a spreadsheet to a word processor document. The cut-and-paste capability of AppleWorks is discussed in Chapter 8.

AppleWorks operates on two distinct levels. The top level of activity we will call the system level. The bottom level we will call the application level. This arrangement of activities is shown in Fig. 1-1.

Figure 1-1 shows the three major blocks of AppleWorks. The Other Activities box is reached from the Main Menu at the system level. The reason this box is broken out and shown here is because there are so many additional activities performed when you are presented with the Other Activities menu screen.

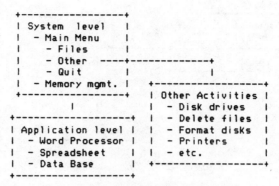

```
+-----------------+
| System level    |
|  - Main Menu    |
|    - Files      |
|    - Other  ----+-------------+
|    - Quit       |             |
|  - Memory mgmt. |     +--------------------+
+-----------------+     | Other Activities   |
        |               |  - Disk drives     |
+-------------------+   |  - Delete files    |
| Application level |   |  - Format disks    |
|  - Word Processor |   |  - Printers        |
|  - Spreadsheet    |   |  - etc.            |
|  - Data Base      |   +--------------------+
+-------------------+
```

Figure 1-1   *AppleWorks Organization*

The system level includes Main Menu activities, various file activities, and, of course, the ability to quit AppleWorks. Section 1.4 discusses the Main Menu in detail. The application level includes the three major program segments of AppleWorks. The Other Activities level will be discussed as you need each of the capabilities of that submenu.

At this point, we would like to introduce the concept of a *Clipboard*. In the context of AppleWorks, the Clipboard is a temporary storage location within the computer's memory. This temporary storage location is used to move information within a file or from one AppleWorks document or file to another. This is shown in Fig. 1-2.

Shown below is a box. We will use a box like this every time we want to warn you, caution you, call your attention to something, or just give you useful tips, notes, or hints on how to make AppleWorks easier to use.

Warning: Because the Clipboard is in memory, if you lose power you will lose the contents of the Clipboard and everything else in memory. It is recommended that you never leave information stored in the Clipboard for very long.

1.2 WHAT IS NEEDED

This section discusses the hardware and software required to take advantage of AppleWorks. We assume that all of the components of your particular computer system are connected correctly. Your computer dealer should have shown you how to do this.

Before you can start using AppleWorks, you will need the following hardware:

- An Apple IIe or Apple IIc computer.
- An Apple 80-column text card, preferably one with extended memory, to

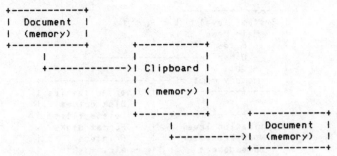

Figure 1-2   *Clipboard Concept*

be installed in the auxiliary slot of the Apple IIe. Since the Apple IIc has
this card already built in, you need not activate the 80-column switch on
the top of the Apple IIc computer.

- A video monitor or screen capable of 80 columns.
- One or more disk drives with the disk controller card installed in slot 6 of
  the Apple IIe. With the Apple IIc, the disk controller card is already built
  in.
- A printer. It is recommended that you select a printer that supports the
  type fonts, styles, and sizes supported by AppleWorks. An ImageWriter or
  ScribeWriter printer is recommended.
- A printer serial interface card installed in slot 1 of the Apple IIe. With the
  Apple IIc, the printer interface card is already built in as port 1.

You will also need the following software diskettes. Fortunately, all of the following,
except the blank diskette, come with AppleWorks:

- The AppleWorks Startup diskette.
- The AppleWorks Program diskette.
- At least one blank diskette.

Notice that the disk controller card should be in slot 6 and the printer interface card
and printer should be in slot 1 for the Apple IIe. These are the normal slot locations for
this equipment. With an Apple IIc, these cards are already installed in the main computer
chassis. Your printer should be connected to port 1 on the Apple IIc. Printer interfacing
and possible printer problems are discussed in Appendix P.

There is some optional hardware that can be effectively used with AppleWorks. You
might find it helpful to use this optional equipment with your system:

- A hard-disk storage device, such as the Apple ProFile. If you are using a
  hard disk, you will need to be familiar with the owner's manual for that

hard disk. If you have a hard-disk drive, the interface card should be installed in slot 5 of the Apple IIe.

- A system clock/calendar interface card installed in slot 4 of the Apple IIe. If you have a clock/calendar card installed you need to be familiar with the owner's manual.

With your computer system hooked up correctly, you are ready to start using AppleWorks.

1.3 GETTING STARTED

Before actually using AppleWorks, it is recommended you make exact copies of the diskettes that came with AppleWorks. Use the copies instead of the originals when working with AppleWorks. In this way, you protect your investment by protecting and storing the original diskettes in a safe place. You may use the FILER program on the ProDOS/USERS.DISK. The specific procedures for making copies are discussed in Appendix F.

To start, use the following procedure:

1. Power up your computer video monitor. You may want to wait about 15 seconds to let the monitor warm up.

2. Insert the AppleWorks Startup diskette into drive 1 of the Apple IIe or the built-in disk drive on the Apple IIc.

3. Power up your computer. If your computer is already turned on, simultaneously press the CONTROL-OPEN-APPLE-RESET keys. It will take a few seconds for the computer to read the necessary information from the Startup diskette.

4. When prompted from the video screen, replace the Startup diskette with the Program diskette. You must place the Program diskette also in drive 1 of the Apple IIe or the built-in disk drive on the Apple IIc. If you do not, the following message will appear when using the Apple IIe.

> Your copy of the AppleWorks program disk *must* be in drive 1 of the Apple IIe or the built-in drive of the Apple IIc. The write-protect notch must be uncovered.

5. From the keyboard, enter the current date using the format shown on the screen, then press the RETURN key. If the date shown is correct, simply press the RETURN key to accept it.

> **Tip:** The RETURN key is used to accept an answer or prompt message, or to make a selection.

6. The video screen will now change and display the Main Menu of AppleWorks. If you are using a two-disk drive system or a ProFile hard disk, it is recommended that you first select option 6, "Select the Standard Location of the Data Disk," from the Other Activities menu. In this way, the program will always know where to find data files.

> **Hint:** If you are using a single drive system, AppleWorks will ask you to exchange the program diskette and the data diskette as AppleWorks requires.

Doing this will become very clear by the time you have finished reading this chapter.

1.4 THE MAIN MENU

This section presents the Main Menu and its options, and discusses what can be done from this menu. The Main Menu screen is shown in Fig. 1-3.

There are five major options available from this screen. The Main Menu is the pivotal part of the system level. You will always start and end work sessions from this part of AppleWorks.

> **Note:** There are a number of different symbols that appear in the lower right-hand corner of the video screen near the question mark symbol, depending upon your particular computer configuration:
>
> 1. The Apple IIc shows a small Apple symbol.
> 2. The Apple IIe, with the current ROM chip set installed, shows an inverse capital A. The Apple IIe, with the upgraded ROM chip set, shows a small Apple symbol. The upgraded ROM chip set for the Apple IIe became available in early 1985.
> 3. The screen printout normally will show an @ symbol.
>
> If there is no file in memory when at the Main Menu, nothing appears in the upper right-hand corner. The source drive for data appears in the upper left-hand corner.

```
Disk: Drive 2                  MAIN MENU                   Escape: "CH1"
 _____
|  Main Menu                    |_____|
| |                                                                     | |
| |   1.  Add files to the Desktop                                      | |
| |                                                                     | |
| |   2.  Work with one of the files on the Desktop                     | |
| |                                                                     | |
| |   3.  Save Desktop files to disk                                    | |
| |                                                                     | |
| |   4.  Remove files from the Desktop                                 | |
| |                                                                     | |
| |   5.  Other Activities                                              | |
| |                                                                     | |
| |   6.  Quit                                                          | |
| |                                                                     | |
| |_____| |
|_____|



Type number, or use arrows, then press Return              @-? for Help
```

Figure 1-3 Main Menu Screen

Now that you have the Main Menu on the screen, a few words need to be said about how to communicate with AppleWorks. In general, there are six major ways of communicating with AppleWorks through keystroke sequences:

1. The ESCape key. This key is located in the upper left-hand corner of the keyboard. Regardless of where you are in the AppleWorks program, you may use this key to move away, escape, or exit from where you are processing. The upper right-hand corner of the screen tells you the return location when you press the ESCape key.

2. The OPEN-APPLE keystroke combination commands. The OPEN-APPLE key, located just to the left of the space bar, is used in combination with other keys. This means that you press and hold the OPEN-APPLE key while pressing another key, then release both keys together. These commands and others are discussed in Chapter 9.

3. The RETURN key. This key, located in the middle of the right side of the keyboard, is used to accept highlighted commands, answer prompt messages, or confirm requensts proposed by AppleWorks.

4. Answer prompt messages. Prompting messages may be answered by typing a number followed by the RETURN key, pressing the RETURN key, entering information from the keyboard, or typing a legal OPEN-APPLE command key combination.

5. Type and edit information. In every application-level program, you will enter, correct, and change information in the application using the keyboard.

6. The AppleWorks Ruler. This is a way to move quickly through any file. It is activated by using the OPEN-APPLE key in combination with the number keys 1 through 9. The OPEN-APPLE 1 keystroke combination is the top of a file, while the OPEN-APPLE 9 keystroke combination is the bottom of a file. See Chapter 9.

Now that you know what keystrokes to use to communicate with AppleWorks, you need to know what can be done from the Main Menu. The next five subsections will discuss each of the options available from the Main Menu.

1.4.1 Adding Files to the Desktop

This option allows you to add one or more files to your Desktop.
To add files:

1. Be sure the Main Menu is displayed. If you do not have the Main Menu displayed, you may get to it by pressing the ESCape key one or more times.

2. Choose option 1, "Add files to the Desktop" from the Main Menu. Use the up/down arrow keys or the number 1 key until this option is highlighted and displayed in inverse video, then press the RETURN key to select this option for processing. The screen display will change as shown in Fig. 1-4.

3. Choose one of the options from the Add Files secondary menu. Use the up/down arrow keys or the number keys until an option is highlighted, then press the RETURN key to accept the highlighted option.

```
Disk: Drive 2                    ADD FILES              Escape: Main Menu
_____

I       Main Menu               I_____
I                                                                   I
I   I       Add Files           I_____I__
I   I                                                                   I
I   I                                                                   I
I   I       Get files from:                                             I
I   I                                                                   I
I   I   1.  The current disk: Drive 2                                   I
I   I   2.  A different disk                                            I
I   I                                                                   I
I   I       Make a new file for the:                                   I
I   I                                                                   I
I   I   3.  Word Processor                                              I
I   I   4.  Data Base                                                   I
I   I   5.  Spreadsheet                                                 I
I __I                                                                   I
I       I                                                               I
I       I_____I

_____
Type number, or use arrows, then press Return            33K Avail.
```

Figure 1-4   Add Files Screen

Note: There will be a different amount of memory available shown in the lower right-hand corner of the video screen, depending upon what is loaded into memory on the Desktop, the number of files on the Desktop, and their individual sizes. The maximum memory available on the Desktop with nothing in memory is 55K bytes.

To retrieve a previously stored file, use either of the "Get files from" options. Select from either the current disk (in Drive 2) or a different disk.

Get files from:

1. The current disk: Drive 2
2. A different disk

The first option is selected most often. Once you have selected that option, all AppleWorks files stored on that diskette are shown on the screen. The stored AppleWorks files are presented in alphabetical order within each AppleWorks application file type. Each file listed shows the file name, type, and size, and the date and time the file was last saved. The time item is shown only when there is a clock/calendar card installed in the computer. The list may contain a maximum of 150 different file names. If there are more than ten file names in the list, the word *More* will appear at the bottom of the screen. In order to scroll through the list of names, use the up/down arrow keys. Each file will be selected in order by highlighting the file name. Multiple files may be selected by using the right/left arrow keys.

If you choose the second option, AppleWorks asks you to specify a new disk drive number. After selecting a new storage disk drive, AppleWorks presents the list of files stored on that disk drive.

Caution: When changing disk drives, make sure that the diskette is inserted in the correct drive, the drive door is closed, and the diskette can accept AppleWorks files on it. If you make a mistake, AppleWorks informs you and lets you correct it.

If you are going to create a new file for the word processor, data base, or spreadsheet, you will be able to use any one of the application files you need at the time. After choosing an option, AppleWorks asks you to either make the new file from scratch or from an existing ASCII file.

Tip: AppleWorks will not let you have more than twelve files on the Desktop. Further, AppleWorks will not let you add more files than allotted in the available memory space. AppleWorks will warn you if either or both of these conditions exists.

You will be required now to name any new file created from scratch. AppleWorks will accept up to fifteen characters as a file name. The first character must be a letter of the alphabet, either upper- or lowercase. Spaces, numbers, and the period can also be used in the name. The following table lists acceptable and nonacceptable file names:

Acceptable names	Nonacceptable names	Comments
net.worth.1985	1985.net.worth	starts with a number
BUSINESS.LETTER	10/15.BUSINESS	starts with a number
PERSONAL WORTH	#4 NET WORTH	special character
personal.worth	personal worth #3	spec. char. & too long
subs list	subcontractor.list	name is too long
Sam.net.worth	Sam.and.Linda.worth	name is too long

After the file has been named, AppleWorks opens a temporary file area in memory for the new application. A blank application will appear on your screen ready for you to start entering information.

1.4.2 Working with One of the Files on the Desktop

This option allows you to shift from one file in memory to another and to work with different files on your Desktop:

1. Be sure you have the Main Menu displayed. If you do not have the Main Menu displayed, you may get to it by pressing the ESCape key one or more times.
2. Select option 2, "Work with one of the files on the Desktop." Use either the up/down arrow keys until the option is highlighted or the number 2 key. Press the RETURN key to select the option. AppleWorks displays the list of files stored on the Desktop.
3. Select the file with which you wish to work. AppleWorks will activate the selected file, change the screen display to that application format, and place the cursor at the last used position in the file or at the beginning of the file.

> **Tip:** Typing OPEN-APPLE and Q keys simultaneously lets you display an index box on the screen. The index box lists the files on the Desktop. Select a file by highlighting it. This is done using the up/down arrow keys. Press the RETURN key to accept that file. The OPEN-APPLE key commands are discussed in Chapter 9.

Most of the time, you probably will be working with only one file on the Desktop. When that is the case, AppleWorks goes directly to that file. If there is more than one file on the Desktop, you will be presented with an index box screen inset that requires you to select the file you want displayed.

1.4.3 Saving Desktop Files to Disk

Selecting this option saves the current file to a diskette. There are times when you will want to save a file to a diskette and still continue to work on it. It is recommended that you save files frequently, just in case of disaster. Murphy has a rule about such things happening.

When you save a file to a diskette, AppleWorks first saves the changed file. Then the old file is erased from the storage diskette. This is a built-in safety feature that prevents the possibility of completely losing a file.

> **Caution:** There should be sufficient room on a storage diskette to hold both the new file version and the old file, at least temporarily, while both files are stored and before the old version is deleted from the storage diskette.

To save a file:

1. Be sure to have the Main Menu displayed. If you do not have the Main Menu displayed, you can get to it by pressing the ESCape key one or more times.

2. Select option 3, "Save Desktop files to disk." Use the up/down arrow keys or the number 3 key to highlight this option, then press the RETURN key to select it. AppleWorks will then display the Save Files menu. This menu is shown in Fig. 1-5.

3. Select the file you wish to save by highlighting that file name.

4. Use the up/down arrows to scroll through the list of files on your Desktop. Each file will highlight as you pass by it. When you reach the name of the

```
Disk: Drive 2                   SAVE FILES              Escape: Main Menu


 I    Main Menu            I
 I  I   Save Files         I                                        I
 I  I   Name               Status     Document type   Size          I
 I  I   ============================================================ I
 I  I   CH9                Saved      Word Processor  22K           I
 I  I                                                               I
 I  I                                                               I
 I  I                                                               I
 I  I                                                               I
 I  I                                                               I
 I  I                                                               I
 I  I                                                               I
 I_I                                                               I
    I                                                               I


Use Right Arrow to choose files, Left Arrow to undo      33K Avail.
```

Figure 1-5 *Save File Screen*

file you want to save, press the RETURN key. AppleWorks will save the selected file to the storage diskette.

5. You may also use the left/right arrows to save more than one file at a time.

There are a number of pieces of information presented about each file that need to be
noticed. The Save File screen tells you the

Name of the file.

Status of the current file.

Document type of the file.

Size of the file.

Memory available on the Desktop. This number will vary depending upon your
computer, files on the Desktop, file sizes, etc.

At this point, you still have another set of choices to make, depending upon whether
the selected file is new, changed, unchanged, or saved. If the file selected is new or
changed, AppleWorks requires you to select either the same storage diskette in the same
directory, the same storage diskette in another directory, or another diskette device and
directory.

If you choose to save the file on the current diskette, you have to specify whether you
want to replace the currently stored file with the new one or to save the file with a different name. If you are changing the file name, enter the new name and press the RETURN
key.

1.4.4 Removing Files from the Desktop

This option allows you to remove a file from your Desktop. When your Desktop becomes full or you are finished working with a file, you may remove it from the Desktop. By removing a file, you will recover that file's memory space. When you remove a file, you will be asked if you want to save the file, if the file has been changed since the last time it was saved, if you want to save the file to a different location, or if you want to throw it away.

To remove a file from the Desktop:

1. Be sure you have the Main Menu displayed. If you do not have the Main Menu displayed, you can get to it by pressing the ESCape key one or more times.

2. Select option 4, "Remove files from the Desktop." Use the up/down arrow keys or the number 4 key to highlight this option, then press the RETURN key to select this option. AppleWorks then displays the Remove Files menu. This menu is shown in Fig. 1-6.

3. Select the file you wish to remove. Use the up/down arrow keys to scroll through the list of files on your Desktop. Files are highlighted as you pass by them. When you reach the file you want removed, press the RETURN key.

4. You may also use the left/right arrow keys to remove more than one file at a time.

At this point, you still have another set of choices to make, depending upon whether the selected file is new, changed, unchanged, or saved.

```
Disk: Drive 2                  REMOVE FILES              Escape: Main Menu
_____

  |   Main Menu          |_____
  |  _____|_____  |
  | |   Remove Files       |                                            |__
  | |  Name                 Status     Document type    Size            |  |
  | | ================================================================  |  |
  | |  CH9                  Saved      Word Processor   22K             |  |
  | |                                                                   |  |
  | |                                                                   |  |
  | |                                                                   |  |
  | |                                                                   |  |
  | |                                                                   |  |
  | |                                                                   |  |
  | |                                                                   |  |
  | |_|                                                                 |  |
  |   |                                                                 |
  |   |_____ |
_____
Use Right Arrow to choose files, Left Arrow to undo            33K Avail.
```

Figure 1-6   *Remove Files Screen*

If the file selected is new or changed, AppleWorks requires you to select either the same storage diskette in the same directory, the same storage diskette in another directory, or another diskette device and directory.

If you choose to remove the file on the current diskette, you will have to specify whether you want to replace the currently stored file with the new one or save the file with a different name. If you are changing the file name, type in the new name and press the RETURN key.

1.4.5 Quitting AppleWorks

This option lets you leave AppleWorks. Using any other procedure to get out of AppleWorks could cause damage to files or inadvertently lose last-minute changes to files.
To quit AppleWorks:

1. Be sure you have the Main Menu displayed. If you do not have the Main Menu displayed, you can get to it by pressing the ESCape key one or more times.
2. Select option 6, "Quit." Use the up/down arrow keys to highlight this option, then press the RETURN key to select it.
3. Select the "Yes" option. AppleWorks lets you change your mind by using the left/right arrow keys.
4. Decide on the disposition of all files on the Desktop. You may:

   Save all files on the current storage diskette.

   Change the storage diskette to a different storage diskette or directory.

   Throw away the file(s).
5. Enter the Prefix of the new program to be executed. If you are not familiar with ProDOS see Appendix F.

Caution: Using the Quit option to leave AppleWorks ensures that you will always think about saving changed files before actually quitting the system.

After you have taken care of all Desktop files, the final screen presentation will be a 40-column sentence that asks you to enter the full name of the next program to be executed. This is shown below. You can now remove all AppleWorks disks and turn off your computer.

```
ENTER PREFIX (PRESS ''RETURN'' TO ACCEPT)
APPLEWORKS
```

You could also change the diskette in drive 1 to the next program package you want to execute, then enter the volume name of the next program.

You also have the following options:

- Press the OPEN-APPLE-CONTROL-RESET. This keystroke combination will cause your computer system to reboot as if you had just powered up.
- Power down your computer system. Wait at least thirty seconds before you power up your system again with the new diskettes installed.
- Press simultaneously the CONTROL-RESET keys. This keystroke combination will interrupt your system and place you in the immediate mode with the Applesoft II BASIC prompt character. Then type PR#6, from the keyboard, to reboot your computer system.

If you are using a hard disk, like the ProFile, you could:

- Press the RETURN key to continue using the same volume name.
- Enter a new volume name, then press the RETURN key. This will change the Prefix and allow you to execute a program stored somewhere else on the hard disk. For example, you might enter /PROFILE, which is the volume name of the ProFile hard disk. Follow this by pressing the RETURN key. The screen will then clear and the following prompt message will appear:

`ENTER PATHNAME OF NEXT APPLICATION`

Now you should type the name of the next program you want to run.

1.5 OTHER ACTIVITIES MENU

This section discusses the Other Activities Menu. It is examined here because you will probably be using it early when working with AppleWorks. The menu is shown in Fig. 1-7.

The last option is also described in Appendix P along with information about printers. The next seven sections will describe each of the options from this menu.

1.5.1 Changing the Current Disk Drive

This option is for the purpose of temporarily changing the location of your data diskette or the location for the storage of a file. This option is only active during your current work session or until you again temporarily change the storage location. You could use it if you have a disk drive failure or if you are saving multiple copies of the same file in different locations on the same storage diskette.

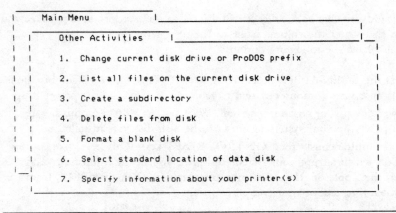

```
 _____
|    Main Menu      |_____
|  _____|_____   |
| |    Other Activities   |_____   |_|
| |                                                       | |
| |   1.  Change current disk drive or ProDOS prefix      | |
| |                                                       | |
| |   2.  List all files on the current disk drive        | |
| |                                                       | |
| |   3.  Create a subdirectory                           | |
| |                                                       | |
| |   4.  Delete files from disk                          | |
| |                                                       | |
| |   5.  Format a blank disk                             | |
| |                                                       | |
| |   6.  Select standard location of data disk           | |
| |_|                                                     | |
|   |   7.  Specify information about your printer(s)      | |
|   |_____|_|
```

```
_____
Type number, or use arrows, then press Return          55K Avail.
```

Figure 1-7   *Other Activities Menu*

To make a change:

1. Be sure you have the Main Menu displayed. If you do not have the Main Menu displayed, you can get to it by pressing the ESCape key one or more times.

2. Select option 5, "Other Activities." Use the up/down arrow keys or the number 5 key to highlight this option, then press the RETURN key to select it.

3. Select option 1, "Change current disk drive or ProDOS prefix." AppleWorks will then display the message, CHANGE CURRENT DISK.

4. Decide on the drive you want. If you are changing floppy disk drives, enter either a 1 or 2 for the number of the drive.

5. Enter the hard disk prefix name if you choose the ProFile or other ProDOS directory.

6. Press the ESCape key to return to the Other Activities Menu.

1.5.2 Listing Files on the Current Disk

It is very convenient to be able to see what AppleWorks files are stored on a disk. This option lets you see all files stored on a current diskette.

To list files:

1. Be sure you have the Main Menu displayed. If you do not have the Main Menu displayed, you can get to it by pressing the ESCape key one or more times.

2. Select option 5, "Other Activities." Use the up/down arrow keys or the number 5 key to highlight this option, then press the RETURN key to select it.

3. Select option 2, "List all files on the current disk drive." Use the up/down arrow keys or the number 2 key to highlight this option. The file names are presented in alphabetical order within the AppleWorks file types. Each file listed shows the name, type, size, and the date and time the file was last saved. The last item is only shown when there is a clock/calendar card installed in the computer. If the list contains more than ten files, you will see the word *more* at the bottom of the screen. You may then scroll through the list by using the up/down arrow keys.

4. Press the ESCape key to return to the Other Activities Menu.

1.5.3 Creating a New Subdirectory

This option allows you to create a new subdirectory either on the current data diskette or on a hard disk. A *subdirectory* is a directory within another directory. The name of the subdirectory becomes a part of a file's pathname. A *pathname* is the series of file names that indicates the entire path from the volume directory name to the file.

To create a subdirectory:

1. Be sure you have the Main Menu displayed. If you do not have the Main Menu displayed, you can get to it by pressing the ESCape key one or more times.

2. Select the "Other Activities" option. Use the up/down arrow keys or the number 5 key to highlight this option, then press the RETURN key to select it.

3. Select option 3, "Create a subdirectory." Use the up/down arrow keys or the number 3 key to highlight this option, then press the RETURN key to select it.

4. Type the complete pathname of the new subdirectory, then press the RETURN key. After the new subdirectory has been created, AppleWorks tells you this by putting the message *Success!* on the screen. For example, change /MYDISK/LETTERS1 to /MYDISK/LETTERS2.

5. Press the ESCape key to return to the Other Activities Menu.

1.5.4 Deleting Files from the Disk

This option allows you to get rid of old files either on the current data diskette or on a hard disk.

To delete files:

1. Be sure you have the Main Menu displayed. If you do not have the Main Menu displayed, you can get to it by pressing the ESCape key one or more times.

2. Select the "Other Activities" option. Use the up/down arrow keys or the number 5 key to highlight this option, then press the RETURN key to select it.

3. Select option 4, "Delete files from disk." Use the up/down arrow keys or the number 4 key to highlight this option, then press the RETURN key to select it.

4. Select the file name to be deleted by using the up/down arrow keys to highlight the name, then press the RETURN key.

5. Press the ESCape key to return to the Other Activities Menu.

Tip: This option also lets you delete a subdirectory, provided it contains no other files.

1.5.5 Formatting a Blank Disk

This option allows you to format a blank diskette as an AppleWorks data diskette or for use with other ProDOS software. Formatting a diskette does not place the operating system on the diskette; rather, it creates more storage space for files. AppleWorks operates only with ProDOS-formatted storage diskettes.

To format a blank diskette:

1. Be sure you have the Main Menu displayed. If you do not have the Main Menu displayed, you can get to it by pressing the ESCape key one or more times.

2. Select the "Other Activities" option. Use the up/down arrow keys or the number 5 key to highlight this option, then press the RETURN key to select it.

3. Select the "Format a blank disk" option. Use the up/down arrow keys or the number 5 key to highlight this option, then press the RETURN key to select it.

4. Enter the volume name of the new diskette, then press the RETURN key. The volume name may contain up to fifteen letters, numbers, or periods but may not contain spaces. The volume name must start with a letter of the alphabet. After the diskette has been formatted, AppleWorks tells you this by putting the message *Success!*, on the screen.

5. Press the ESCape key to return to the Other Activities Menu.

ProDOS is the Apple II Plus, Apple IIe, and Apple IIc operating system. If you are not familiar or comfortable with its capabilities, it is recommended that you read Appendix F and/or *Inside Apple's ProDOS,* by J.L. Campbell.

Caution:	AppleWorks formats diskettes in the ProDOS format. This format is different from the DOS 3.3 format. The two formats are not compatible. DOS 3.3 disks cannot be used with AppleWorks. Remember, when you format a diskette, all files previously on that diskette are erased.

Now would be a good time to format a blank diskette. Power up your system using the procedure in Section 1.3, then use the above procedure. Make sure that you DO NOT format your copy of the AppleWorks program diskette. Name the new volume BLANK00 or a name of your choosing. After the diskette is formatted, use it to store all of the examples shown in this book.

1.5.6 Selecting the Standard Location of a Disk

AppleWorks always looks for a standard location for the storage of files. This option allows you to set a standard storage diskette for data files. Information is saved from one work session to another. The standard location will remain in effect until it is later changed.

To select the standard location of a data diskette:

1. Be sure you have the Main Menu displayed. If you do not have the Main Menu displayed, you can get to it by pressing the ESCape key one or more times.

2. Select the "Other Activities" option. Use the up/down arrow keys or the number 5 key to highlight this option, then press the RETURN key to select it.

3. Select option 6, "Change standard location of data disk." Use the up/down arrow keys or the number 6 key to highlight this option, then press the RETURN key to select it.

Tip:	When starting AppleWorks, the standard data drive is drive 1. If you are going to use two disk drives, you should change the standard storage disk location of the data disk to drive 2 or to the ProFile hard disk.

4. AppleWorks presents you with another screen that allows you to select either a disk drive or a ProFile or other ProDOS directory.
5. Press the ESCape key to return to the Other Activities Menu.

1.5.7 Specifying Printer Information

This option allows you to modify and change printers, printer specifications, and printer types. AppleWorks has the capability to support a number of different printers; however, it is necessary that you tell AppleWorks about the printer you are using.

To specify printer information:

1. Be sure you have the Main Menu displayed. If you do not have the Main Menu displayed, you can get to it by pressing the ESCape key one or more times.
2. Select the "Other Activities" option. Use the up/down arrow keys or the number 5 key to highlight this option, then press the RETURN key to select it.
3. Select option 7, "Specify information about your printer(s)." Use the up/down arrow keys or the number 7 key to highlight this option, then press the RETURN key to select it.
4. AppleWorks presents you with another screen that allows you to:

   Change standard values. By choosing this option, you can change the printer where you want a screen display to be printed.

   Add or remove a printer.

   Change printer specifications.

5. Press the ESCape key to return to the Other Activities Menu.

1.6 FILE SOURCES

In addition to being able to create files from scratch using the word processor, the spreadsheet, or the data base, AppleWorks lets you use files created by many other programs. These file sources are:

The Clipboard
ASCII text file
Quick File
DIF
VisiCalc

The Clipboard is used to move data and information from one file to another. Normally you will use the Clipboard when you are cutting something from one file and pasting it in another. This was shown in Fig. 1-2. Cutting and pasting will be discussed in detail in Chapter 8.

ASCII text files can be sources for the word processor or the data base application files. An ASCII text file is one that has been created using a word processor such as AppleWriter II or IIe or some data base program. ASCII files have the characteristic that all stored information is stored in text form. All characters are stored using the ASCII character set rather than binary or machine code characters.

Quick File can be a source for the data base application. Quick File is a software database package.

The DIF (Data Interchange Format) file first appeared as a means of moving VisiCalc file information between spreadsheets. AppleWorks allows you to use this information in the spreadsheet application.

VisiCalc templates and files can be used by the Spreadsheet portion of AppleWorks.

1.7 SUMMARY

This chapter has given you a first look at the AppleWorks integrated software program. The makeup, capabilities, and features of this program were described so that you will know what this program can do.

You were told what computer equipment is required and how to get started using AppleWorks. Once you have all of the equipment installed properly, you are ready to use AppleWorks.

The Main Menu screen was discussed in detail in Section 1.4. It is from this screen presentation that you begin and end all work sessions. The Main Menu acts like the executive manager for all of AppleWorks.

The Other Activities Menu was discussed in Section 1.5. This secondary menu is very important. It performs many utility functions that will be used repeatedly. This menu allows you to perform many disk file manipulations.

AppleWorks lets you use files created by many other software programs. These other sources of files are:

The Clipboard—Files or file portions from other portions of AppleWorks.

ASCII text file—Files from other word processors or data bases.

Quick File—Data base files from Quick File.

DIF—Files or file portions from other spreadsheet programs such as VisiCalc.

VisiCalc—Files or file portions from VisiCalc directly.

Essentially, this chapter has given you all of the basic information needed to get started using AppleWorks.

PART TWO

Ever since thoughts and words have been written on parchment, it seems that man has been processing those words in some form or another. They have been misspelled, respelled, rearranged, edited, modified, copied, typed, retyped, typeset, printed. The next two chapters discuss how the word processor processes words electronically.

CHAPTER TWO

The Word Processor

Words from the thread on which we string our experiences.
ALDOUS HUXLEY, 1937

2.0 OVERVIEW

This chapter discusses the first of the application-level programs in AppleWorks, the word processor. The processing of words electronically is one of the most widely used microcomputer applications. A word processor program is a computer program whose primary purpose is to take in characters, words, sentences, paragraphs, punctuation marks, and formatting commands; place all of these items on a video screen according to the entered punctuation and formatting commands; and present the finished product either to a screen or to a printer.

Actually, with the development of word processors, it has become very easy for someone to write letters, memos, manuscripts, reports, or term papers. Written communications of all kinds have become much easier to create, write, edit, and print.

There are six basic steps involved in doing word processing. These are:

- *Creating*. The starting from scratch and the naming of a new word processing file.
- *Typing*. The entering of the words, phrases, sentences, and paragraphs as text into a document. The great majority of your word processing time will be spent typing text.
- *Saving*. The storing of a document on a diskette.
- *Loading*. The retrieving of a copy of a saved file from a diskette and placing it in memory.
- *Editing*. The correcting, changing, or rearranging of the text in a document.
- *Printing*. The transferring of your document onto paper using a printer.

27

When you know how to do all of these steps using the word processor portion of AppleWorks, you are processing words electronically. This chapter discusses these capabilities, functions, and activities.

Section 2.1 discusses how to get started with a new piece of electronic paper. You will be shown how to create a new document, load a previously created document, and save your work.

Section 2.2 discusses how to enter text material into a new or existing document. This section will also discuss how to edit information that already exists.

Section 2.3 discusses how to manipulate text material within a document. This section includes how to copy, move, and delete text plus how to search for, find, and replace words or phrases.

Section 2.4 summarizes the information in this chapter.

2.1 WORKING WITH A DOCUMENT

Before you create or enter text material into a new document, it is usually a good idea to plan out the physical characteristics of your final manuscript, letter, memo, report, etc. After all, when you first create a new document, all you have is a blank sheet of electronic paper. Oh yes, there is a ruler near the top of the Desktop display and a line of prompt messages and information at the top and bottom of the Desktop screen. Other than that, a very dull, blank screen greets you. That makes things very uninteresting, but very easy to describe.

Therefore, this section discusses some of the planning needed to help transform the blank screen into something that exhibits a logical, interesting form. You will be shown how to get a fresh sheet of electronic paper and to start to enter text material, to load a document previously created and put away, and to save a new document to your storage disk.

After you know how to perform all these very basic functions, you will be ready to proceed to entering and editing text into the new document you have created.

2.1.1 Document Planning

When starting a new document you should decide its general characteristics before you start entering text. For example, a business letter may have different margin settings and line spacings than a book manuscript, a dissertation, an office memo, a business report, or a screenplay. With all of the things you can do with the word processor application of AppleWorks, it is necessary that you know something about the physical characteristics of such things as your printer, your paper size, and character set size. For example, a letterhead paper might have different margin settings, both horizontally and vertically, than a memo or a thesis paper.

Printers that handle a maximum paper width of 9½", including the printer tractor feed, paper gear feed, and perforations, usually have a platen printer carriage roller length of about 10 to 11". However, you can only use about 8½" of this horizontal space on the platen because this is the tear size of the paper. Further, each document will usually require that there be some margin sizes specified on both the left and right side of the paper.

Another consideration to be decided upon early is the number of characters to be printed on each horizontal line of print. In a number of cases, this is dictated by the physical ability of the printer you are using. For example, daisy-wheel printers require that a print wheel be installed before you are able to print. Each print wheel, in conjunction with the daisy-wheel printer settings, will print a specified number of characters per inch. This could be 10 or 12 characters per inch or be proportionally spaced. Appendix P discusses printers, printer differences, and possible printer problems.

> **Note:** The two-letter abbreviations shown in the following explanations refer to the printer option entry codes that are entered from the printer options menu presentations.

Therefore, if you have set the following from the options menu:

Left margin (LM) = 1″
Right margin (RM) = 1″
Platen width (PW) = 8″
Characters per inch (CI) = 10

you will get a maximum of 60 characters, including spaces, printed on each horizontal line. The above specifications are the default settings when a new document is first created. Assume that you set the characters per inch (CI) option to 12. This would mean that a maximum of 72 characters could be printed on a horizontal line. See OPEN-APPLE O in Chapter 9.

The word processor lets you specify the range of characters per inch from 4 to 24. Most daisy-wheel printers will not support such a wide range of character sizes. However, dot-matrix printers may be able to support this wide range of character sizes.

The mathematics involved so that you can figure this out for yourself are:

Mathematics	Example #1	Example #2
+ Platen width	+8 inches	+8 inches
− Left margin	−1 inch	−1 inch
− Right margin	−1 inch	−1 inch
= Text width	6 inches	6 inches
Text width	6 inches/line	6 inches/line
× Characters per inch	× 10 C/inch	× 12 C/inch
= Characters per line	60 C/line	72 C/line

The next consideration is to specify the vertical spacing of text in a document. Normally, the most commonly used paper size is 8½ " wide by 11" long which is known as letter-size paper. Another common size is legal-size paper, 8½ " wide by 14" long. Other paper sizes are 8" wide by 10" long and 8½ " wide by 5½ " long.

Assume that you will be using letter-size paper. Like specifying the left and right margins, you will probably want to specify a top and bottom margin. The top margin might be long enough to skip over a possible preprinted letterhead at the top of a page. The bottom margin is usually specified so that text material is always printed down to the same place on a page and does not run to the very last possible line. Besides, any document looks better and more professional if there is both a top and bottom margin.

Therefore, if you have set the following from the options menu:

Top margin (TM) = 1"
Bottom margin (BM) = 1"
Paper length (PL) = 11"
Lines per inch (LI) = 6

you will get a maximum of 54 lines, including blank lines, printed on each page. The above specifications are the default settings when a new document is first created. Now, let us assume that you set the bottom margin option to 2". This would mean that a maximum of 48 lines could be printed on a page. See OPEN-APPLE O in Chapter 9.

The mathematics involved so that you can figure this out for yourself is:

Mathematics	Example #1	Example #2
+ Paper length	+11 inches	+11 inches
− Top margin	−1 inch	−2 inches
− Bottom margin	−1 inch	−1 inch
= Text length	9 inches	8 inches
Text length	9 inches/page	8 inches/page
× Lines per inch	× 6 lines/inch	× 6 lines/inch
= Lines per page	54 Lines/page	48 Lines/page

The next page and paragraph formatting that needs to be specified early is the line justification and line spacing you want for your printed text material. Both line justification and line spacing are specified using the options menu presentation. See the OPEN-APPLE O command.

Unjustified (UJ)—even left margin, uneven right margin.
Justified (JU)—even left and right margins.
Centered (CN)—centered on a horizontal line.

The default value for a new document is unjustified. If you change the line justification somewhere in a document, it remains in effect until it is later changed.

The final specification necessary when you start a new document is:

Single spacing (SS)—no spaces between lines of text.

Double spacing (DS)—a single line between lines of text.

Triple spacing (TS)—a double line between lines of text.

The default value for a new document is single spacing.

Tip: Even though you might specify double or triple spacing for a document, all text material will be shown single spaced on the video screen Desktop.

The word processor uses the above defaults until you change them by using the OPEN-APPLE O option menu.

You need to be familiar with the above information so that you can design your document to be consistent with the physical characteristics of the paper you are using in your printer and the capability of your printer to print the final document.

If you have a number of letters or documents that use the same formatting settings, then you may find the next tip very handy and helpful.

Tip: Create a word processor file that contains all of the page formatting you use frequently and save it to disk. Then, when you need to start a new document, use that file as the starting point. Before you save the new file, change its name using OPEN-APPLE N. In this way, you have a document preplanned, preformatted, and ready to be used quickly.

2.1.2 Creating a Document

Now, get a new document started. See Section 1.4.1 for the detailed procedure. The abbreviated procedure is shown here for quick reference.

To create a new document:

1. Choose option 1, "Add files to the Desktop" from Main Menu.

2. Choose option 3, "Word Processor" from "Add files" screen.

3. Choose option 1, "From scratch."

4. Name the new document.

Once you have selected to start a file from scratch, you will be asked to type in the new file name. AppleWorks file names can contain up to 15 characters, must start with a letter of the alphabet, and may contain both upper- and lowercase letters, numbers, periods, and spaces. ProDOS file names can contain 15 characters, must start with a letter of the alphabet, may contain numbers and periods, but cannot contain spaces.

When you are not using AppleWorks, the Apple IIc accepts lowercase letters in file names but converts them to uppercase before writing the name to the diskette. As of this writing, the Apple IIe will accept only uppercase letters as file names. Soon there will be a ROM chip set modification for the Apple IIe that will allow lowercase file names to be entered. In all cases, however, the file name is converted to upper case before being written to the diskette. This new ROM chip set will convert your Apple IIe to the Enhanced Apple IIe.

You also have the capability to create new AppleWorks word processor files from text files developed using other word processor programs, such as Apple Writer II/IIe, Apple Writer III, the Pascal Editor, and others. This can be done using the following abbreviated procedure:

1. Convert the ASCII file from other sources to a ProDOS diskette file. Use the CONVERT program on the ProDOS diskette.

Then within AppleWorks:

2. Choose option 1, "Add files to the Desktop" from Main Menu.
3. Choose option 3, "Word Processor" from Add Files screen.
4. Choose option 2, "From a text (ASCII) file."

The word processor allows you to use ASCII text files located on any ProDOS formatted diskette as the source for its new documents. The file on the diskette must be stored as an ASCII text file. It is recommended that you check the owner's manual of other word processors to determine whether or not they are stored in an ASCII text file format.

> **Caution:** You must first convert text files stored on DOS 3.3 diskettes to ProDOS. This is done by using the CONVERT program on the ProDOS User's Disk for converting stored files. This procedure is discussed in Appendix F.

After you have properly converted a stored word processor file created through other word processor programs, you can load it into the word processor as an ASCII file, then rename, edit, and save it. This new file name must be different from the ASCII name.

2.1.3 Loading a Document

Use the procedure in Section 1.4.1 to load a file into the Desktop. This is the first step required before you can make any changes to a stored file.

The loading of a file into the Desktop involves a number of selections. The storage disk of the file is selected, the files stored on a data disk are presented to the video screen, the file to be loaded must be selected from the files presented, the file is loaded, and finally, the word processor is activated so that you can work on the loaded file.

All of these things become very routine after you have loaded several files. You will really not even think about what is happening, you will just do it.

2.1.4 Saving a Document

Use the procedure in Section 1.4.3 to save a file that is on your Desktop. This step should be performed often when changes are made.

When you save a file there are a number of pieces of information presented about each file that need to be noticed. This Save Files screen tells you the

- Name of the file.
- Status of the current file, saved, changed, or unchanged.
- Document type of the file (WP, SS, or DB).
- Size of the file, expressed in thousands (K) of bytes.
- Memory available in the Desktop. This number will vary depending upon your machine.

The Save Files screen presentation tells you the disk drive where the file will be saved; the use of the ESCape key to return to the Main Menu; the memory available on the Desktop; and the process of selecting a file to be saved, if there is more than one on the Desktop.

2.2 ENTERING TEXT AND EDITING A DOCUMENT

It is relatively easy to enter new text material into a word processing document and to later edit that material for mistakes and typographical errors. It's a good thing that correcting errors is easy because everyone makes typing and spelling errors.

As you are typing text information into a document, each line will be formatted according to the margin settings you have defined or according to the default margins for that document. As you come to the end of a line and you are in the middle of a word, the entire word will be automatically moved to the beginning of the next line. This feature is known as *word wraparound*.

Now would be a good time to start entering some text material into a new document. Power up your system, get AppleWorks running, and start a new word processing document from scratch. Use the procedures in Sections 1.3 and 1.4.1.

If you have a two-drive system, the AppleWorks program diskette is in disk drive 1 and the formatted blank diskette in disk drive 2. If you have a one-drive system, the program disk in disk drive 1 is replaced with the formatted blank diskette.

Name the new file POEM. At this point, do not worry about any special page formatting. Use all of the defaults. Start typing the poem in Fig. 2-1 at the cursor position at the top left edge of the screen. Press the RETURN key once so that the text material will start on the second line of the screen. Type the poem title and author line. Then continue entering the rest of the poem as shown.

The first thing to notice is that the first character of the text is placed along the left edge of the screen regardless of the left margin setting. The left and right margin settings will become active when the poem is printed.

As you are entering the poem, do not worry about typing errors. How to correct errors is explained very shortly. For now, just type each line of the poem. At the end of each line press the RETURN key. You may want to zoom in, using OPEN-APPLE Z, so that you can see where the RETURN symbols are placed.

After entering the poem, reformat the screen presentation. Move the cursor to the top line of the screen and reset the left margin setting to .5″. Press OPEN-APPLE O. Enter LM followed by the RETURN key in response to the "Option" prompting. Then enter .5 followed by the RETURN key in response to the "Inches" prompting. Press the ESCape key to exit from the options screen. Now, place the insert cursor under the O in Open on the first line of the poem. Press OPEN-APPLE O again. Reset the left margin (LM) to 1.5″, the right margin (RM) to 1.5″, and indent (IN) characters to 5. After all that has been done, the screen presentation should look like Fig. 2-2.

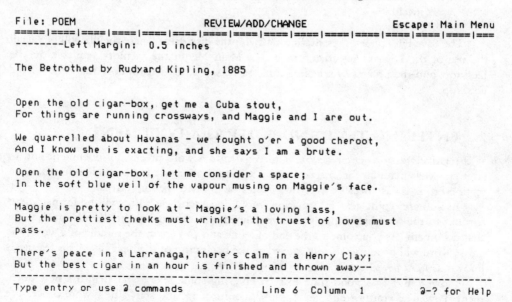

```
File: POEM                    REVIEW/ADD/CHANGE              Escape: Main Menu
=====|====|====|====|====|====|====|====|====|====|====|====|====|====|====|
--------Left Margin:  0.5 inches

The Betrothed by Rudyard Kipling, 1885


Open the old cigar-box, get me a Cuba stout,
For things are running crossways, and Maggie and I are out.

We quarrelled about Havanas - we fought o'er a good cheroot,
And I know she is exacting, and she says I am a brute.

Open the old cigar-box, let me consider a space;
In the soft blue veil of the vapour musing on Maggie's face.

Maggie is pretty to look at - Maggie's a loving lass,
But the prettiest cheeks must wrinkle, the truest of loves must
pass.

There's peace in a Larranaga, there's calm in a Henry Clay;
But the best cigar in an hour is finished and thrown away--
-------------------------------------------------------------------
Type entry or use a commands          Line 6  Column  1        a-? for Help
```

Figure 2-1   *Unformatted Poem by Rudyard Kipling*

```
File: POEM                    REVIEW/ADD/CHANGE              Escape: Main Menu
=====|====|====|====|====|====|====|====|====|====|====|====|====|====|===
--------Left Margin:  0.5 inches

The Betrothed by Rudyard Kipling, 1885


--------Left Margin:  1.5 inches
--------Right Margin:  1.5 inches
--------Indent: 5 chars
          Open the old cigar-box, get me a Cuba stout,
          For things are running crossways, and Maggie and I
              are out.

          We quarrelled about Havanas - we fought o'er a
              good cheroot,
          And I know she is exacting, and she says I am a
              brute.

          Open the old cigar-box, let me consider a space;
          In the soft blue veil of the vapour musing on
              Maggie's face.
-------------------------------------------------------------------------
Type entry or use ⌐ commands             Line 2  Column 11      ⌐-? for Help
```

Figure 2-2   *Modified Poem Presentation*

By doing the margin settings, you are able to control the length of horizontal lines. By specifying the indenting of characters for any line of poetry greater than a single line of text, you can control and format any words that are wrapped around to the next line. If there is no RETURN character on the line above, the subsequent lines will be indented as specified. The default indentation is 0 characters.

Since the POEM file is entered and formatted, use the procedure in Section 1.4.3 to save the file on the blank diskette. You now have an exact copy of the file in memory stored on this diskette.

Another way to control word wraparound is by using sticky spaces. Sticky spaces are not like the normal spaces that exist between words or groups of characters; they can be inserted between words or groups of characters by using the OPEN-APPLE-SPACE BAR keystroke combination to insert a space between words or groups of characters. The difference is that AppleWorks inserts a CARET (^) symbol in the nromal space position between words or groups of characters. This signifies that the words or group of characters are to be placed upon a single line when the document is printed.

This is a very hand feature because there are times when you want to have names, titles, or phrases appear on one line of text and not be separated between lines. For example, the titles, Commander in Chief, Commander in Chief Pacific Fleet need to be all on a single line. Entering sticky spaces into a document is shown, in zoomed-in form, in Fig. 2-3.

When typing text material, you can separate paragraphs by pressing the RETURN key one or more times. You can use the RETURN key to

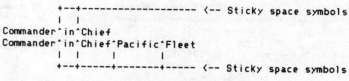

Figure 2-3   *Sticky Space Example*

- end a paragraph,
- create one or more blank lines, or
- end and/or separate subject material.

You can add information anywhere within a word processing document using the insert cursor. The insert cursor is a blinking underline bar. Anything typed while using the insert cursor will be added at the cursor position within the document. All text material and the cursor is moved to the right and/or down as you type the new material.

If you would rather overstrike information, change to the overstrike cursor. The overstrike cursor is an inverse blinking box. Anything typed with the overstrike cursor changes the current text material to the newly typed material. In this case, all text to the right and down is not moved or disturbed. Use the OPEN-APPLE E keystroke combination to change the cursor from the insert cursor to the overstrike cursor or vice versa. See Section 9.1.5.

There are a number of ways to edit, change, or correct text material which already exists. When editing information, you can use:

- DELETE key—This key erases one displayed text character each time you press it. The character deleted is just to the left of the current cursor position.

- CONTROL Y—This keystroke combination allows you to delete all text material from the cursor position to the end of the current screen line or to the next carriage return, whichever comes first. All of the empty space is closed up automatically.

- Arrow keys—Remember that you can use the arrow keys to move around within a document or reposition the cursor.

- OPEN-APPLE E—This keystroke combination changes the cursor from an insert cursor to an overstrike cursor or vice versa. See Section 2.1.3.

- OPEN-APPLE R—This keystroke combination allows you to search for, find, and replace characters, words, or phrases. See Section 9.4.3.

Tip: It is recommended that you zoom in when making a large number of editing changes or editing large blocks of text material. This allows you to see all of the printer option commands easily.

Finish making any corrections to the POEM file and save your final version. You have now successfully completed your first word processing document.

Essentially, the word processor conforms to the rule that "what you see is what you get." This is especially true when you use 10 characters per inch type size and have a horizontal text line less than 79 characters, the screen width. With this in mind, it is easy to get a pretty good idea of what your final document will look like when it is printed. Of course, for every rule there always seem to be exceptions. These are:

- If you have specified that your document is to be printed using either of the proportional spacing fonts, P1 or P2, what you see on the screen is not what you will get on a printed page. Everything on the screen is presented in a fixed-font size, each character occupying the same horizontal space.
- Any printer options that are presented on the video screen, such as the CARET, will not be present in the final printed document.
- Double and triple spacing is not shown on the video screen.
- Page headers and footers are not shown on each page of the video screen.
- If you specify that the font size is to have a low numeric value or a high numeric value, the video display will seem distorted. However, the word processor is just accounting for the final printing of the document.
- Text will always start at the left edge of the screen for the smallest left margin setting. For example, if you have a left margin setting of 1" as the smallest setting, all text with a left margin setting of 1" is displayed starting at the left edge of the video screen. All other larger margin settings are moved to the right accordingly.

2.3 MANIPULATING A DOCUMENT

Once you have entered text material, there are many ways to rearrange it. This section discusses how to copy, move, delete, and replace blocks of text.

2.3.1 Copying Text

The copying feature allows you to duplicate paragraphs, sections, or words easily. This feature is very handy if you need to duplicate similar sections of large documents or manuscripts. See Section 9.1.3, the OPEN-APPLE C command. You are allowed to copy a total of 250 lines of text at any one time.

2.3.2 Moving Text

Being able to move text makes it very easy to rearrange elements in a document without a lot of headaches. Section 9.1.13 discusses the OPEN-APPLE M command. You are allowed to move a total of 250 lines of text at one time.

When you are in the move mode, you cannot move the cursor or text beyond where you have already entered text. It is necessary that you make some room for text to be moved beyond the present end of the text.

2.3.3 Deleting Text

Deleting text from a document is discussed in Section 9.1.4. Since you can delete anything from a single character to large blocks of information and move and copy text material, you are able to rearrange the contents of any document without much problem.

There are three ways that you can delete text material from a document. The first way is by using the DELETE key. The use of this key was discussed previously. Deleting always works backwards, that is, to the left of the cursor. Remember, anything that is deleted is gone forever.

Another way to delete text is to use CONTROL-Y to delete from the cursor to the end of a screen line.

The third way to delete text material in large blocks is to use the OPEN-APPLE D keystroke combination. See Section 9.1.4.

2.3.4 Finding Text

The AppleWorks word processor lets you search for and find five different types of information within any document. See Section 9.1.6.

When you want to find specific text, AppleWorks will start at the cursor position and search forward in the document until a match is found. The maximum number of characters that can be matched is 30. After the first match has been found, you can ask for the next occurrence of the same information.

2.3.5 Replacing Text

The OPEN-APPLE R (replace command) allows you to search for, find, and replace text within a document. You can replace one or several occurrences of a character, word, or phrase. Further, you are allowed to replace all occurrences at once or just one at a time, depending upon the choices you make from the prompting messages. OPEN-APPLE R is discussed in Section 9.1.18.

The OPEN-APPLE F (find command) only lets you search for, find, and review the occurrences of items within a document. By combining the use of these commands, you are able to both find and replace items, review what has been written, and review and check embedded printer options.

2.4 SUMMARY

This chapter explained the six basic steps performed when doing word processing. These are:

- Creating. The starting from scratch and the naming of new word processing files.
- Typing. The entering of all of the words, phrases, sentences, paragraphs, and text into a document. The great majority of your word processing time will be spent typing text.
- Saving. The storing of a document on a diskette.
- Loading. The retrieving of a copy of a saved file from a diskette and placing it in memory.
- Editing. The correcting, changing, or rearranging of the text document.
- Printing. The transferring of your document onto paper using a printer.

This chapter amplified on these six steps by giving you the basic skills necessary to create, load, save, edit, print, and start using the word processor portion of AppleWorks.

The first section outlined how to plan the physical characteristics of a document, and create, load, and save it. It showed you the commands available to format a page of printed output. This included specifying

- The left and right margins.
- The top and bottom margins.
- The spacing of each line.
- The justification of lines of text.

You were also given the procedures for

- Creating a new document.
- Loading an existing document.
- Saving a document.
- Manipulating text within a document.
  Copying text.
  Moving text.
  Deleting text.
  Finding text.
  Replacing text.

Additional Word Processor Features

*Man does not live by words alone, despite the fact that
sometimes he has to eat them.*
ADLAI STEVENSON, 1952

3.0 OVERVIEW

This chapter continues with a discussion of the word processor portion of AppleWorks. It describes a number of the capabilities of the application that were not fully explained in Chapter 2, which concentrated primarily on explaining the skills, procedures, and mechanics of operating the word processor.

We will be outlining some of the common practices that are used in offices for correspondence, interoffice memos, financial statements, manuscripts, etc. It is not our intention to teach a typing course, but to simply give you some of the generally accepted ways of outlining, formatting, and entering information into these various documents. The information in this chapter should give you some ideas on how to make your written materials more effective and professional-looking.

Section 3.1 discusses the ubiquitous memorandum.

Section 3.2 gives pointers on using the word processor to develop business letters.

Section 3.3 describes creating financial statements using the word processor.

Sections 3.4 and 3.5 give tips on organizing newsletters, articles, manuscripts, and theses.

Section 3.6 wraps up this chapter with a summary.

3.1 INTEROFFICE MEMOS

The memorandum is probably the most informal communications document in an office. The formatting of the memo and the entering of information into it involves the easiest, most straight-forward word processing. That makes it a good place to start.

Begin by creating and formatting a blank word processor document. This can be done by using the procedure in Section 2.1.2. Name the document MEMO. It should look like the one shown in Fig. 3-1.

```
File: MEMO                      REVIEW/ADD/CHANGE              Escape: Main Menu
=====|====|====|====|====|====|====|====|====|====|====|====|====|====|====|===
```

```
-----------------------------------------------------------------------------
Type entry or use @ commands              Line 1  Column  1        @-? for Help
```

Figure 3-1   A Blank Memo

Notice that the top of the new blank document identifies the file name, MEMO, and tells you that you are in the REVIEW/ADD/CHANGE mode. The horizontal Ruler shows the predefined tab settings. At the bottom of your Desktop is a dashed line and a prompt line. The prompt line tells you that you may either type an entry or use an OPEN-APPLE command, the line number, and the column number position of the cursor. Finally, you may use the OPEN-APPLE ? help command to get the help screen contents. Now that you know what a blank sheet of electronic paper and Desktop screen look like, we can proceed to the creation of a memo.

Every memo usually has a number of identification lines at the top of the document. There are many possible arrangements for these identification lines; we are going to show and discuss only one arrangment. These lines include the type of document; a date line; and From, To, Subj(ect), Ref(er to), and Via (intermediary addressees) lines.

All of these items are usually aligned along the left margin of the page. An example of this is shown in Fig. 3-2.

The first things to specify for the new memorandum are all of the initial physical characteristics of the document, assuming you will not be using the default values. Some of these default values were given in Chapter 2.

Notice in Fig. 3-3 that, in some of the cases, the default printer option settings have been used while other options have been changed to meet the requirements for the memorandum being created. Although it is not necessary to respecify the default settings embedded within a document, you want to have all of the printer options actually within the document itself. Then, when you zoom in with OPEN-APPLE Z, you can see exactly what you have specified and where it is in the document. (Remember, the printed @ symbol is the Apple symbol on the screen.)

Memorandum _____

Date:

From:

To:

Subj:

Ref:

Via:

(Body of the memorandum)

Figure 3-2   *An Example of One Arrangement of Identification Lines*

Next, notice that the line with the word "Memorandum" on it is going to be printed using a 4-characters-per-inch font size. This means that a 7″ line length may contain only 28 characters including any printer option characters such as CARETS. This is derived from the following simple mathematics:

```
+ Platen width, PW = 8.5 inches        +------>  Line length      = 7.0 inches
- Left margin, LM  = 0.5 inch          |        X Char per inch (CI) = 4.0
- Right margin, RM = 1.0 inch          |        ======================
====================                   |        = Characters/Line   = 28.0
= Line length = 7.0 inches  ---------+
```

There are two pairs of carets shown in Fig. 3-3, one pair to the left of the word "Memorandum," the other pair at the end of the line. The first caret tells the word processor to begin underlining (UB). The last caret tells it to end underlining (UE). The second caret instructs the word processor to print boldface (BB). The third caret tells it to end boldface (BE).

What all of this means is that the word "Memorandum" plus the remainder of the blank spaces on that same line is to be printed using 4-characters-per-inch font size, in boldface, and underlined. A dot-matrix printer is best for this type of printing. All of the other carets used in this example are for boldface printing. Remember, CARETs mark where printer option commands are inserted, but they are not shown when the document is printed.

All of the other formatting lines are to be printed in boldface using 10-characters-per-inch font size.

> **Tips:**
> 1. An easier method of placing the boldface-begin and boldface-end carets in text is to use CONTROL-B. With this keystroke combination, the first entry on a line will be interpreted as the boldface-begin point and the second one as the boldface-end point.
> 2. An easier method of placing the underline-begin and underline-end carets in text is to use CONTROL-L. With this keystroke combination, the first entry on a line will be interpreted as the underline-begin point and the second one as the underline-end point.

All of the other formatting items, done by spacing over using the SPACEBAR, are aligned vertically so that information can be easily aligned. The rest of the first page is left blank for the contents of the memo.

> **Tip:** It is recommended that you have a preformatted memorandum stored on a diskette. Then when you need to create one, just load the preformatted memo into your Desktop, enter the information, and save the new memo to another disk under a different name. Do this before you print the memo. In this way, you will always have a supply of blank memos available.

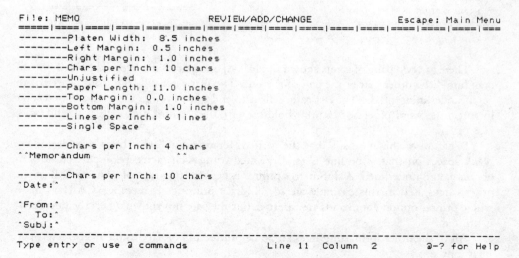

```
File: MEMO                    REVIEW/ADD/CHANGE              Escape: Main Menu
=====|====|====|====|====|====|====|====|====|====|====|====|====|====|====|===
--------Platen Width:  8.5 inches
--------Left Margin:  0.5 inches
--------Right Margin:  1.0 inches
--------Chars per Inch: 10 chars
--------Unjustified
--------Paper Length: 11.0 inches
--------Top Margin:  0.0 inches
--------Bottom Margin:  1.0 inches
--------Lines per Inch: 6 lines
--------Single Space

--------Chars per Inch: 4 chars
^^Memorandum              ^^

--------Chars per Inch: 10 chars
^Date:^

^From:^
^  To:^
^Subj:^
-------------------------------------------------------------------------------
Type entry or use a commands          Line 11  Column  2        a-? for Help
```

Figure 3-3 *Memorandum Physical Settings*

Memorandum

Date: 08/28/84

From: Harry Hardcase
  To: All employees
Subj: Annual company picnic

 Ref:
 Via: All department heads

1. The company picnic this year will be held at my brother's ranch,
    the same as it was last year.

2. The fee for parking automobiles and trucks this year, however,
    will be $4.00 per vehicle instead of the $2.50 charged last year.
    The barbecue dinner will be $7.50 per person this year.

3. It is imperative that all employees attend this gala event. Last
    year's attendance was slack and my brother lost money. All heads
    of departments will make every effort to have a good attendance.

4. Hope to see y'all there!

                         Harry

Figure 3-4   Filled-in Memorandum

Figure 3-4 is a filled-in memorandum. Now, finally, you can start entering information into a blank sheet called MEMO. As you type, you will notice that the character entered is actually to the left of the cursor even though you entered the character at the cursor position. The reason for this is because the cursor immediately moves to the right as soon as you enter a character. Also notice that when you enter a printer option command, it is entered on the line *above* the line of the cursor position and at the left edge of the Desktop screen, regardless of the position of the cursor on any horizontal line.

Some general typing and formatting tips for memos and similar documents:

There are 70 characters printed on a line with a characters-per-inch setting of 10 and a line length of 7″. There are 84 characters printed on a line with a characters-per-inch setting of 12 and a line length of 7″. (See Section 2.1.1 for figuring characters per line.) A 6.5″ or 7″ is considered standard.

Place two spaces after a period that signifies the end of a sentence. A period at the end of an abbreviation is followed by only one space. Periods always go inside closing quotation marks.

Use only one space after a comma, colon, or semicolon. Colons and semicolons go outside of closing quotation marks, commas are placed within.

When a hyphen is used in a compound word, no spaces are used either before or after the hyphen. Hyphens and dashes are created by typing the minus sign on the keyboard. There are rules for dividing words at the end of a line. For instance, a compound word should be divided between its parts. Never divide a contraction. Divide words only between syllables. If you are not sure of syllabication, consult a dictionary.

Abbreviations may be typed in lowercase letters, with periods (etc., i.e.), or in capital letters (A.M.). Many abbreviations for organizations are typed in solid capitals without periods (UNICEF).

The subject line is used to preview the contents of the memorandum. The preferred position is to have a double line after the subject line. It may be either at the left margin or centered on the line.

3.2 BUSINESS LETTERS

There are probably as many different formulas for business letters as there are businesses operating. However, there are a few general formatting requirements that seem to be used by all of the letters. This section will discuss these as a sample business letter is entered.

In general, the opening paragraph of a business letter should explain the reason for writing it. (See Fig. 3-5.) The next paragraph(s) should contain the subject of the letter.

```
                                        3101 Pioneer Ave.
                                        Waco, Texas 76710
                                        April 5, 1984



Mr. John L. Campbell
507 E. Woodside Ave.
South Bend, Indiana  99999

Dear Mr. Campbell:

When we talked at the office automation clinic last Thursday,
I promised to send you a letter done on my word processor in
blocked form.  Well, sir, here is the letter.

All lines begin at the left margin except the date line,
which is moved to the right margin, and the principle closing
lines, which begin at the center of a line.  I centered the
closing line using the printer options feature.

If there is anything else that you would like me to explain,
please let me know.

                    Very sincerely,



                    Training Instructor
```

Figure 3-5 *Sample Business Letter*

The last paragraph is the closing. It should be generally pleasant and urge whatever action that needs to be taken.

Figure 3-6 shows the printer options that were used to create the initial format of the letter.

As the letter was entered, the only formatting done was the vertical spacing of lines. The reason for this is because, at this point, you are more concerned with getting the words entered and not making typographical errors. Once you have all of the text entered, go back and insert the horizontal formatting. Remember, you have already specified the major formatting, so the word processor will do most of the work for you.

For example, the return address and the date at the top of the letter were first entered along the left margin. Then the cursor was placed at the left edge of one of the lines and the space bar was used to move that line to the right margin. This was done for all three lines.

Notice that the closing lines are centered. This was done using printer option command CN. Since the closing phrase, "Very sincerely," is a different length than the title of the writer, it is necessary to pad blank spaces after the closing so that the carriage-return character for that line is in the same position horizontally on both lines. By doing this, both lines will align on the left. It is recommended that you do this in the zoomed-in mode so that you can easily see the carriage returns. This is shown in Fig. 3-7.

When doing business letters, you might be using single sheets of letterhead paper instead of tractor-fed paper. In this case, it is very handy to be able to stop the printing of multiple-page letters between pages to change the paper in the printer. This can be done by using either the Pause Here (PH) or Pause Each Page (PE) capability from the printer options menu, OPEN-APPLE O. The Pause Here option allows you to interrupt printing while you change printer paper, check the letter, or check the formatting. The Pause Each Page option interrupts the printing of a document at the end of each printed page. While

```
File: CH4                     REVIEW/ADD/CHANGE              Escape: Main Menu
=====|====|====|====|====|====|====|====|====|====|====|====|====|====|===
--------Left Margin:   1.2 inches
--------Right Margin:  1.3 inches
--------Platen Width:  8.5 inches
--------Paper Length: 11.0 inches
--------Chars per Inch: 10 chars
--------Indent: 0 chars
--------Unjustified
--------Top Margin:   1.0 inches
--------Bottom Margin: 1.0 inches
--------Single Space




                                  3101 Pioneer Ave.
                                  Waco, Texas 76710
                                  April 5, 1984



--------------------------------------------------------------------------
Type entry or use ∂ commands          Line 392  Column  8      ∂-? for Help
```

Figure 3-6 *Sample Letter Printer Options*

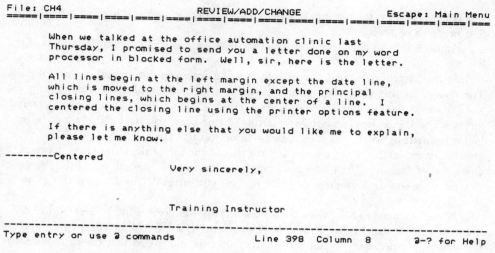

Figure 3-7   Sample Closing Format

> **Tip:** When you format a section of a document horizontally, it is recommended that you start at the end of the document and work toward the beginning. The reason for this is because all the remainder of a document is reformatted. Formatting takes effect from the cursor position to the end of a document. If the document is very long, this will take time to accomplish.
>
> For example, you may want to change from unjustified to centered for only one paragraph and then back to unjustified. When you tell AppleWorks you want the document centered, all of the rest of the document will be centered or until the next line-formatting command.

printing is interrupted, you can change the letterhead paper or do anything else needed. Use the following procedure:

1. Calculate the page breaks in a document using the OPEN-APPLE K command.
2. Place the cursor just after a page break in the document.
3. Press OPEN-APPLE O options command.
4. Enter PH option in response to the prompt message. Use the ESCape key to exit from the options menu.

Some general typing and formatting tips for business letters follow:

On January 1, 1967, the Postal Service instituted the Zoning Improvement Program (ZIP) and introduced the zip code. Originally this was a five-digit code. The first digit of the code refers to a specific region of the country, the next two digits to a specific city. The last two digits identify a specific post office branch. An additional four-digit suffix to the original zip code is being introduced to provide post office box and other information.

A set of accepted abbreviations for each of the states, plus protectorates, territories, and districts, is also used. The inclusion of the zip code and state abbreviation in an address should help your letter be processed more quickly. No side comments. That was what we were told by the Postal Service.

Always use the appropriate personal title on an envelope addressed to an individual. The current tendency is to omit business titles in addresses. Envelope mailing labels are easily created using the data base. (See Chapters 7 and 8.)

When writing the name of a business, always use the official name and follow the company's style for spelling, punctuation, capitalization, and spacing.

If the name of a building is indicated in the address, type it on a line by itself. Always type the street address on a line by itself. The city, state, and zip code are typed on the last line of the address.

Depending upon the size of a one-page business letter, it may be necessary to readjust all margins in order to fit the letter neatly in the center of the page. This gives the letter a well-balanced appearance. As a general rule, the longer the letter, the smaller the margins that are used.

The salutation of a business letter may be followed by a colon or by no punctuation at all. Titles should be capitalized. The salutation should be preceded and followed by a blank line.

There are a number of styles for business letters. If you begin every line in a letter at the left margin, the style is called full blocked. If you indent the date and the closing line, the style is called blocked or modified block. If you also indent the first line of each paragraph, the style is semiblocked. If you also indent the lines of the inside address and closing, the style is called indented.

The most acceptable style is the full-blocked letter. The most popular business letter is the blocked style.

The close of a business letter is typed on the second line below the last line of the body of the letter. It may begin at the left margin, centered on the line, or at the point where the date entry was made.

Business titles are frequently used to identify the signer of a letter. When a title is used, it may follow the name separated by a comma, or it may be used in place of the name. The title may also be placed on the next line.

Enclosure notations should be below the complimentary close of the letter and separated by at least one line space.

The distribution of the letter should be shown by the cc notation typed under any enclosure notations.

3.3 INVITATIONS

There comes the time when it is necessary to invite a group to a social function, a fund raiser, or a festive gathering. For example:

```
        Mr. and Mrs. John Campbell
      requests the pleasure of your company
     at dinner, on Wednesday, January the tenth
              at seven o'clock
                Brazos Landing
                404 River Road
```

Creating an invitation with the word processor is relatively easy. Entering an invitation is essentially the same as entering a business letter. First do all of the vertical formatting, then do the formatting of those horizontal lines that require it.

What has been shown is only one possible format for an invitation. Most of the time, offices, printers, and others may have a specific format that you may want to follow. However, every invitation does essentially the same thing: it lists the date, hour, and place of the event. It may also note if confirmation is required, if formal or informal attire is expected, and if any charges are involved.

Figures 3-8, 3-9, and 3-10 show how invitations may be formatted.

Some general typing and formatting tips for invitations:

If the purpose of your invitation is not clear, the response may be minimal.
    Invitations need not always be centered on the paper. It might be much easier to create a friendly, personal letter that states the invitation purpose clearly.

```
        Mr. and Mrs. John Campbell

      requests the pleasure of your company

     at dinner, on Wednesday, January the tenth

              at seven o'clock

                Brazos Landing

                404 River Road
```

Figure 3-8   *Dinner Invitation*

```
                You are invited
              To an Important Meeting
            of the Easter Seal Telethon
              Fund Raising Committee

                January Fifteenth
            6 to 8 pm     Refreshments

            Huaco Convention Center
              414 Washington Ave.
```

```
R.S.V.P. 752-4481
```

Figure 3-9   *Fund-raising Invitation*

```
             Mr. and Mrs. Sam Redden
         request the pleasure of your company
                  at the Garden Room

          on Friday evening, May twenty-fifth
                     at 6 P.M.

                  Hilton Hotel
                333 Columbus Ave.

Dinner and Dancing                      R.S.V.P. 752-4481
```

Figure 3-10 *Dinner and Dancing Invitation*

Important parts of an invitation should be highlighted in some way: bold print, underlined, or larger font sizes.

Above all, the date, time, and place of the event must be made very clear. It might even be necessary to repeat these items at the end of an invitation.

Invitations and responses to invitations are good candidates for general formats that may be filled in later.

3.4 NEWSLETTERS AND ARTICLES

Other documents that can be created easily with the word processor are the newsletter and magazine or newspaper article. All of these documents have a few things in common: they need to be written in an interesting manner, be formatted to meet the requirements of the publisher, and cover specific topics. These documents also are normally typeset. When any document is typeset, a lot of formatting that is done is beyond the capabilities of AppleWorks.

However, there are many things that you can do with the word processor that makes the creation, development, and eventual publication of a newsletter or article easier. For example, using the word processor, you can make the vertical spacing of lines, the print size, the margin settings, and the general document organization conform to the requirements of the publisher.

The following excerpt is from an article about the Lisa computer.

The ROOTS of Lisa
by
John Campbell

"The shell must break before the bird can fly."
ALFRED, LORD TENNYSON, 1885

Every once in a while, an idea comes along that completely changes the way we think about things. For those of us that fool around with computers, these ideas have been few and far between, but have had a major impact on the industry.

Probably the most influential idea was John von Neumann's stored-program concept, which stated that both a program and the data upon which the program acted could be simultaneously resident in a common storage media, the memory. This concept, first put forth in 1946, is the basis of all of our present-day computers.

The next major idea was the institution and implementation of the subroutine. A subroutine is a portion of a program that performs a specific task necessary for the execution of the entire program. A subroutine represents a unique implementation of a process that is utilized many times in a program.

In the mid-Sixties the first monolithic integrated circuits appeared commercially. These allowed for multiple functions to be performed within the same electronic circuitry. This signaled the transition from discrete, single-function devices to the multi-device, multi-function circuit capability.

The concept of structured programming was first introduced in a series of articles by Dijkstra published in 1968. The high-level language Pascal, developed by N. Wirth in the early Seventies, illustrated many of these structured-programming techniques.

I realize that there were numerous ideas that contributed to the present-day microcomputer industry. However, most of them were extensions rather than revolutionary departures from the accepted way of doing things. For example, the development of software for microcomputers closely followed the development of software for mainframes.

In January of 1983, Apple Computer Inc. introduced Lisa, a computer that integrated hardware, operating system, languages, and utilities into one complete system. . . .

To create this article, information was first entered without attention given to the physical layout of the piece. The emphasis was on the content, organization, and wording. After the article was entered into the word processor, it was edited for spelling errors and typographical errors. Finally, the article was formatted to meet the requirements of the publisher.

3.5 RESEARCH PAPERS

Research papers seem to be the nemesis of every school student. These kinds of documents range from book reports to term papers and dissertations. They can range from a few paragraphs to hundreds of pages in length. By using a word processor, you can spend more time on the content of the manuscript than on the mechanics and form of entering the words.

One of the characteristics of all of these documents is the use of superscripts and subscripts. A superscript is a distinguishing symbol (usually a letter or numeral) written above the line of print. A subscript is a character printed below the line. Superscripts and subscripts are used to refer to footnotes or bibliography items. They are also used in mathematical formulas.

To insert a superscript or subscript:

1. Position the cursor at the point you want to place a superscript or subscript.
2   Press OPEN-APPLE O. This will give you the printer options.

3. Select the option you want:
    Begin superscript = +B
    End superscript = +E
    Begin subscript = −B
    End subscript = −E

4. Press the ESCape key to return to the REVIEW/ADD/CHANGE screen and your document.

For example, a superscript may be used in the following way:

$$Y = X^3 + X^2 + X + 5$$

or

"The machine, yes the machine—
never wastes anybody's time—
never watches the foreman—
never talks back."[1]

[1]Carl Sandburg, *The People, Yes* (1936)

```
File: CH3.5                    REVIEW/ADD/CHANGE              Escape: Main Menu
=====|=====|=====|=====|=====|=====|=====|=====|=====|=====|=====|=====|=====|=====|===

For example, a superscript may be used in the following way.

--------Left Margin:  2.0 inches
--------Indent: 0 chars
             Y = X^3^ + X^2^ + X + 5


        or

--------Chars per Inch: 8 chars
             ^"The machine, yes the machine --^
             ^ never wastes anybody's time --^
             ^ never watches the foreman --^
             ^ never talks back."^1^^

             1 - CARL SANDBURG, ^The People, Yes^ (1936)
--------Chars per Inch: 12 chars
--------Left Margin:  0.5 inches


---------------------------------------------------------------------------
Type entry or use a commands          Line 88   Column   1        a-? for Help
```

Figure 3-11 *Superscript Formatting*

A subscript may be used as follows:

$$Y = 5X_2 + 3X_1 + X_0 + 5$$

```
File: CH3.5                    REVIEW/ADD/CHANGE              Escape: Main Menu
====|====|====|====|====|====|====|====|====|====|====|====|====|====|====|===

A subscript may be used as follows:

--------Left Margin:  2.0 inches
--------Indent: 0 chars
              Y = 5X^2^ + 3X^1^ + X^0^ + 5


              or


--------Chars per Inch: 8 chars
              ^"I finally know what distinguishes^
              ^ man from the other beasts:^
              ^ financial worries."^2^^

              2 - JULES RENARD, ^Journal^ (1887-1910)
--------Chars per Inch: 12 chars
--------Left Margin:  0.5 inches



---------------------------------------------------------------------------
Type entry or use @ commands              Line 122  Column  1        @-? for Help
```

Figure 3-12 *Subscript Formatting*

or

   "I finally know what distinguishes man from the other beasts: financial worries."$_2$
   2—Jules Renard, *Journal* (1887–1910)

   Notice in Figs. 3-11 and 3-12 that a number of CARETs are spread throughout the
screen. Some of the CARET pairs signify boldface printing, others signify underlining,
and others represent superscripting or subscripting.
   What Figs. 3-11 and 3-12 really show is how you may combine the different capabilities of the word processor to effect different and sometimes dramatic presentations of text
material in a document.

Caution: Your printer must be able to support both superscripting and
subscripting. This means that the printer roller, paper, and tractors
must be able to be repositioned vertically through software control.

   Another characteristic of research papers is the use of page headers and footers. A
page header is a single line of text that appears within the specified top margin setting. A

page footer is a single line of text that appears within the bottom margin setting. Of course, anything you want can appear on these lines. Normally, manuscript identification information will be placed in headers and footers. For example, you could use any or all of the following:

- Document identification. This entry identifies the complete document, such as a book title.
- Document section. This entry identifies the particular section of the document. This could be the chapter or section name.
- Date and time information. This entry could be the date the document is first created, modified, or printed.
- Page number.
- Author.
- Document classification. This entry identifies the document classification, such as CONFIDENTIAL, SECRET, etc.

To specify headers, footers, and page numbers:

1. Place the cursor where you want the headers, footers, and page numbers to be positioned.
2. Press OPEN-APPLE Z (zoom-in command).
3. Press OPEN-APPLE O. This activates the printer options menu.
4. Enter PN (page numbers option) in response to the prompt message and press the RETURN key. Enter the page number in response to the prompt message. Use the ESCape key to exit from the printer options menu.
5. Enter HE (page header option) in response to the prompt message and press the RETURN key. Use the ESCape key to exit from the options menu. Enter the header line immediately after the page header options entry.
6. Enter FO (page footer option) in response to the prompt message and press the RETURN key. Use the ESCape key to exit from the options menu. Enter the footer line immediately after the page footer options entry. In the case of the example in Fig. 3-13, place the cursor on the line where you want the page number printed. Use the options menu selection PP to have the page number printed at that position on the footer line.

```
--------Page Number: 1
--------Page Header
Appleworks Book              Chapter 3              Date: 04/25/84
--------Page Footer
                             Page 3- ^
```

Figure 3-13 *Page Header, Footer, and Number Example*

Examples of headers, footers, and page number entries are shown in Fig. 3-13.

Although header, footer, and page number entries may be placed anywhere within a document, it is recommended that they be placed at the beginning of the document with all of the other printer option information. The caret in the page footer line is for the printing of page numbers. It is recommended that you calculate page numbers, using OPEN-APPLE K, so you will know where to place headers and footers. Once you have placed a header or footer into a document, it remains in effect, during printing, until you make a change to the header or footer.

Another very handy feature of the word processor is the grouping option. Grouping text means placing information on one page or on adjacent pages. AppleWorks will calculate the amount of space required to hold the grouped information. If the information can be placed on the current page, it is placed there. If not, the grouped information is started on the next page.

To specify groups:

1. Place the cursor where you want the grouping to begin.

2. Press OPEN-APPLE O. This activates the printer options menu.

3. Enter GB (Group Begin) in response to the prompt message and press the RETURN key. Use the ESCape key to exit from the printer options menu.

4. Place the cursor where you want the grouping to end.

5. Enter GE (Group End) in response to the prompt message and press the RETURN key. Use the ESCape key to exit from the options menu.

Hanging paragraphs or bulleted paragraphs are often used for presenting lists. To create hanging paragraphs:

1. Place the cursor along the left margin, where the list is to begin.

2. Press OPEN-APPLE Z. This will put you in the zoom-in mode.

3. Press OPEN-APPLE O. This will activate the printer options menu.

4. Specify the new left margin for the list where each item in the list will start. Use the LM printer option.

5. Define the number of characters the body of the text should be indented on each line of a paragraph. Use the IN printer option.

6. Start each item in the list with a lower case o, a plus sign (+), a minus sign (−), an asterisk (*), or a number.

Some general typing and formatting tips for research papers follow:

When typing one-page reports, arrange the material so that it will be proportional to the dimensions of the paper. The side margins should be equal. The bottom margin should be a little larger than the top margin.

The top margin on the first page and chapter pages of an unbound manuscript is normally 2″, 1″ on other pages. The minimum side and bottom margins are usually

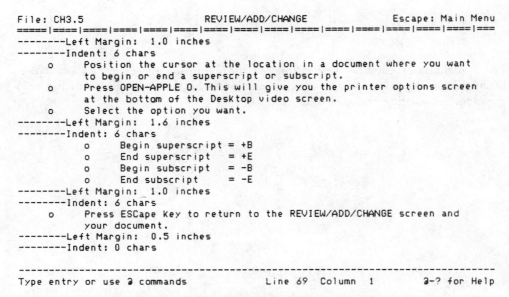

```
File: CH3.5                    REVIEW/ADD/CHANGE              Escape: Main Menu
=====|====|====|====|====|====|====|====|====|====|====|====|====|====|====|===
--------Left Margin:  1.0 inches
--------Indent: 6 chars
     o      Position the cursor at the location in a document where you want
            to begin or end a superscript or subscript.
     o      Press OPEN-APPLE O. This will give you the printer options screen
            at the bottom of the Desktop video screen.
     o      Select the option you want.
--------Left Margin:  1.6 inches
--------Indent: 6 chars
            o     Begin superscript = +B
            o     End superscript   = +E
            o     Begin subscript   = -B
            o     End subscript     = -E
--------Left Margin:  1.0 inches
--------Indent: 6 chars
     o      Press ESCape key to return to the REVIEW/ADD/CHANGE screen and
            your document.
--------Left Margin:  0.5 inches
--------Indent: 0 chars


-------------------------------------------------------------------------------
Type entry or use ∂ commands           Line 69  Column  1        ∂-? for Help
```

Figure 3-14 *Hanging Paragraphs Example*

1″. If the manuscript is to be bound at the top, the first page should have a top margin of 2½″ with all continuation pages having a top margin of 1½″. If the manuscript is to be bound on the left edge, the left margin should be set to 1½″.

You should triple space after the heading on any page and before any major sub-heading. The body of the manuscript should generally be double spaced. Quotations, tables, and footnotes are normally single spaced.

When typing a report or research paper, get manuscript specifications. Some instructors prefer specific margin settings, footnote styles, etc.

Reports and manuscripts that are to be done on "blue line" paper must always correspond to the margin constraints. Blue line means paper that has a solid blue line around the edges, specifying margin settings.

Footnotes that go at the bottom of a page should be single spaced with a blank line above and below the footnote. Footnotes can be further separated from the body of the text by an underscore across the bottom of the page.

3.6 SUMMARY

This chapter described how to format a number of different documents using the word processor. These documents were:

- Interoffice memos
- Business letters
- Invitations

- Newsletters and articles
- Research papers

Additional capabilities were introduced, including tabbing, adding headers, footers, and page numbers, grouping, pausing, superscripting and subscripting, underlining, bold-facing, and hanging paragraphs.

PART THREE

A man has one hundred dollars and you leave him with two dollars, that's subtraction.
MAE WEST, 1940

Solving mathematical problems using computers has been around since the development of the first computer. Solving extensive mathematical problems were still tedious and time consuming, however. Each problem required a new, distinct computer program. With the development of spreadsheet programs, solving mathematical problems using computers has been greatly simplified. Part 3 explains the spreadsheet.

CHAPTER FOUR

The Spreadsheet

*My life is a bubble; but how much solid cash it costs to keep
that bubble floating.*
LOGAN PEARSALL, 1931

4.0 OVERVIEW

This chapter examines the second of the AppleWorks application programs, the spreadsheet. You can use the spreadsheet to prepare financial summaries, balance checkbooks, calculate taxes, solve equations, estimate costs, project sales, or perform almost any form of mathematical manipulation.

Working with a spreadsheet is one of the most versatile means of solving complex mathematical functions on your computer. But it does require you to learn to develop templates.

A template defines the set of instructions to the spreadsheet program. The program in turn uses these instructions to perform the specified mathematics; to manipulate the predefined values, formulas, or mathematical functions; and to generate a product or answer for the task to be accomplished or the problem to be solved. In this chapter we will refer to the uncompleted template as a worksheet.

This chapter discusses the techniques used in building templates. It shows you the commands needed to get the Spreadsheet on the Desktop screen, and manipulate it to produce some useful work. You will build your first template in this chapter and become familiar with making entries into the spreadsheet program.

4.1 WHAT IS A SPREADSHEET?

A spreadsheet is an electronic sheet of ledger paper that lets you work with numerical information. It contains columns and rows of blank cells, each of which may contain labels, numbers, mathematical formulas, or functions. The Spreadsheet program can maintain up to 999 rows and up to 127 columns of information. This corresponds to 126,873 empty cells that will accept individual entries.

One of the advantages a spreadsheet has over a structured, stand-alone program package is the ability to recalculate automatically when new information is supplied. This allows you to change the information in the spreadsheet over and over, until you have the results that you want or until you have explored numerous possibilities. The modified spreadsheet immediately recalculates, giving a new result as soon as an entry is made in a cell. A stand-alone program package usually allows for only limited recalculation capability.

The spreadsheet has the following addressing scheme for rows, columns, and cells: Every column is designated by a letter of the alphabet. Each row is designated by a number. The intersection of a column with a row is a cell. All cells are designated by their column–row designators. For example, the upper left-hand corner cell of a spreadsheet is A1. The cell located at the intersection of the sixth column with the twelfth row is designated F12. (See Fig 4-1.)

The activity flow of the spreadsheet program is shown in Fig. 4-2.

The spreadsheet allows you to review, add, or change the contents of cells. Normally, you will enter all of the information first and then format the printed report. When all of this work is done, you have a template.

A template for a spreadsheet program does not need to be reproduced every time you want to do calculations. Only the numeric values may need to be changed as conditions change. This will save you a lot of work and time in performing mathematical tasks. If

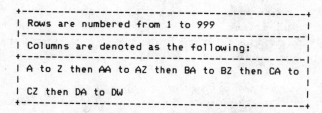

Figure 4-1 *AppleWorks Cell Designators*

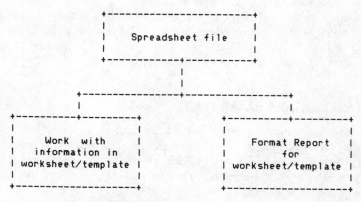

Figure 4-2 *Activity Flow Chart*

your template designs have been completed correctly, you will find yourself using just a few templates to complete all of your tasks.

A well-designed template should include all the capabilities needed to create master templates. Master templates should include all of the mathematics, functions, and pointers needed to perform the task, but should not have any numerical values entered. Values should be entered only when a computation is needed.

4.2 PLANNING A SPREADSHEET TEMPLATE

Planning the form of the problem presentation and actually implementing the plan is as important as, if not more important than, entering the data.

When you plan a worksheet/template, you must decide several things:

- What task is to be performed?
- What answer do you expect or require?
- What values, formulas, functions, and/or procedures will produce the required results?
- What display format is to be used with values, formulas, and functions?
- What order is to be used for calculations?
- How will the printed report look?
- How will the screen format look?
- What documentation is required to support your template?

These questions will be discussed in detail as we get into the designing of templates. To help in the designing, several useful figures are given throughout the chapter.

Of course, before you can design a template, you must know what task or function you wish the program to do, as well as how to obtain the results. Then, to get the program to execute the function, you need to write a formula. A *formula* is simply a "sentence" telling the program which mathematical operations to perform on a given set of numbers.

One of the first steps in planning a template is to know what answers, for a simple case, you require. Knowing the answer, for a simple case, will make all of the succeeding steps a lot easier. Most of us, who want to start using the spreadsheet, already know the answers wanted or required to the problem. What you hope to accomplish is a faster, more accurate means of completing the work without having to duplicate and repeat everything each time.

Step two is to define and specify the mathematics to be used to perform your work and solve the task at hand. This includes the defining of labels, values, formulas, pointers, and functions that will be needed to compute the problem solution:

- *Labels* are alphabetic or numeric characters used to identify information or titles within a template.

- *Values* are numerical information, including numbers, pointers, formulas, and functions within a template.
- *Pointers* are values that lead to other value constants in a template. They are preceeded by either a + or − sign. They are normally a cell location designator.
- *Formulas* are mathematical statements representing combinations of values, pointers, and functions. They define the desired set of calculations to be performed within a template.
- *Functions* are code symbols that represent a set of spreadsheet built-in mathematical calculations.

Step three is to define the format for the numbers used as values and formulas. These formats define the number of decimal places in a number, justification left or right in a cell, and the column width to be used in each cell element of a template.

Step four is to define the order of the calculations to be performed. Order refers to whether to perform calculations on columns or rows, the line of calculations, and the frequency of calculations. The line of calculation is either from top left to bottom right when using the column order or left to right when using the row order. The frequency of calculations means whether calculations are automatic or manual. The default settings are column calculations carried out automatically.

Step five is to define the printed report. This design consideration is placed before the screen formatting considerations because you want your work to look nice and neat, page breaks to be located correctly, and important data to be printed on specific lines.

Steps six and seven define the screen formatting of information and the documentation included in the template. Here you are concerned with the readability and understandability of your template, as well as the instructions on how to use the template. No matter who you are, if you do not use your template frequently, you will forget the purpose of your template and what it accomplishes. So, documenting the template, within the template, is very important when planning, designing, and implementing spreadsheet templates.

If you are new to using spreadsheet programs, worksheets, or templates, you need to learn how to start building a worksheet or template from scratch. A template, in its simplest form, is like a ledger sheet or piece of paper with rows and columns that are used to enter data. Each row and column is usually given a title or label that identifies the information entered into each element in the ledger sheet.

To generate a worksheet or template you should follow some sort of an outline. This has been the general thrust of giving you specific steps to follow. By following the preceding steps, your thought processes are structured and, hopefully, the outline for the template will become clear. This outline will reflect, of course, the task or job you plan on accomplishing.

As an example, assume the task to be accomplished is a personal financial statement for your banker. The design considerations for the personal financial statement are:

- First, you will need a template header or title. A header identifies the template. The header is normally centered horizontally on the page in the top margin. A three-or-four-line header should normally be sufficient. The template instructions location may also be included in the header.

- You will have at least four parts in your financial statement. These are header, current assets, current liabilities, and owner's equity.

- The labels column, usually along the left edge of the template, should be wide enough to handle the longest label, about thirty characters wide in this case.

- Two columns of numbers will be required, a detail column and a total column, with a width of ten to fifteen characters, including two decimal places and a decimal point. The final width depends upon the maximum size of the dollars and cents amounts to be entered in these two columns.

- The display format for numbers will contain a decimal point and two decimal places because of the nature of the numbers being entered.

- You will need to determine the mathematical functions to be used. For example, you will need to add and subtract groups of numbers.

Figure 4-3 shows the personal financial statement formatting that has just been described.

Instructions for the use of the template:

1. Enter the name and current date of the financial statement.

2. Enter all of your asset dollar amounts.

3. Enter all of your liability dollar amounts.

The specific cell entries for this template will be shown later.

4.3 STARTING A SPREADSHEET TEMPLATE

To start using the spreadsheet program, you must first learn how to load it into memory from the AppleWorks Main Menu. Once you have loaded the program you can begin entering information into a worksheet or template. We will use the template outline discussed above.

To start a worksheet, start at the Main Menu of AppleWorks. (See Section 1.4.1.) Your display will be as shown in Fig. 1-3. The abbreviated procedure is given here for quick reference.

To create a new spreadsheet:

1. Choose option 1, "Add files to the Desktop" from Main Menu.

2. Choose option 5, "Spreadsheet" from Add Files screen.

```
For spreadsheet template instructions, Press OPEN-APPLE 9.
==================================================================
                        Personal Financial Statement

                            Sam & Linda Redden

                                   As of

                            January 1, 1984


            ASSETS:

    Current Assets

                    Income....................    $0.00
                    Commissions...............    $0.00
                    First Saving and Loan......   $0.00
                    Stocks and Bonds..........    $0.00
                    Waco Bank and Trust - Auto    $0.00
                    Pioneer Saving Home Loan...   $0.00
                    Waco Bank and Trust - Auto    $0.00
                    Waco Bank and Trust - Auto    $0.00
                    Computer and equipment.....   $0.00
                    Home furinure.............    $0.00
                                                -------------
    Total Assets.......................................   $0.00
                                                =============


                        LIABILITIES :

    Current Liabilities

                    Waco Bank and Trust - Auto    $0.00
                    Waco Bank and Trust - Auto    $0.00
                    Pioneer Saving Home Loan...   $0.00
                                                -------------
    Total Liabilities.................................   $0.00
                                                =============


                        OWNER'S EQUITY :

    S. R. REDDEN EQUITY...............................   $0.00
                                                -------------

    TOTAL NET WORTH AND LIABILITIES...................   $0.00
                                                =============


    _____              _____
        Signature                                   Date
```

Figure 4-3   *Net Worth Statement Template*

3. Choose option 1, "From scratch."

4. Name the new document.

The spreadsheet, like the word processor, will accept up to fifteen characters as a file name. No special characters are allowed. It is recommended that you use periods to separate parts of file names. Enter the name for the personal financial statement and press the RETURN key.

After the file has been given a name, AppleWorks creates a temporary file in memory for the new worksheet. A blank worksheet will appear on your video screen ready for you to start entering information, as shown in Fig. 4-4.

You are almost ready to make entries into the worksheet on the Desktop.

4.4 THE CURSOR

Before making entries into cells, you need to know about the cursors used within the spreadsheet.

There are three cursors used in the spreadsheet program:

- The large rectangular cursor highlights the intersection of a row and column, a cell. This is your current location in the worksheet. This cursor is the width of a column (nine characters) when starting the worksheet from scratch.

```
File: BLANK                    REVIEW/ADD/CHANGE                 Escape: Main Menu
========A=======B=======C=======D=======E=======F=======G=======H===
  1|
  2|
  3|
  4|
  5|
  6|
  7|
  8|
  9|
 10|
 11|
 12|
 13|
 14|
 15|
 16|
 17|
 18|
----------------------------------------------------------------------
A1

Type entry or use 크 commands                              크-? for Help
```

Figure 4-4   Blank Spreadsheet Screen

- The second cursor is the blinking underline bar, known as the insert cursor.
- The third cursor is the blinking rectangular cursor, known as the overstrike cursor.

The last two cursors mark the location where all new entries will occur on the command line. You may switch between these two cursors by using OPEN-APPLE E, editing command. (See Section 9.1.5.)

The cursor at the bottom of the screen display requires a response from the operator. It is always one character wide. It can be either the insert or overstrike cursor, depending upon which you have selected.

- When you see the blinking underline bar (insert cursor), whatever character you type is moved to the left of the cursor position and all other characters to the right of the cursor are moved one position to the right along with the cursor. That is, the character that is typed is moved to the left as the cursor is moved to the right along with all other characters.
- When you see the blinking rectangle (overstrike cursor), whatever character you type replaces the character under the cursor. The cursor is then moved to the right one character.

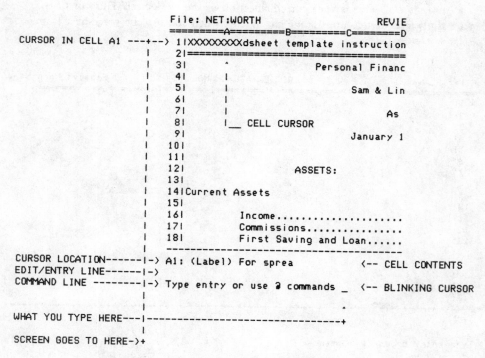

Figure 4-5 *Cursor Locations*

Whatever you type into the bottom display also is placed into the cell marked by the highlighted cursor in the worksheet. If you type more characters than there are spaces in that cell, the highlighted cursor moves to the next cell on the right and will become highlighted. If you try to enter characters into a protected cell, the spreadsheet will halt at that cell and accept no more information. A protected cell is one that will not accept new information. See Fig. 4-5 for cursor locations.

Most of the cursor movement keystrokes in the spreadsheet are the same as in the data base and the word processor. There are three ways to move around in a spreadsheet worksheet or template: You can use the arrow keys or the Ruler, or you can specify the coordinate location of a cell.

The arrow keys are located on the bottom line of keys near the right-hand corner of the keyboard. To use the arrow keys, press the key that corresponds to the direction you want to move. This will move the cursor one cell at a time in that direction.

If you press the OPEN-APPLE arrow-key keystroke combination, the cursor will move to the edge of the screen. (See Sections 9.2.2 through 9.2.5.) By repeating the keystroke combination, the cursor will jump a full screen in the arrow-key direction. These methods of cursor movement are shown in the table below.

KEYSTROKE	KEYSTROKE MEANING	CURSOR MOVEMENT
←	Left arrow	Left one position
→	Right arrow	Right one position
↑	Up arrow	Up one screen line
↓	Down arrow	Down one screen line
O-A ←	O-A Left arrow	Left edge of screen
O-A →	O-A Right arrow	Right edge of screen
O-A ↑	O-A Up arrow	Top of screen
O-A ↓	O-A Down arrow	Bottom of screen
O-A 1	O-A number 1	Top of template
O-A 5	O-A number 5	Middle of template
O-A 9	O-A number 9	Bottom of template

You can use the Ruler to move several cells at a time. Press and hold the OPEN-APPLE number keystroke combination. This is the Ruler command. (See Section 9.2.1.) You can now move proportionally through the worksheet. If you are at cell location A1 and press the OPEN-APPLE 5 keystroke combination, you will move to the middle of your template. The Ruler capability moves in only two directions—up and down. The Ruler capability is a fast way to scroll back and forth through your worksheet. If you want to go to cell location A1, use OPEN-APPLE 1; to go to the bottom of the worksheet, use OPEN-APPLE 9.

The coordinate method capability is used to define the cell location you want to find directly. This is done by using the OPEN-APPLE F, find command. (See Section 2.1.6.) You are then presented a command line at the bottom of the screen which asks for an entry. Choose *Coordinates,* then enter the coordinates of the cell and press the RETURN key. The cursor will be immediately placed at that cell location.

4.5 THE WINDOW

When you talk about a window in the spreadsheet you are describing the cells that contain information seen on the video screen. The spreadsheet allows a maximum of 126,873 cells. With this many cells, there is no way to display the entire worksheet all at once. So you must look at only segments or portions of the worksheet, the size of a window. The maximum size of a single window can be 72 characters wide by 18 lines deep. Figure 4-6 shows a possible single-window worksheet.

You can also have two windows, split screens, presented at the same time, either

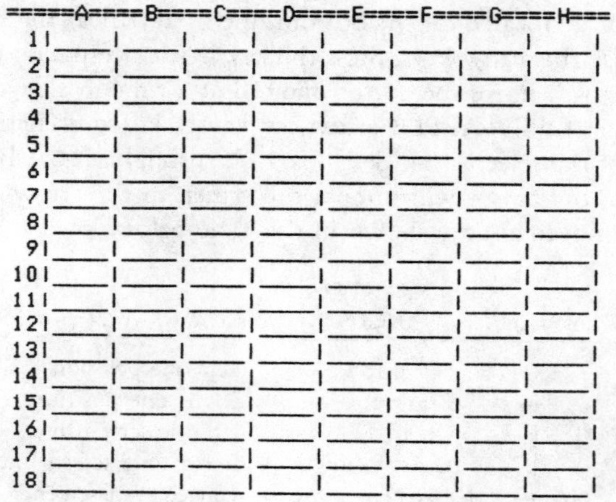

Figure 4-6   Single Window Worksheet

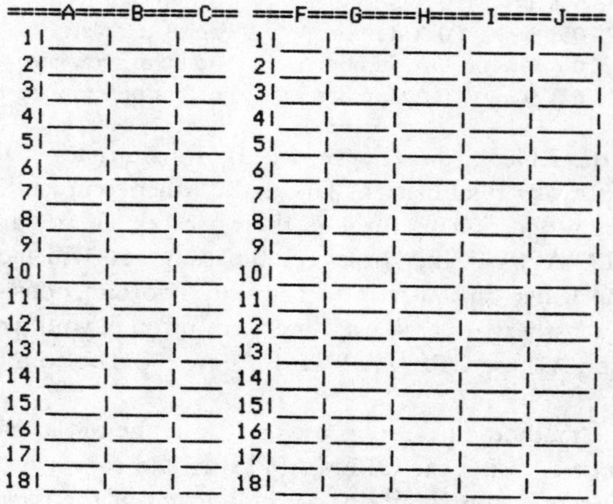

Figure 4-7   Side-by-Side Windows

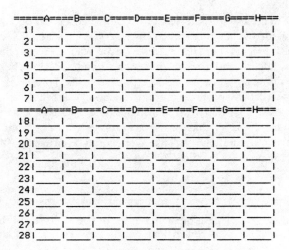

Figure 4-8   *Top-and-Bottom Windows*

side-by-side windows or top-and-bottom windows. For example, you can have windows that look like those shown in Figs. 4-7 and 4-8.

By being able to split the screen presentation into windows, you are able to see different portions of a template at the same time. This is handy when you are entering information into a template that depends upon previous information located a large distance from the present information being entered. For example, if you are entering information into column L and you need to see the labels in column A, split the screen vertically.

When you have finished making entries in one window, you may want to make or edit entries in the other window. As you scroll the cursor within a window, you may also want to have both windows scroll in-step, synchronized. This is done by using the OPEN-APPLE W command to activate the split-screen capability, and then using OPEN-APPLE W again to cause both windows to scroll synchronously. You can jump between windows by using the OPEN-APPLE J command. When you want to return to unsynchronized windows, use the OPEN-APPLE W command again. (See Chapter 9 for these procedures.)

4.6 MAKING ENTRIES

The spreadsheet cell display can hold any one of the five different types of entries—labels, values, formulas, functions, or cell pointers.

4.6.1 Entering Labels

A label is a piece of information which does not represent a numeric value, and therefore cannot be used in mathematical operations. Labels are used mainly for column and row headings.

A label may contain any set of letters of the alphabet, capital or lowercase, and numbers 0 through 9, or any of the other special characters, such as !@#$%^&*()(+?><, that can be generated from the Apple IIe or Apple IIc keyboard. (See Appendix G.)

All entries that start with letters of the alphabet and contain other letters are labels. Only letters of the alphabet can be directly accepted as labels. To use any other character as the first character of a label, you must first enter a quotation mark before the rest of the entry will be accepted as a label. This signals that you are starting a label with a character not normally considered a label character. For example, you may want 1984 to be a column label rather than a numeric value. That label would be entered as "1984. Examples of labels are shown in Figs. 4-3, 4-5, and 4-14.

Tip: When entering labels, press any letter of the alphabet as the first character of the label. If you make a typing mistake, use the DELETE key.

If a label is too long to fit into just one cell, AppleWorks will automatically expand the entry into the next cell and continue doing so until it reaches a maximum length of 72 characters. If AppleWorks encounters a protected cell, it will not expand the entry any further. When making cell entries, the cell pointer at the bottom left of the screen indicates that the entry made into the cell is a label.

Label formats are available as either left- or right-justified or centered. (See Fig. 4-9.) These may be set using the OPEN-APPLE L or OPEN-APPLE V commands. (See Chapter 9.)

4.6.2 Entering Values

A value is a numeric piece of data which can be used in mathematical operations.

Numeric entries are directly accepted as values. That means, if you enter 123 into a cell location, it is placed into that cell as a value without any format conversions. Values must start with any one of the digits, 0 through 9, or a plus sign, a minus sign, or a decimal point. For example, 9876, +234, —9876, and .54 are all valid value entries.

```
+-----------------------------------------------------+
|    Format       |      Examples                     |
|-----------------------------------------------------|
| Left justified  |January                            |
|                 |                                   |
| Right justified |                          January  |
|                 |                                   |
| Centered        |            January                |
+-----------------------------------------------------+
```

Figure 4-9 *Label Formats*

```
+--------------------+
| Values  | Pointers |
|--------------------|
| 123.00  | +A12     |
| 123     | +E12     |
| -123    | -H12     |
| .123    | -E12     |
+--------------------+
```

Figure 4-10 *Values and Pointers*

4.6.3 Entering Pointers

A pointer specifies, or points to, another cell in a worksheet or template. The pointer instructs the program that a value from some cell within the worksheet will be used to do a calculation in another cell. AppleWorks takes the value in the cell being pointed to and places it into the current cell. That means, AppleWorks takes the value from one cell and duplicates the exact information into the cell you specify. Pointers require a plus or minus sign before the cell coordinates of the cell being pointed to. For example, +A1, +E155, and —C88 are all valid pointer entries. (See Fig. 4-10.)

Tip: After you have entered the plus or minus sign entry you are allowed to use the arrow keys to point to a cell. Then press the RETURN key or another plus or minus sign. In this way, you may build up a formula easily and quickly. When finished, press the RETURN key.

4.6.4. Entering Functions and Formulas

The spreadsheet can perform simple or complex functions through the use of codes entered by the template designer. Functions built in to the program include the integer (whole number) value of a numeric quantity (INT), the logarithm (LOG), and the total of a range of numbers (SUM).

A function entry is made up of three parts: the @ function header, the function code that represents the function, and the function arguments. A listing and explanation of the built-in functions are found in Chapter 5.

To enter functions into templates, first enter the header character symbol. Next, enter the function code. Finally, enter any required function arguments enclosed in parentheses. For example, see the functions entered in Fig. 4-11.

```
+------------------------------------+
| 1.  @SUM(A12...A32)                |
|                                    |
| 2.  @MAX(A12,B12)-@MIN(A12,B12)    |
+------------------------------------+
```

Figure 4-11 *Function Examples*

The last type of value that can be used in a template is the formula. Formulas are mathematical statements that are used to calculate number values. Formulas may consist of any combination of two or more of the following:

Numbers. For example, 123, 45.67, or 44.3456.

Arithmetic operators. For example, addition (+), subtraction (−), multiplication (*), division (/), and exponentiation (^).

Pointers. For example, +A1, −B45, +C22.

Functions. For example, @AVG(123,+A22,44.67), @INT(123.45).

Formulas do not require a lead-in or header character. Formulas must begin with a plus sign, a minus sign, a decimal point, the digits 0 through 9, a left or right parenthesis, or the "at" sign (@). The cell indicator, in the lower left portion of the screen, tells you that a formula is a value and is being entered. Examples of formulas are shown in Fig. 4-12.

Notice that a formula may contain one or more functions. There is a set order in which these operations are performed. Working from the left to the right of the formula, exponentiation is performed first. Next, multiplication and division are executed, then addition and subtraction. Operations contained within parentheses are performed first; then the standard order of operations is followed. (See Fig. 4-13.)

Tip: If you want to see all of the formulas in every cell, use the OPEN-APPLE Z, zoom-in command. (See Section 9.1.25.) However, only that portion of a formula that fits within the width of a cell is shown. Using OPEN-APPLE Z again returns the template cells to their normal appearance.

```
+----------------------------------------+
| 1.    125.50 * 120 / 12 + A14          |
|                                        |
| 2.    ((12 X 35) - 18 * 18) - C32      |
|                                        |
| 3.    @SUM(C11...C44) + B22 - F12      |
+----------------------------------------+
```

Figure 4-12   *Formula Examples*

```
+----------------------------------+
| 1.  +A15 * +B33 / +A12 + C22     |
|                                  |
| 2.  -A15 * +B33 * +A12 + C22     |
+----------------------------------+
```

Figure 4-13   *Pointer Examples*

Now that you have a small glimpse into what can be entered into worksheet or template cells, look again at the blank worksheet in Fig. 4-4. This is what the spreadsheet worksheet looks like when it first appears on the screen. The large cursor will be located in cell A1, the row 1-column 1 cell position. The top line of the screen shows the name of the file in the upper left-hand corner. The bottom portion of the screen shows you that the OPEN-APPLE ? keystroke combination, the help command, is active, the cursor is at cell A1, and you can type an entry or use the OPEN-APPLE command keys. This last item on the screen is the command line. All data entered into a worksheet is first placed on this line until the RETURN key is pressed.

Figure 4-14 shows a practical, partial master template that could be called NET.WORTH or FINANCIAL.STMT. The asset dollar column is set to two decimal places and has only zero's entered. The total assets row has the @SUM function entered which will total the asset column of numbers. This is done so that later, you can use the template for any net worth calculations or for a personal financial statement. In this case you would only have to change the template header which identifies whose statement it is and the date of preparation.

> **Tip:** Notice that the @SUM function includes all of the individual ASSET items plus an additional item. The reason for this is so that you may add more individual items, starting in row 26. The @SUM function arguments will then automatically readjust for the added items.

4.6.5 Editing Entries

Since everyone makes typing errors, the editing capability of individual cell entries is very handy. Anytime you need to edit the contents of a cell, place the cursor on that cell, using

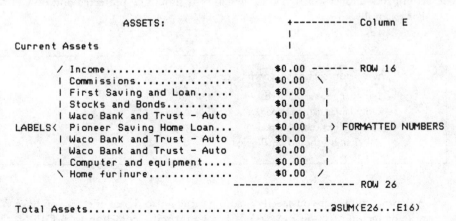

Figure 4-14 Practical Master Template

the arrow keys, and then use the OPEN-APPLE U, edit command. (See Section 9.1.21.) The cursor will then be placed at the beginning of the cell entry on the edit line of the video screen. You may now use either of the normal cursors to edit the cell entry. When you have finished making changes to the cell contents, press the RETURN key. The template is then recalculated automatically. You are then ready to continue editing or adding entries.

Before proceeding further with the development of the personal financial statement template, we would like to digress a bit and discuss standard values and individual cell layouts.

4.7 STANDARD VALUES

Like the word processor described in the last two chapters, there are certain default settings active when the spreadsheet is first activated. These default settings are called *Current setting of standard values.* These can be seen by using the OPEN-APPLE ? keystroke combination. See Fig. 4-15.

Scroll to the bottom of the help screen, using the up/down arrow keys. As you scroll down the list, you will be moving through all of the help screen commands. All of these commands are preceded by the OPEN-APPLE key plus a letter. They may be used directly from the REVIEW/ADD/CHANGE screen. That is, as you enter data into your template you can call on any of these commands by entering the OPEN-APPLE command plus the letter required for that command. These commands are explained in Chapter 9.

Each of the above standard value settings will be discussed in the next few paragraphs.

- Protection is set to ON. This prohibits certain kinds of changes to be made to cell contents in a template. The OPEN-APPLE L, record layout command, allows you to specify which cells should be protected and how. For example:

Tip: The option settings allowed are:

—No changes are allowed.
—Only labels can be typed.
—Only values can be typed.
—All changes should be allowed.

Any protection that you specify is automatically placed into effect if you have not changed protection to "No." When you specify protection with OPEN-APPLE L, only those cells with entries or layouts will be protected.

- The labels format is set to left justify for all entries in a cell.
- The values format is set to fixed decimal with zero decimal places. This means that all entries in a cell will be displayed exactly as you entered them. There are no global numeric formats to be set.
- The default frequency is set to recalculate all entries automatically when an entry is made. The option for the frequency of recalculation can be either automatic or manual.
- The default calculation order is set to columns. This means that calculations will be from the first entry in the first column on the left, down the first column to the bottom. Then, move to the top of the next column on the right, calculating entries to the bottom of that column. Continue until all columns have been recalculated.

Changing any of these settings must be done while you are working on a template. Remember, you can always check the standard values that are in effect by using the OPEN-APPLE ? command.

In addition, you can use the OPEN-APPLE V, standard value command, to change standard values that affect an entire template. This command makes global changes. Other spreadsheet programs use the term global for making changes that affect an entire template.

4.8 CELL LAYOUTS

The OPEN-APPLE L, layout command, lets you change the standard settings of cell layouts individually, in columns, in rows, or in blocks of cells.

Six value formats are available for a spreadsheet template or worksheet—standard, appropriate, fixed, dollars, commmas, and percent. *Standard* format resets individual cells or groups of cells back to the standard number display for the template. *Appropriate* format displays numbers just as you enter them. Numbers are left justified in their columns with a blank in the leftmost column, and trailing zeroes dropped. *Dollars* format sets numbers to include two decimal places and a decimal point. The *commas* format displays numbers with commas in their appropriate places, if the number is large enough. *Percent* formats a

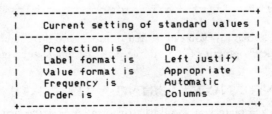

```
+------------------------------------------+
|   Current setting of standard values     |
|------------------------------------------|
|   Protection is        On                |
|   Label format is      Left justify      |
|   Value format is      Appropriate       |
|   Frequency is         Automatic         |
|   Order is             Columns           |
+------------------------------------------+
```

Figure 4-15   *Current Setting of Standard Values*

```
+-------------------------------------------------------------------+
| Format      | Examples of usage | Description of the format       |
+-------------+-------------------+---------------------------------+
| Fixed       |      123.00       | Contains a fixed number of      |
|             |      123          | decimal places, 0-7.            |
|             |     1234.5678     |                                 |
|             |   12345.6789012   |                                 |
|             |                   |                                 |
| Dollars     | $123,000.00       | Same format as commas           |
|             |    ($123.00)      | except dollar sign is added     |
|             |     $123.00       | to the number format.           |
|             |        $.13       | Negative numbers are shown      |
|             |  ($1,234.56)      | placed in brackets.             |
|             |                   |                                 |
| Commas      |  123,000.00       | Places commas between           |
|             |     (123.00)      | thousands. Negative numbers     |
|             |      123.13       | are placed in brackets and      |
|             |    1,234.56       | contain fixed decimal           |
|             |   12,345.56789    | places 0-7.                     |
|             |                   |                                 |
| Percent     |     123.13%       | Percentage sign added and       |
|             |      -1.23%       | contains the set number of      |
|             |      50.0%        | decimal places.                 |
|             |                   |                                 |
| Standard    |      1234         | Columns are 9 spaces wide.      |
|             |      1234.5       | Fixed decimal, 0 decimal        |
|             |      1234.56      | places.                         |
|             |      Scores       | Labels are left justified.      |
+-------------+-------------------+---------------------------------+
```

Figure 4-16   Value Format Examples

number with a percentage sign following the number. Figure 4-16 shows you examples of formats.

Column widths can be set in the spreadsheet from 2 to 75 characters.

Tip: It is recommended that you make your columns wide enough to accommodate the maximum number you expect to handle in that column, including characters like the decimal point, comma, and dollar sign. If a column width is too narrow for the number, then a series of pound signs, # # # #, are placed in that cell location.

Now that you know how you can format numbers and how standard values work, we can return to the development of the sample personal financial statement.

4.9 DESIGNING AND ENTERING A TEMPLATE

When designing a template you should list information in the order it will be needed. This is the presentation or appearance order of the template.

```
+----------------------------------------------------+
I o Location of the template instruction.            I
I                                                    I
I o Name of the template.                            I
I                                                    I
I o Who is the financial statement for?              I
I                                                    I
I o Date of the statement.                           I
I                                                    I
I o Categories of the financial data.                I
I                                                    I
I o Individual titles for each of your categories.   I
I                                                    I
I o Individual titles for your dollar amounts.        I
I                                                    I
I o Signature and date line at the bottom            I
I   of your financial statement.                     I
+----------------------------------------------------+
```

Figure 4-17   Information List

You should begin at the top and work down to the end of the template.

The list shown in Fig. 4-17 is the complete personal financial statement outline that is going to be entered as a template. Sometimes, it is easier to enter information for the first time if you have some sort of guide to follow. Look at Fig. 4-18 before you start to make entries.

Refer to Section 4.3 for instructions on how to start a template from scratch. First, enter all of the label information found in Fig. 4-18. Then enter the mathematics to be performed, cell layouts to be used, and the funcions into your template. Information can be entered into a template either by rows or columns. We have found that entering information by columns is easier for us. You may find entering complete rows is easier.

Follow the outline of Fig. 4-19 and start entering information into the template.

4.10 IMPLEMENTING THE TEMPLATE DESIGN

What is "implementing"? The dictionary defines it as "putting into effect according to a procedure." What you are doing with your template is implementing the design. You are setting up the procedure that AppleWorks is to follow in the template to produce the required results.

The task at hand will be solved with labels, formulas, functions, values, and pointers. This alone may give the results and answers to your problems, but are they the correct ones? Chances are, you will obtain the correct results because you usually already know the results you want. There are a few procedures that, if followed, will help obtain results that are correct, clearly understood, and easily modified. A few of these procedures are explained below.

Personal Financial Statement

Sam & Linda Redden

As of

January 1, 1984

ASSETS:

Current Assets

```
        Income...................... $22,000.00
        Commissions................  $4,800.00
        First Saving and Loan......  $5,700.00
        Stocks and Bonds...........  $3,300.00
        Waco Bank and Trust - Auto  $12,000.00
        Pioneer Saving Home Loan... $95,000.00
        Waco Bank and Trust - Auto   $5,600.00
        Waco Bank and Trust - Auto  $10,500.00
        Computer and equipment.....  $5,200.00
        Home furinure..............  $15,000.00
                                    --------------
Total Assets.....................................  $179,100.00
                                                   ==============
```

LIABILITIES :

Current Liabilities

```
        Waco Bank and Trust - Auto    $3,400.00
        Waco Bank and Trust - Auto    $8,200.00
        Pioneer Saving Home Loan...  $68,000.00
                                    --------------
Total Liabilities................................   $79,600.00
                                                   ==============
```

OWNER'S EQUITY :

```
S. R. REDDEN EQUITY...............................   $99,500.00
                                                   --------------

TOTAL NET WORTH AND LIABILITIES...................  $179,100.00
                                                   ==============
```

_____   _____

        Signature   Date

Instructions for the use of the template:

1. Enter the name and current date for the financial statement.
2. Enter all of your asset dollar amounts.
3. Enter all of your liability dollar amounts.

Figure 4-18 *Completed Master Template*

80

```
+---------------------------------------------------------------------+
| 1.  Move the cursor to cell A1 and enter the text header line,      |
|     "For Spreadsheet template instructions, Press OPEN-APPLE 9.",   |
|     across row 1.                                                   |
|                                                                     |
| 2.  Place the cursor at the correct cell, A2, within the template.  |
|                                                                     |
| 3.  Press the quotation mark key. This tells AppleWorks that you are|
|     entering a label. Press the equal sign, =, key and hold down until|
|     the cell is filled. This gives you a double dashed, barrier line |
|     that separates information in the template.                     |
|                                                                     |
| 4.  You are now going to copy your first entry into another set of cell|
|     locations in your template. Press OPEN-APPLE C keystroke combination|
|     for the copy capability. See Section 9.1.3. You will be asked where|
|     to copy to. Select Within worksheet. Now, highlight the source of |
|     the information to be copied, set to inverse, then press the RETURN|
|     key. Use the right arrow key to highlight to column C, then press |
|     the RETURN key. At this point in the copying process, you are asked|
|     to move to the new location. Continue copying cell A2 into cells B2|
|     through H2.                                                     |
|                                                                     |
| 5.  Move the cursor to cell C3 and enter the name of the template,  |
|     "Personal Financial Statement". Do the same thing for rows 5,7, and|
|     9 of your template, entering the appropriate labels. Use the    |
|     information in Figure 4-18 to complete all of the labels, down   |
|     through row 11.                                                 |
|                                                                     |
| 6.  Move the cursor to cell C12 and enter the label, "ASSETS:" in   |
|     upper case letters. Then move the cursor to cell A14 and enter the|
|     label "Current Assets".                                        |
|                                                                     |
| 7.  Move the cursor to cell B16 and enter the individual label titles|
|     for each of your asset categories. Do not enter any dollar amounts|
|     into cells at this time. These will be entered after all labels have|
|     been completed.                                                |
|                                                                     |
| 8.  Continue entering all of the remainder of the labels, rows 17   |
|     through 47, as shown in Figure 4-18.                           |
|                                                                     |
| 9.  Finish the template by entering the labels in rows 52 and 54 and |
|     the template instructions in rows 57 through 61.                |
+---------------------------------------------------------------------+
```

Figure 4-19   *Outlined Information of the Template*

- Define the total number of columns and the width of each column. Not all columns need to be the same width. Those columns that contain labels may need more space for characters than those columns that have dollar amounts entered. Those columns that use standard values may use less space.
- Define the format for representing numeric and dollar values in your columns. Refer to Section 4.8.

- Define the order of calculation. If it is by row, then calculations are started at the far left-hand corner cell, A1, and continue to the end of that row. Then the next row is calculated and continues to the end of that row. Calculations are continued until all rows have been calculated. If calculations are done by columns, they start with the first cell, A1, and proceed from that cell to the bottom of the A column. Calculations then move back to the top of the next column, B, and continue until all columns have been calculated.

- Define the type of procedures to use that will ensure correct calculations. This is the most important consideration concerning your template. *If you are performing calculations by rows or columns, do not use pointers to cell information that has not yet been calculated.* If you do, you are leaving yourself open for errors in your calculations or you may need to recalculate your template.

- Define which cells are to be protected to prevent the over-writing of important values, functions, formulas, or pointers. A master template will have columns and rows that produce values from pointers. These are the areas that need protection from over-writing.

- Use a structured approach in the use of pointers and other special techniques to ensure that calculations are correct. Do not point to cells for values that have not yet been calculated. Restructure your column values or row values to help prevent this from occurring.

If you have entered all of your labels into the template, you can begin your cell layouts. Follow the outline in Fig. 4-20 to enter your cell layout options.

4.11 DOCUMENTING THE TEMPLATE

One of the most powerful design techniques used in computer programming is top-down structured programming.

Top-down programming is a programming discipline in which the major steps to be accomplished are first identified, programmed, and tested; substeps are added to the program as they are written and tested. This same design technique is used to develop templates:

- The first line of text in a template should give the location of the instructions for the template.

- Instructions should be placed at the end of the template.

- Use parentheses in mathematical formulas, so that the mathematics is performed in the order you require.

- Format template instructions so that they can be easily read and understood.

```
-----------------------------------------------------------------------------
1.    Setting column widths :
      To set column widths, move to column E and press OPEN-APPLE L for the layout
      options. See Section 4.13.5. You will be given a command line that states
      Layout? Select columns. Another command line will tell you to use the cursor to
      highlight the column(s) to be widened or shortened. Press the RETURN key for
      column E. You will then see the Layout? question again. Select column width, to
      increase the column to 13 spaces from 9 spaces wide and then use OPEN-APPLE
      right arrow key 4 times.

      1a.   Perform the same procedure for column F. Set column F to a width of 3
            characters. Set column G to a width of 14 characters.

2.    Setting dollar values:
      To set dollar values move to column E and press OPEN OPEN L for the layout
      options. You will be given a command line that states Layout? Select value.
      Another command line will tell you to use the cursor to highlight the columns.
      Press the RETURN key for column E. You will then see the Layout? question
      again. Select Dollars. You are then asked how many decimal places. Select 2
      decimal places.

      2a.   Perform the same procedure for column G.

3.    Using the @SUM function:
      To use the @SUM function move to cell G27. Enter the following function at cell
      G27, @SUM(E26...E16).

      3a.   Move to cell G39. Enter the following function at cell G39,
            @SUM(E38...E35).
      3b.   Move to cell G44. Enter the following formula at cell G44, +G27-G39.
      3c.   Move to cell G47. Enter the following function at cell G47, @SUM(G44..G39)

4.    Protecting columns:
      To set column protection, move to column E and press OPEN-APPLE L for the
      layout options. You will be given a command line that states, Layout? Select
      columns. Another command line will tell you to use the cursor to highlight the
      column(s) to be protected. Press the RETURN key for column E. You will then see
      the Layout? question again. Select Protection. Then select nothing from the
      command line.

      4a. Perform the same procedure on column G.
-----------------------------------------------------------------------------
```

Figure 4-20   *Cell Layout of Financial Statement*

- Use indentation in the instructions to show the template structure and flow of operations.

If you follow these principles when you prepare your template, you will produce a worksheet that is easily read and understood by others. Templates are only good if they contain the correct mathematics, structure, and the proper documentation to instruct the user in its operation and function.

```
File: BLANK                    PRINTER OPTIONS        Escape: Review/Add/Change
===============================================================================

-------Left and right margins--------      ------Top and bottom margins-------
PW: Platen Width          8.5 inches      PL: Paper Length         11.0 inches
LM: Left Margin           0.0 inches      TM: Top Margin            0.0 inches
RM: Right Margin          0.0 inches      BM: Bottom Margin         0.0 inches
CI: Chars per Inch        10              LI: Lines per Inch        6

    Line width            8.5 inches          Printing length      11.0 inches
    Char per line (est)   85                  Lines per page        66

    ----------------------Formatting options--------------------
    SC:  Send Special Codes to printer                        No
    PH:  Print report Header at top of each page              Yes
         Single, Double or Triple Spacing (SS/DS/TS)          SS


    "Specify information about your printer" (on menu of Other
    Activities) gives you additional control over printers.
-------------------------------------------------------------------------------
Type a two letter option code                                   55K Avail.
```

Figure 4-21   Printer Opton Menu

4.12 PRINTER OPTIONS

There are a set of printer options that are also standard when a worksheet or template is started. These are listed on the Printer Options Menu. You enter the Printer Options screen by pressing the OPEN-APPLE O keystroke combination, the options command.

The Printer Option Menu is a list of the default values used by the spreadsheet. These values may be changed to meet the requirements of your printer as well as the requirements for your printed report. The screen is broken into three main parts—left and right margins, top and bottom margins, and report formatting options.

- Platen width (PW) is set to 8.0″. The paper width seting should correspond to the paper size.
- Left margin (LM) is set as 0.0″. This means there is no left margin.
- Right margin (RM) is set as 0.0″. This means there is no right margin.
- Characters per inch (CI) is listed as 10. This specifies the number of characters printed per inch of paper width.
- The line width and characters per line setting are calculated by AppleWorks, using the above entries. These calculations were shown in Section 2.1.1.
- Default paper length (PL) is set to 11″.
- Top margin (TM) is set as 0.0″. This specifies the amount of space left blank at the top of the printed page.

- Bottom margin (BM) is set as 0.0″. This is the amount of space left blank at the bottom of the printed page.
- Lines per inch (LI) is set to 6.
- Printing length is set to 11″. This is the length of text, not the paper length.
- Lines per page is set to 66. This is calculated using the above entries. These calculations were shown in Section 2.1.1.
- SC means *send special codes* to a printer. The default answer is *No*.
- PH means *print report header* at the top of the page. A *Yes* answer means that a report header will be printed. A *No* answer means the report header will not be printed. The default is *Yes*.
- The last option is to define the line spacing of a printed report. You may select single, double, or triple space. The default is single spacing.

Figure 4-21 shows the options that are in effect when the spreadsheet program is started. You can make changes while you are developing a template.

4.13 SUMMARY

This chapter introduced you to the spreadsheet portion of AppleWorks. It also introduced you to the concept of a template. A template, in this context, is a guide which you will later use to enter information.

This chapter also covered the basic skills necessary to create a spreadsheet template from scratch. You were shown all of the mechanics and keystroke combinations used to format cells, to enter information, and to create an entire template.

Additional Spreadsheet Features

If a man's wit be wandering, let him study mathematics.
FRANCIS BACON, 1625

5.0 OVERVIEW

This chapter discusses additional features and techniques used in spreadsheet templates. You will see applications and examples of all the functions of the spreadsheet. You will learn the purpose of function arguments. You will also be introduced to logical operators, master headers, and special functions.

You will learn the uses of the copy feature in designing and building templates. You will see how to repeat labels, headers, pointers, formulas, and mathematical functions in your template; how to move or copy information from cell to cell; how to move or copy groups of cells; and how to move or copy the contents of a cell depending on its new position in the template.

You will learn about the Data Interchange Format (DIF), where it originated, and how it is used. You will see how to move information from a spreadsheet using the DIF to other parts of AppleWorks and how this information could be moved to other programs.

This chapter includes seven application examples that can be used as is to meet your needs. Entering these templates should give you the understanding needed to build and enter your own templates.

5.1 FUNCTIONS IN THE SPREADSHEET

Functions are codes that stand for a set of calculations built into the spreadsheet. When entering a function into a cell, you are calling for a formula that operates on the specified cell(s) and/or the values and arguments supplied within the function.

All function entries start with the "at" (@) sign function header and are followed by the function code. Finally, any required function arguments are enclosed in parentheses. For example, @SUM (A1 . . . A6) is a valid expression.

This section discusses and defines the terms associated with functions.

5.1.1 Value

An argument in a function is the independent variable upon whose valuation a function depends. It can be a number (123) or a cell coordinate (B43). If it is a cell coordinate position, you may precede the cell location with either a plus or minus sign like all pointers, but it is *not* required.

5.1.2 Range

The range entry for a function refers to a sequence of cell locations that begin and end with cell coordinate positions. The beginning and ending cell coordinates are separated by three periods. The referenced cells must be adjacent row cells, such as A12 . . . A50, or adjacent column cells, such as A12 . . . H12. Do not group different rows, such as A12 . . . H13, or different columns, such as A12 . . . B50, as these entries will cause an error condition to develop. Argument ranges *cannot* include blocks of rows or columns. The range arguments tell a function where to begin and end finding values.

5.1.3 List

Some functions refer to arguments as a list. A list may be any combination of expressions, values, or ranges of numbers. Each item in the list is separated from the others by a comma. You can use rows, columns, and/or individual items when defining information to a function. A list may be a group of coordinates in either rows or columns, such as the column arguments A12 . . . A25,H25 . . . H48, or row arguments A12 . . . E12,H15 . . . K15. The list may include individual cell and value entries such as H22,15,B43,23. The argument list tells a function where to find the values required to perform the function.

Figure 5-1 summarizes the types of arguments covered thus far.

5.1.4 Rate

Rate refers to the discount rate or the cost of money. The cost of money may be viewed as the interest rate paid when you borrow money or the annual inflation rate. Regardless of how you view the cost of money, it means that an amount of money received today has greater buying power than the same amount of money received next year, because today's money has not been devalued by the inflation rate or you have not paid the interest

```
+------------------------------------------------------------+
| Argument      Examples                                     |
|------------------------------------------------------------|
| Value         123 or +A12 or -A12 or 56.43                 |
|                                                            |
| Range         A12...A50 or A12...H12                       |
|                                                            |
| List          A12...A25,A25...H25 or A12,123,H12           |
+------------------------------------------------------------+
```

Figure 5-1   *Function Arguments*

charged. Therefore, any money received in the future must be discounted by this rate to determine the actual buying power value of the money, if it were received today.

The @NPV (Net Present Value) function requires the use of rate. (See Section 5.3.)

5.1.5 Logical Operators

A logical operator is a symbol or combination of symbols that defines the relationship between two values. There are six different logical operator relationships that are recognized by the spreadsheet.

Logical operator relationships are created with the following operators:

Operator	Meaning	Examples	Results
<	less than	2 < 3	True = 1
		3 < 2	False = 2
>	greater than	3 > 2	True = 1
		2 > 3	False = 2
=	equal to	3 = 3	True = 1
		2 = 3	False = 2
<=	less than or equal to	3 <= 3	True = 1
		2 <= 3	True = 1
		3 <= 2	False = 2
>=	greater than or equal to	3 >= 3	True = 1
		3 >= 2	True = 1
		2 >= 3	False = 2
<>	not equal to	3 <> 2	True = 1
		2 <> 3	True = 1
		3 <> 3	False = 2

If a logical expression is true, a value of 1 is returned to the spreadsheet. If a logical expression is false, a value of 2 is returned to the spreadsheet.

Logical operators are used to evaluate the @IF function. (See Section 5.4.)

5.2 ARITHMETIC FUNCTIONS

Some arithmetic functions perform calculations on values in the form of numbers, pointers, or formulas, while other functions perform calculations on lists of numbers or pointer coordinates. With other functions, you may select from a set of alternatives by using special functions, such as @LOOKUP and @CHOOSE. Figure 5-2 shows types of functions, their arguments, and the functions themselves.

Note: Individual argument entries in a function are separated by commas.

```
| Type of Function    Argument(s)    Function              |
|----------------------------------------------------------|
| Arithmetic          Value          @ABS  @INT  @SQRT     |
|                                                          |
|                     List           @AVG  @COUNT  @MAX    |
|                                    @MIN  @SUM            |
|                                                          |
|                     Range          @CHOOSE  @LOOKUP      |
|                                                          |
|                     Range or List  @ERROR  @NA           |
|                                                          |
| Financial           List           @NPV                  |
|                                                          |
| Logical             List           @IF                   |
+----------------------------------------------------------+
```

Figure 5-2 *Types of Functions and Arguments*

The next sections describe each of the built-in functions in the spreadsheet.

5.2.1 @ABS(value)

@ABS(value) finds the absolute value of a number. An absolute value is the numerical value of a number regardless of its sign. For example, the absolute value of +3 and −3 is 3.

You may substitute cell coordinates for value in an @ABS function. For example, if cell A1 has the value 1.23456, and you enter the function @ABS(A1) at location A10, the value 1.23456 would be returned to cell A10. If cell A1 contains the value −1.23456, then cell A10 will still contain 1.23456 (the sign is dropped).

Figure 5-3 gives a few more examples of the @ABS function.

5.2.2 @SQRT(value)

The @SQRT(value) function finds the square root of the argument value. A square root is the second root of a number and is equivalent to raising a number to the ½ power. Figure 5-4 shows what is returned in cell A9 when a value of 123 is in cell A5 and an entry of @SQRT(A5) is in cell A9.

5.2.3 @INT(value)

The @INT(value) function returns the integer portion of a value. An integer is a whole number or the whole number portion of a real number. Entering 10.50 at cell A11 and @INT(A11) at cell A5 returns the value 10. Additional examples are shown in Fig. 5-5.

5.2.4 @AVG(list)

The @AVG(list) function is used to average a list of values in a column, row, and/or individual cell and value entries. The value returned is the equivalent to the @SUM func-

```
+-------------------------+
| Function      = Value   |
+-------------------------+
| @ABS(3)       = 3       |
| @ABS(-3)      = 3       |
| A12           = 1.23456 |
| @ABS(A12)     = 1.23456 |
| A14           = -4.56   |
| @ABS(A14)     = 4.56    |
| @ABS(A12+A14) = 3.32544 |
+-------------------------+
```

Figure 5-3   @*ABS Function*

```
+--------------------------------+
|                                |
| =====A======B======C======D===== |
|  4|                            |
|  5|   123                      |
|  6|                            |
|  7|   25                       |
|  8|                            |
|  9|     <--- @SQRT(A5) = 11.09053 |
| 10|                            |
| 11|     <--- @SQRT(A7) =  5     |
| 12|     <--- @SQRT(A5+A7) = 11.318 |
+--------------------------------+
```

Figure 5-4   @*SQRT Function*

```
+--------------------------------+
|                                |
| ====A======B======C======D===== |
|  4|                            |
|  5| 10.50                      |
|  6| 12.60                      |
|  7| 13.87                      |
|  8|                            |
|  9|                            |
| 10|     <-------- @INT(A5+A6) = 23 |
| 11|     <-------- @INT(A5)    = 10 |
| 12|     <-------- @INT(A6)    = 12 |
| 13|     <-------- @INT(A7)    = 13 |
+--------------------------------+
```

Figure 5-5   @*INT Function*

tion divided by the @COUNT function. There is no limit to the number of elements in a list, except for the limits on the number of rows or columns in a worksheet. An argument list of cells must be in the form @AVG(A5 ... A7,B13,100,A5 ... C5). The @AVG function does not allow for the combining of different rows and/or columns, such as @AVG(A12 ... B12); this will cause an error because blocks of cells cannot be specified as a single argument. You can combine cell values from different columns or rows into

```
+-----------------------------------+
|                                   |
|  ====A======B======C======D====== |
| 4|                                |
| 5|   100     400     700          |
| 6|   200     500     800          |
| 7|   300     600     900          |
+-----------------------------------+
|10|    <-- @AVG(A5...A7)    = 200   |
|11|    <-- @AVG(A5...C5)    = 400   |
|12|    <-- @AVG(C7,A6,C5)   = 600   |
|13|    <-- @AVG(1000,B6,C7) = 800   |
|14|    <-- @AVG(A5...C7)    = ERROR |
+-----------------------------------+
```

Figure 5-6   @AVG Function

the list, provided they are specified individually. Figure 5-6 shows examples of the @AVG function.

5.2.5 @COUNT(list)

The @COUNT(list) function returns the number of non-zero cell entries in a list. The @COUNT function does not add or sum up the values in cells, but merely counts the number of entries in a given range. For example, @COUNT(B12 ... B30) returns a count of 19, if all cells in the list are filled. Figure 5-7 shows examples of this function.

There are a number of additional combinations and mixtures that may be used in the @COUNT argument list that have not been shown. You may want to experiment with this powerful function.

5.2.6 @MAX(list)

The @MAX(list) function finds the maximum value in a range of numbers. For example, if you enter the values 100, 200, and 300 at cells A5, A6, and A7 with the function entry

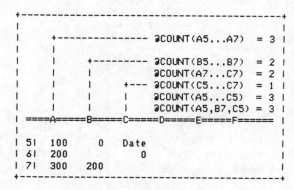

Figure 5-7   @COUNT Function

```
+------------------------------------------+
|                                          |
|      +--------- @MAX(A5...A7) = 300       |
|      |     +--- @MAX(B5...B7) = 600       |
|      |     |    @MAX(A5...C5) = 700       |
|      |     |    @MAX(A7...C7) = 900       |
|      |     |    @MAX(A5,C7)   = 900       |
|  ====A=====B=====C=====D=====E=====       |
| 4|   0     0     0                        |
| 5|   100   400   700                      |
| 6|   200   500   800                      |
| 7|   300   600   900                      |
+------------------------------------------+
```

Figure 5-8   *@MAX Function*

@MAX(A5 . . . A7) in some other cell, the value 300 will be returned as the largest value of the list. Figure 5-8 shows examples of the @MAX function.

5.2.7 @MIN(list)

The @MIN(list) function finds the minimum value in a range of numbers. For example, if you enter the values 100, 200, and 300 at cells A5, A6, and A7 with the function entry @MIN(A5 . . . A7) in some other cell, the value 100 will be returned as the smallest value of the list. Figure 5-9 shows examples of the @MIN function.

5.2.8 @SUM(list)

The @SUM(list) function finds the total of a range of numbers. For example, if column B contains values at cells B5, B6, and B7 of 100, 200, and 300, respectively, and cell B10 contains the function @SUM(B5 . . . B7), the value 600 would be returned in cell B10. Examples of @SUM are shown in Fig. 5-10.

The @SUM function entered into a cell might also be as complicated as:
@SUM(250,450,B14,D22,C5 . . . C20,F33/F22,C4+C6)

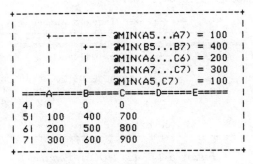

```
+------------------------------------------+
|                                          |
|      +--------- @MIN(A5...A7) = 100       |
|      |     +--- @MIN(B5...B7) = 400       |
|      |     |    @MIN(A6...C6) = 200       |
|      |     |    @MIN(A7...C7) = 300       |
|      |     |    @MIN(A5,C7)   = 100       |
|  ====A=====B=====C=====D=====E=====       |
| 4|   0     0     0                        |
| 5|   100   400   700                      |
| 6|   200   500   800                      |
| 7|   300   600   900                      |
+------------------------------------------+
```

Figure 5-9   *@MIN Function*

```
+--------------------------------------+
|                                      |
|    +--------- @SUM(A5...A7) =  600   |
|    |    +--- @SUM(B5...B7) = 1500    |
|    |    |    @SUM(A6...C6) = 1500    |
|    |    |    @SUM(A7...C7) = 1800    |
|    |    |    @SUM(A5,C7)   = 1000    |
| ====A=====B=====C=====D=====E=====   |
| 4|  0      0      0                  |
| 5|  100    400    700                |
| 6|  200    500    800                |
| 7|  300    600    900                |
+--------------------------------------+
```

Figure 5-10   @SUM Function

5.2.9 @CHOOSE(value, list)

The @CHOOSE(value,list) function can be used to select alternatives for calculations. The @CHOOSE function takes the first value element in the list of values as the index value to select the value to be returned by the function. If the first argument is 0 or less, or if the value is greater than the number of remaining arguments in the list, then @CHOOSE is evaluated to NA (Not Available). Figure 5-11 shows an example of the @CHOOSE function.

5.2.10 @LOOKUP(value,range)

The @LOOKUP(value,range) funtion can be used to select alternatives for calculations in a template or to transfer data from one section of a template to another.

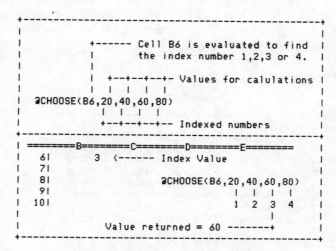

```
+--------------------------------------------------+
|                                                  |
|         +------ Cell B6 is evaluated to find     |
|         |       the index number 1,2,3 or 4.     |
|         |                                        |
|         |  +--+--+--+- Values for calulations    |
|         |  |  |  |  |                            |
|  @CHOOSE(B6,20,40,60,80)                         |
|            |  |  |  |                            |
|         +--+--+--+- Indexed numbers              |
+--------------------------------------------------+
| ========B========C========D========E========     |
|   6|    3  <------ Index Value                    |
|   7|                                              |
|   8|              @CHOOSE(B6,20,40,60,80)         |
|   9|                       |  |  |  |             |
|  10|                       1  2  3  4             |
|                               |                   |
|         Value returned = 60 -------+              |
+--------------------------------------------------+
```

Figure 5-11   @CHOOSE Function

To use the @LOOKUP function set up two tables. The first table can be either a column or a row table. The second table should be either a column to the right of the first table column or a row below the first row table. The @LOOKUP function takes the value argument supplied for the first table as the search value. The function then searches for the largest value in the first table that is equal to or less than the search value. When the function finds the correct value, it returns the corresponding value from the second table. An example set of row tables is shown below.

```
                                  +----+              +----+----+----+
First table: search value =       | 10 | values =     |  7 |  9 | 11 |
                                  +----+              +----+----+----+
Second table:                                values =  | 12 | 13 | 14 |
                                                       +----+----+----+

                         Possible cell entry = @LOOKUP(10,C11...C13) or
                         for a column table  = @LOOKUP(10,C11...E11)
```

If the search value is smaller than the first entry in the first table, NA (Not Available) will be returned. If the search value is larger than any of the entries of the first table, the last value in the table will be returned. Further, the values in the first table must be in ascending order. A possible implementation of this function is shown in Fig. 5-12.

A special use of the @LOOKUP table lets you transfer information from one area of a template to another. This area could be used for entering data into the template. This would make the uses of the template easier to operate. Figure 5-13 shows the @LOOKUP function to be used in this transfer.

An example of this is found in a Project cost template (see Fig. 5-14). Here we transfer data from the "change orders" column to the main section of the template. This allows the end user of the template to make just one entry at a time. Without this function, the user of the template would have to use the edit function of the spreadsheet program to make more than one entry into the main template area.

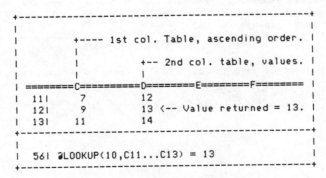

Figure 5-12 Column @Lookup Table

```
+-------------------------------------------------------------------+
|                                                                   |
|       +----+--- Looks for the value at B16 at location B41 through B57. |
|       |    |                                                      |
|       |    |    +----- If value is the same then returns the value |
|       |    |    |      in the corresponding cell in the second table. |
|       |    |    |                                                 |
|       |    |    |   +---- Sums the values in D41+E41+F41 to the second |
|       |    |    |   |     table value and returns the total to E16. |
|       |    |    |   |                                             |
| ƏLOOKUP(B16,B41...B57)+(+D41+E41+F41)   <-- Function entered in cell E16. |
+-------------------------------------------------------------------+
```

Figure 5-13   *Transfer Formula*

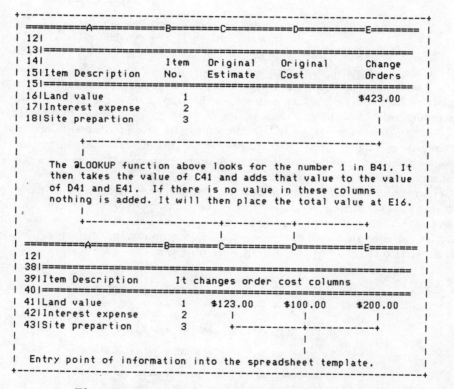

Figure 5-14   *Data Entry Transfer Section of Spreadsheet*

5.2.11 @ERROR

The @ERROR function causes the word ERROR to be displayed at the cell location where the function is entered and at all other cell locations that refer to that cell. This function is useful as an argument in @LOOKUP tables and in the @IF logical function. This function is also useful as a check-out mechanism when you are developing a template.

5.2.12 @NA

The @NA (Not Available) function is used to fill in a cell when a value needs to be entered but is not yet available. When AppleWorks calculates a value that refers to a cell that contains the @NA function, the NA text value is placed in that cell. (Text values are words placed in a cell.) The @NA function will help you keep track of the cells that require values or formulas to be completed.

5.3 FINANCIAL FUNCTION

The @NPV(rate,range) (Net Present Value) function calculates the present value of future cash flows discounted by the cost of money. The first value of the function is the discount rate, or cost of money used to discount the future cash inflows or outflows. The second value entered is a range of cell locations that include the cash inflows and outflows. A cash inflow is entered as a positive number and a cash outflow is entered as a negative number. The formula for the @NPV function is:

$$\text{Net Present Value} = \sum_{t=1}^{n} \frac{R_t}{(1+i)^{\wedge^t}} - C$$

Where
R_t = cash flow for period t
n = number of time periods
C = initial project investment
i = discount rate, interest
t = time period, usually a year

The internal rate of return of an investment is equal to the discount rate that produces a Net Present Value of 0. Notice that the internal ate of return is a modifcation to the function formula for net present value.

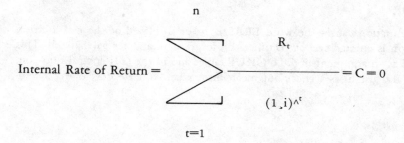

$$\text{Internal Rate of Return} = \sum_{t=1}^{n} \frac{R_t}{(1.i)^{\wedge t}} = C = 0$$

R_t = cash flow for period t
n = number of time periods
C = initial project investment
i = discount rate, interest
t = time period, usually a year

When calculating the net present value of an investment, certain numeric information must be supplied, including the interest rate, the expected cash inflows and outflows for each time period, and the dollar amount of the initial investment. The following table shows the net present value of an investment. The implementation of this template is shown in Figs. 5-26a and 5-26b.

$50,000 = initial investment in property
10% = discount rate of money on investment

Net Present Value Analysis

Year	Date	Cash Flow
1	1984	2000—1st year cash flow on investment
2	1985	5000—2nd year cash flow on investment
3	1986	20500—3rd year cash flow on investment
4	1987	−15000—4th year cash flow on investment
5	1988	90000—5th year proceeds from sale on investment

Net Present Value $16,990

Tip: General formulas for Net Present Value:

NPV = Present value of the annual net cash inflows or outflows, using the present discount rate of money to calculate the present value of the future cash inflows or outflows.

NPV = Present value of the annual net cash flows from operations and property sale less the initial cost of the property.

Figure 5-15 shows the completed template for the net present value analysis as it would look on the screen. The OPEN-APPLE Z command is in effect to show the @NPV function used to calculate the net present value of the investment. The OPEN-APPLE Z command shows all of the pointers, values, and functions. If there are more than nine characters per cell, you must increase the column width to see the complete cell entry.

5.4 Logical @IF Function

The logical @IF function takes three values. The first value must be a logical operator relation. That means an expression is entered into the function to be evaluated as either a true (1) or false (2) relationship. The second and third argument values can be any value, formula, or another function to be evaluated. For example, for @IF(logical value#1,-value#2,value#3):

- If the logical value#1 is true, then the function returns the #2 value to the cell.
- If the logical value is false, then the function returns the #3 value to the cell.

Logical operators are used to define and evaluate the relationship between both sides of the expression to be either true or false. Depending upon valuation of the logical value, true returns value#2, false returns value#3. (See Section 5.1.5 for information on logical operators.)

For example, the function entry @IF(C170,>D17/C17,0) means: if the value in cell C17 is greater than 0, then take the value in cell D17 and divide it by the value in cell C17. Place the result in the cell containing the @IF function. If the value in cell C17 is equal

```
File: NET.PVALUE                REVIEW/ADD/CHANGE              Escape: Main Menu
==========A=========B=========C=========D=========E=========F=========G=========H====
  1|
  2|50000        Initial Investment of Property
  3|
  4|10       % Discount Rate of money
  5|-------------------------------------------------------------------
  6|         Cash Flow of Investment
  7|
  8|Year     Date     Cash Flow
  9|-------------------------------------------------------------------
 10|1        1984     2000      - Cash Flow of Investment
 11|2        1985     5000      - Cash Flow of Investment
 12|3        1986     20500     - Cash Flow of Investment
 13|4        1987     -15000    - Cash Flow of Investment
 14|5        1988     90000     - Proceeds from Sale of Investment
 15|-------------------------------------------------------------------
 16|Net Present value  -A2+@NPV(
 17|                   =========
 18|
-------------------------------------------------------------------
C16: (Value, Layout-DO)  -A2+@NPV(A4/100,C10...C14)

Type entry or use @ commands                              @-? for Help
```

Figure 5-15 *OPEN-APPLE Z Presentation for @NPV Function*

to, or less than 0, then place a 0 in the cell containing the @IF function. The evaluation rules for the @IF function are shown in Fig. 5-16.

> Tip: The above @IF function is a good way to prevent a division by zero or a negative number from happening with a template.

Value of First Argument	Evaluates to
True	Value of second argument
False	Value of third argument
NA	NA
Not logical or ERROR	ERROR

Now that the discussion of the built-in functions is completed, we can get back to describing the spreadsheet and creating templates.

5.5 MASTER HEADERS

A master header is any template that can be loaded before the main part of the template is completed. For example, the name and address of your business could be placed in a master header. The date, telephone number, or any other information identifying the form's use would also be appropriate.

5.6.1 Master Forms

Master forms are designed to be used as more or less permanent forms that allow the recording of varying data. They contain only the constant values, pointers, functions, and formulas needed to do the calculations. The data are supplied by the user. The templates shown in Section 5.9 are master forms.

As we discussed in Chapter 4, once a well-designed template has been created, it should be documented for future use, otherwise the commands and operation requirements may be forgotten.

```
+---------------------------------+--------------------------------------+
| Value of First Argument  |   Evaluates To                       |
|---------------------------------+--------------------------------------|
| True                     |   Value of second argument           |
| False                    |   Value of third argument            |
| NA                       |   NA                                 |
| Not logical or ERROR     |   ERROR                              |
+---------------------------------+--------------------------------------+
```

Figure 5-16   Evaluation Rules for @IF

Each time you begin a new report that requires information from another template, you can place it in the Clipboard before the new template is added to the Desktop. You can then copy information from the Clipboard to the new template. For example, you may want to include the name and address of your business in the new template. This is shown in Fig. 5-17.

5.7 COPYING SPREADSHEET INFORMATION

The spreadsheet copy feature makes it easy for you to create templates. You can quickly make an exact copy of labels, numbers, pointers, formulas, and functions from one cell to another. You can make the copies reflect their new location. That means you can make many similar calculations depend on one original formula, but modified to perform correctly, relative to the new location.

Before you do any copying, you should consider the following:

- From what cell(s) are you copying information?
- To what cell(s) are you copying information?
- Do you want exact copies, or is the copy dependent on the new cell position?

All of this leads to the conclusion that you need to exercise a little caution before copying anything. Use the copy procedure discussed in Section 9.1.3.

5.7.1 Copy from Cells

You can copy from one cell or from a range of cells to another cell or range of cells. The only requirement is that the cells being copied from must be adjacent in the same row or column, as shown in Figs. 5-18a and 5-18b.

You can copy from one range of cells to another range of cells. You can copy from rows to rows or columns to columns, but not from rows to columns or columns to rows. Copying from rows to columns can only be accomplished by copying individual cells.

5.7.2 Copy to Cells

You can copy from one cell to another cell or to a range of cells. When you copy a single cell to multiple cells, the copy-to cells must be adjacent. You are allowed to copy rows to rows and columns to columns, but not rows to columns or columns to rows. See Fig. 5-19.

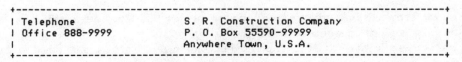

```
+-------------------------------------------------------------------------+
| Telephone            S. R. Construction Company                         |
| Office 888-9999      P. O. Box 55590-99999                              |
|                      Anywhere Town, U.S.A.                              |
+-------------------------------------------------------------------------+
```

Figure 5-17   Master Header

```
+-----------------------------------------------------+
|                                                     |
|=========A===========B============C==========|       |
| 1|Supplier                  Supplier          |
| 2|        |                 |                 |
| 3|        |                 |                 |
| 4|        |                 |                 |
| 5|        +-- Copy from Cell    +-- Copy to Cell  |
| 6|                                             |
|           Copy from cell A1 to cell C1.        |
+-----------------------------------------------------+
```

Figure 5-18(a)   Copy from Cell

```
+-----------------------------------------------------+
|                                                     |
|=========A===========B============C==========|       |
| 1|Supplier                  Supplier          |
| 2|Ace Supply Co.            Ace Supply Co.     |
| 3|Beta Distributor          Beta Distributor  |
| 4|        |                 |                 |
| 5|        +-- Copy from Cells   +-- Copy to Cells |
| 6|                                             |
|        Copy from cells A1...A3 to cells C1...C3 |
+-----------------------------------------------------+
```

Figure 5-18(b)   Copy from Cells

```
+-----------------------------------------------------+
|                                                     |
| =========A===========B============C==========       |
| 11|@ABS(A5)     @ABS(B5)      @ABS(C5)          |
| 12|        |           |           |           |
| 13|        |           +-------------+          |
| 14|        |                       |           |
| 15|        +-- Copy from Cell    +-- Copy to Cells |
| 16|                                             |
|         Copy from cell A1 to cells B1 and C1.  |
+-----------------------------------------------------+
```

Figure 5-19   Copy to Cells

5.7.3 Copy Cells Exactly

When you copy the contents of a cell into another cell exactly, labels, numbers, pointers, formulas, and functions are copied in their exact form, with no changes. See Fig. 5-20.

5.7.4 Copy Cells Relative to the New Position

You can copy cells into other cells and modify the new cell's contents to reflect its location. This is called making a relative copy. See Fig. 5-21.

For example, the @SUM function used in column A of Fig. 5-21 is modified to show that you want to sum the contents of both the A and C columns using the same function, but modified for each column. Therefore, the contents of cell A21 are copied relative to

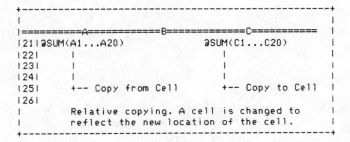

Figure 5-20   *Copy Exactly*

```
+-------------------------------------------------+
|                                                 |
|==========A============B============C=========== |
|21|@SUM(A1...A20)          @SUM(C1...C20)         |
|22|      |                       |               |
|23|      |                       |               |
|24|      |                       |               |
|25|      +-- Copy from Cell      +-- Copy to Cell |
|26|                                               |
|         Relative copying. A cell is changed to  |
|         reflect the new location of the cell.   |
+-------------------------------------------------+
```

Figure 5-21   *Copy Depending on Position*

cell C21. The copy feature prompts you to determine whether the cell references should be modified relatively. By being able to copy cells quickly, you can be more productive in developing templates.

5.8 MOVING INFORMATION

You are allowed to move up to a maximum of 250 rows or a maximum of 125 columns from one location to another in a spreadsheet template. To use the move command, follow the procedure shown in Section 9.1.13.

Tip: A significant amount of movement and adjustment takes place when moving cells within a template.

1. Spaces are closed or opened up for the columns or rows moved.
2. Columns are relettered and rows are renumbered according to the new template organization.
3. Formulas and functions are adjusted so that the references to the moved columns or rows will still refer to the cells that were originally referenced before the move.

5.9 APPLICATION EXAMPLES

This section contains six sample master forms or templates. Although these examples may not be directly applicable to your needs, they will give you an idea of how to design your own templates. You also may be able to adopt them to your own specifications.

The forms are:

Loan Payoff
Draw Report
Door Comparison
NPV Function
Project Cost
Budget

5.9.1 Loan Pay Off

Figure 5-22 shows the completed template for a loan payoff calculator as it would look when the required data has been supplied and the template completed. This calculator may be used for almost any loan you are paying off.

Some lending institutions use the Rule of 78's for paying off loans. This rule states that more of the interest is earned in the earlier months of a loan's life. To compute the amount of payoff on a loan, the number of the months in the term of the loan must be totaled. In a twelve-month loan the total is 78, the name of the rule. That is:

$$12 + 11 + 10 + 9 + 8 + 7 + 6 + 5 + 4 + 3 + 2 + 1 = 78.$$

A lending institution uses 12/78 of the principal to compute the first month's interest for payoff purposes; in the second month, 11/78; in the third month, 10/78, etc. This is continued to the end of the loan. The rule of 78's essentially says that you must pay more of the remaining interest due on the loan than with other methods.

Ask your lending institution if they use this rule. The Rule of 78's template is shown in Fig. 5-23. Another method of calculating the Rule of 78's was shown in Fig. 5-22. The primary difference in these two template methods is that the second one does not require that you know the interest rate but does require that you know the total principal plus interest amount to be paid on the loan. Normally, short-term loans, such as automobile, appliance, and furniture loans use the Rule of 78's.

5.9.2 Draw Report

Figure 5-24 shows a draw report template. (A draw is money borrowed against a prearranged line of credit.) This type of template can be used by contractors for the purpose of tracking money drawn from a lending institution during the construction of a building. This type of template, in modified form, could be used by any project manager charged

```
========A========B========C========D========E========F========H====
 1|====================================================================
 2|For spreadsheet template instructions, Press OPEN-APPLE 9.
 3|====================================================================
 4|
 5|             :::::::  Loan Pay Off Calculator  :::::::
 6|
 7|--------------------------------------------------------------------
 8|
 9|
10|     Principal amount of loan            1500
11|     Annual interest rate                12.75
12|     Terms in months                     24
13|     Last payment number made            19
14|     Monthly payment                     71.14
15|
16|--------------------------------------------------------------------
17|                                                          Notes:
18|     Total interest paid at full term    207.36      <---  1
19|
20|     Total of remaining payments         355.7       <---  2
21|     Interest rebate due                 10.368      <---  3
22|                                         ----------
23|     Payment required to retire loan     345.332     <---  4
24|                                         ==========
25|--------------------------------------------------------------------
26|
27|
28|Instructions for the use of the template:
29|
30|The Loan Pay Off Calculator simply calculates the remaining loan balance
31|after a given number of payments have been made. The user must supply the
32|information on the loan. Prinicpal loan amount, interest, terms in years
33|or months, number of payments that have been made, and the dollar amount
34|of those payments.
```

Notes: 1. Cell F18 = (F14*F12)-F10
       2. Cell F20 = (F12-F13)*F14
       3. Cell F21 = ((F12-F13)*(F12-F13+1))/((F12^2)+F12)*F18
       4. Cell F23 = +F20-F21

Figure 5-22 *Loan Payoff Calculator*

with the responsibility of tracking project costs and bank borrowing. You may want to refer to Fig. 5-29 for a comparison of the two templates.

The month labels and the draws remaining label are right-justified in their cells. The labels along the left edge, column A, are left-justified and 20 characters wide. The rest of the columns are 12 characters wide. All number values are formatted as dollars with two decimal places.

The mathematics performed by this template is very easy to enter and understand. The draws made for each month are added to get the total amount of that month's draws. For example, the two entries for the month of January are totaled in cell B19

```
========A========B========C========D========E=========F========G=======
 1 |=======================================================================
 2 |For spreadsheet template instructions, Press OPEN-APPLE 9.
 3 |=======================================================================
 4 |
 5 |              ::::::::  Rule of 78's Loan Payoff ::::::::
 6 |
 7 |-----------------------------------------------------------------------
 8 |
 9 |         Number of installments to pay        24
10 |
11 |         Amount to be repaid               1707.36
12 |         Amount of loan                    1500.00
13 |                                           ---------           Notes
14 |         Finance charge                     207.36         <--- 1
15 |
16 |
17 |         Number of payments made              19
18 |
19 |         Payment amount of loan             71.14         <--- 2
20 |         Number of months remaining in loan     5         <--- 3
21 |                                           ---------
22 |         Balance of loan now due           355.70         <--- 4
23 |         Unearned interest                  10.37         <--- 5
24 |                                           ---------
25 |         Loan payoff amount                345.33         <--- 6
26 |                                           =========
27 |-----------------------------------------------------------------------
28 |
29 |
30 |Instructions for the use of the template:
31 |
32 |1. Enter the number of payments in cell F9.
33 |2. Enter the amount to be repaid, including interest in cell F11.
34 |3. Enter the amount of the loan in cell F12.
35 |4. Enter the number of the payments made in cell F17.
36 |5. The remainder of the template is automatically computed.
```

Notes: 1. Cell F14 = +F11-F12
      2. Cell F19 = +F11/F9
      3. Cell F20 = +F9-F17
      4. Cell F22 = +F19*F20
      5. Cell F23 = +((F9-F17+1)*(F9-F17))/((F9^2)+F9)*F14
      6. Cell F25 = +F22-F23

Figure 5-23 *Rule of 78's for Loan Payoff Calculations*

(@SUM(B16 . . . B18)). This is done for each of the month columns B through D, the first quarter.

Then each quarter's draws are added to get the total amount of the draws made for that quarter. For example, the entry for the first quarter of the year is +B11 — @SUM(B19 . . . D19). This formula takes the total credit loan amount for the job, +B11, subtracts the total amount drawn for the quarter, and places the result in the correct cell, +E19, for the first quarter. At the end of the next quarter the remaining draw amount

```
File:   DRAW.REPORT


===========================================================
For spreadsheet template instructions, Press OPEN-APPLE 9.
===========================================================
                    S.R. Redden Construction Company
                    P. O. Box 99999-9003
                    Anywhere Town, U.S.A.
===========================================================
Construction Draw Report                 Job Address
===========================================================
Loan Number  --    C1-1900      -------  3101 Pioneer Circle
Loan Amount  --        $0.00    -------  Anywhere Town, U.S.A.


===========================================================
      Month of        January   February     March

1st of the Month       $0.00      $0.00      $0.00
15th of the Month      $0.00      $0.00      $0.00
                    ----------------------------------     Draw
Total for Month        $0.00      $0.00      $0.00   $0.00 Remaining
===========================================================
      Month of         April       May        June

1st of the Month       $0.00      $0.00      $0.00
15th of the Month      $0.00      $0.00      $0.00
                    ----------------------------------     Draw
Total for Month        $0.00      $0.00      $0.00   $0.00 Remaining
===========================================================
      Month of          July     August    September

1st of the Month       $0.00      $0.00      $0.00
15th of the Month      $0.00      $0.00      $0.00
                    ----------------------------------     Draw
Total for Month        $0.00      $0.00      $0.00   $0.00 Remaining
===========================================================
      Month of        October   November   December

1st of the Month       $0.00      $0.00      $0.00
15th of the Month      $0.00      $0.00      $0.00
                    ----------------------------------     Draw
Total for Month        $0.00      $0.00      $0.00   $0.00 Remaining
===========================================================
```

Instructions for the use of the template:

1. Enter the name and address of your company in cells C4 through E6.
2. Enter the loan number in cell B10.
3. Enter the loan amount in cell B11.
4. Enter the address of the construction job in cells D10 through E11.
5. Enter the draws made in the appropriate cell locations for the
   months and date cells.

Figure 5-24   Draw Report

For spreadsheet template instructions, Press OPEN-APPLE 9.

Door price comparision list

Door sizes	Style	Unit cost	Unit cost	Unit cost	
Ash	Slab	Supplier 1	Supplier 2	Supplier 3	Cost variance
DOOR 2/0		0.00	0.00	0.00	0.00
DOOR 2/8		0.00	0.00	0.00	0.00
DOOR 3/0		0.00	0.00	0.00	0.00
DOOR 4/0		0.00	0.00	0.00	0.00
DOOR 5/0		0.00	0.00	0.00	0.00
DOOR 6/0		0.00	0.00	0.00	0.00
Door sizes	Style	Unit cost	Unit cost	Unit cost	
Masonite	Slab	Supplier 1	Supplier 2	Supplier 3	Cost variance
DOOR 2/0		0.00	0.00	0.00	0.00
DOOR 2/8		0.00	0.00	0.00	0.00
DOOR 3/0		0.00	0.00	0.00	0.00
DOOR 4/0		0.00	0.00	0.00	0.00
DOOR 5/0		0.00	0.00	0.00	0.00
DOOR 6/0		0.00	0.00	0.00	0.00
Door sizes	Style	Unit cost	Unit cost	Unit cost	
Brich	Slab	Supplier 1	Supplier 2	Supplier 3	Cost variance
DOOR 2/0		0.00	0.00	0.00	0.00
DOOR 2/8		0.00	0.00	0.00	0.00
DOOR 3/0		0.00	0.00	0.00	0.00
DOOR 4/0		0.00	0.00	0.00	0.00
DOOR 5/0		0.00	0.00	0.00	0.00
DOOR 6/0		0.00	0.00	0.00	0.00

Instructions for the use of the template:

1. Enter the prices for the door style and size in the appropriate
   cell. Do this for each of three possible suppliers.
2. The template will calculate the variance in price between the
   most expensive and least expensive door size and style for the
   three suppliers prices chosen.

Figure 5-25(a)   *Price Comparison List*

```
 1|=========\===============\=================================================
 2|For spread\  instructions,\Press OPEN-APPLE 9.
 3|=========\===============\=================================================
 4|           \                \
 5|           \                \
 6|           \                \
 7|----------\---------------\-------------------------------------------------
 8|Door sizes\Style Unit Cost\Unit Cost
 9|----------\---------------\-------------------------------------------------
10|Ash        \  Supplier 1  \upplier 3  Cost variance
11|----------\---------------\-------------------------------------------------
12|Door 2/0  \         0.00 \    0.00  @MAX(B12,C12,D12)-@MIN(B12,C12,D12)
13|Door 2/8  \         0.00 \    0.00  @MAX(B13,C13,D13)-@MIN(B13,C13,D13)
14|Door 3/0  \         0.00 \    0.00  @MAX(B14,C14,D14)-@MIN(B14,C14,D14)
15|Door 4/0  \         0.00 \    0.00  @MAX(B15,C15,D15)-@MIN(B15,C15,D15)
16|Door 5/0  \         0.00 \    0.00  @MAX(B16,C16,D16)-@MIN(B16,C16,D16)
17|Door 6/0  \         0.00 \    0.00  @MAX(B17,C17,D17)-@MIN(B17,C17,D17)
18|----------\---------------\-------------------------------------------------
```

Figure 5-25(b)   *Price Comparison Segment*

becomes the new total outstanding loan amount. For example, the draws-remaining formula for the second quarter is +E19−@SUM(B26 ... D26). This means that, as you make draws for a construction job, the template keeps track of the dollar amounts available for future draws. The mathematics for the rest of the template is a repeat of the mathematics already shown for the other quarters.

5.9.3 Price Comparison

The price comparison template shows one way of recording and comparing prices from different sources. The final column in a row gives the cost variance between the highest and lowest price, in this case for a particular door size and style. The mathematics used in that column of cells is the @MAX function minus the @MIN function for the prices entered from three suppliers. For example, the contents of cell E12 = @MAX(B12,C12, D12)−@MIN(B12,C12,D12). This formula is then copied, relatively, for all rows that need the formula—rows 12–17, rows 23–28, and rows 34–39. See Fig. 5-25a.

Figure 5-25b shows a partial section of the door price comparison template with some of the mathematics. Normally if you print a screen presentation, you will not be able to see the mathematics because of the length of the formulas.

5.9.4 NPV Function

The next template, Figs. 5-26a and 5-26b, is a slight modification on the template shown on page 00. The mathematics involved and formula for NPV were shown and discussed in Section 5.3. This template shows you how the NPV function operates and illustrates one way to organize the function data.

The only formula used in the template is located in cell C16. The contents of this cell is −A4+@NPV(A6/100,C12 ... C16). The result of this calculation is displayed as

```
File:    NET.PVALUE


$50,000    Initial Investment of Property

       10% Discount Rate of money
------------------------------------------------------------
          Cash Flow of Investment

Year    Date    Cash Flow
------------------------------------------------------------
1       1984         2000 - Cash Flow of Investment
2       1985         5000 - Cash Flow of Investment
3       1986        20500 - Cash Flow of Investment
4       1987       -15000 - Cash Flow of Investment
5       1988        90000 - Proceeds from Sale of Investment
------------------------------------------------------------
Net Present value  $16,990
                   =========
```

Figure 5-26(a)   *Net Present Value*

```
========A========B=========C=========D=========E========F========G=========
 1|=========================================================
 2|For spreadsheet template instrictions, Press OPEN-APPLE 9.
 3|=========================================================
 4|$50,000    Initial Investment of Property
 5|
 6|       10% Discount Rate of money
 7|------------------------------------------------------------
 8|          Cash Flow of Investment
 9|
10|Year    Date    Cash Flow
11|------------------------------------------------------------
12|11      1984         2000 - Cash Flow of Investment
13|12      1985         5000 - Cash Flow of Investment
14|13      1986        20500 - Cash Flow of Investment
15|14      1987       -15000 - Cash Flow of Investment
16|15      1988        90000 - Proceeds from Sale of Investment
17|------------------------------------------------------------
18|Net Present value  $16,990      <-- -A4+@NPV(A6/100,C12...C16)
19|                   =========
20|
21|Instructions for the use of the template.
22|
23|1. Enter the amount of the initial investment is cell A4.
24|2. Enter the discount rate of money or interest rate in cell A6.
25|3. Enter all of the yearly dates, as labels, in cells B12 - B16.
26|4. Enter the individual cash flows into cell C12 - C16.
```

Figure 5-26(b)   *Net Present Value Template*

$16,990.00. What this tells you is that you have received, over the five-year run of this spread, a buying power profit equivalent to $16,990 in today's dollars. Your total investment, in absolute dollars, for this project is $65,000 = $50,000 + $15,000 added in 1987. The total revenues, in absolute dollars, from this project is $117,500 = $2,000 + $5,000 + $20,500 + $90,000.

5.9.5 Project Cost

The project cost template tracks the costs associated with a project. In this case, we are using a simulated residential home construction project. We realize that the template is not necessarily complete, but it is very representative. This same general form can be used for almost any project, from recording the costs involved in producing a consumer item to those involved in creating an advertising campaign. The template not only keeps track of the original, anticipated costs of an item, bu it uses the function @LOOKUP to track the costs of possible change orders. Figure 5-27 shows the completed project cost template.

Figure 5-27a shows the first 18 rows of the template. This area of the template provides all of the identifying or title information. The first row, as usual, tells you where the template instructions are located. The rest of this figure is the start of the main body of the template.

The rest of the main body of the template is shown in Fig. 5-27b. This includes rows 13 through 35.

The entries in rows 17 through 19 are shown in Fig. 5-27c. The cells and their widths, types, and contents are shown.

Within this template, there are two identical lists of component items that make up the total project. The first list is the controlling list. This list requires the entry of the original cost estimate for each item in the project plus the original cost amount expended. If during the completion of any item, changes are required which cause additional money expenditures, they are entered into the second list in the appropriate column.

For example, the formulas and functions used in row 17 are shown in Fig. 5-27c. The formulas and functions used in row 17 are replicated through row 35 using relative copying modifications. The instruction placed in cell E17 is:

```
@LOOKUP((B17,B41 . . . B57)+(D41+E41+F41)
```

This instruction says to look at the index value in cell B17 = 1. Match that value with the table in cells B41 through B57. The table consists of elements, B41 = 1 through B57 = 17, and fulfills the requirements for a lookup table. The value returned by the @LOOKUP function is the value in cell C41. Then, the values in cells D41, E41, and F41 are added to the value in cell C41. The sum is then returned to cell E17. This value represents the original investment plus all change orders entered in row 41. This is a standard implementation of the @LOOKUP function. Now, in order to cut down on the search time and speed up the alculation, a slight modification to this has been implemented. Each succeeding row entry reduces the search table size of the second table. This can be seen in

```
For spreadsheet template instructions, Press OPEN-APPLE 9.
```

```
                              S.R. Construction Company
                              P.O. Box 999
                              Anywhere Town, U.S.A.
```

```
                                       Address of Job
Project Name -:- Garden Apartments -------  1000 Garden Oaks Dr.
Project number - L10234            -------  Anywhere Town, U.S.A.
Job Start Date - 04/01/84          -------
```

Item Description	Item No.	Original Estimate	Original Cost	Change Orders	Actual Cost	Percent Complete	Variance in Job
Land value	1	$0.00	$0.00	$0.00	$0.00	0%	$0.00
Interest expense	2	$0.00	$0.00	$0.00	$0.00	0%	$0.00
Site prepartion	3	$0.00	$0.00	$0.00	$0.00	0%	$0.00
Land scaping cost	4	$0.00	$0.00	$0.00	$0.00	0%	$0.00
Plans	5	$0.00	$0.00	$0.00	$0.00	0%	$0.00
Permit fees	6	$0.00	$0.00	$0.00	$0.00	0%	$0.00
Utility services	7	$0.00	$0.00	$0.00	$0.00	0%	$0.00
Bath acc.expense	8	$0.00	$0.00	$0.00	$0.00	0%	$0.00
Mirror expense	9	$0.00	$0.00	$0.00	$0.00	0%	$0.00
Appliance expense	10	$0.00	$0.00	$0.00	$0.00	0%	$0.00
Drape expense	11	$0.00	$0.00	$0.00	$0.00	0%	$0.00
Lighting expense	12	$0.00	$0.00	$0.00	$0.00	0%	$0.00
Mortar mix expense	13	$0.00	$0.00	$0.00	$0.00	0%	$0.00
Mortarsand expense	14	$0.00	$0.00	$0.00	$0.00	0%	$0.00
Brick labor	15	$0.00	$0.00	$0.00	$0.00	0%	$0.00
Concrete expense	16	$0.00	$0.00	$0.00	$0.00	0%	$0.00
Concrete labor	17	$0.00	$0.00	$0.00	$0.00	0%	$0.00
		$0.00	$0.00	$0.00	$0.00	0%	$0.00

Item Description	Item	Change order cost columns			
Land value	1	$0.00	$0.00	$0.00	$0.00
Interest expense	2	$0.00	$0.00	$0.00	$0.00
Site prepartion	3	$0.00	$0.00	$0.00	$0.00
Land scaping cost	4	$0.00	$0.00	$0.00	$0.00
Plans	5	$0.00	$0.00	$0.00	$0.00
Permit fees	6	$0.00	$0.00	$0.00	$0.00
Utility services	7	$0.00	$0.00	$0.00	$0.00
Bath acc.expense	8	$0.00	$0.00	$0.00	$0.00
Mirror expense	9	$0.00	$0.00	$0.00	$0.00
Appliance expense	10	$0.00	$0.00	$0.00	$0.00
Drape expense	11	$0.00	$0.00	$0.00	$0.00
Lighting expense	12	$0.00	$0.00	$0.00	$0.00
Mortar mix expense	13	$0.00	$0.00	$0.00	$0.00
Mortarsand expense	14	$0.00	$0.00	$0.00	$0.00
Brick labor	15	$0.00	$0.00	$0.00	$0.00
Concrete expense	16	$0.00	$0.00	$0.00	$0.00
Concrete labor	17	$0.00	$0.00	$0.00	$0.00
		$0.00	$0.00		

Figure 5-27 *Project Cost Template*

For spreadsheet template instructions, Press OPEN-APPLE 9.

S.R. Construction Company
P.O. Box 999
Anywhere Town, U.S.A.

Address of Job
1000 Garden Oaks Dr.
Anywhere Town, U.S.A.

Project Name --- Garden Apartments ----------
Project number - L10234 ----------
Job Start Date - 04/01/84 ----------

Item Description	Item No.	Original Estimate	Original Cost	Change Orders	Actual Cost	Percent Complete	Variance in Job
Land value	1	$1,000.00	$1,250.00	$0.00	$1,250.00	125%	($250.00)
Interest expense	2	$0.00	$0.00	$0.00	$0.00	0%	$0.00
Site prepartion	3	$0.00	$0.00	$0.00	$0.00	0%	$0.00
Land scaping cost	4	$0.00	$0.00	$0.00	$0.00	0%	$0.00
Plans	5	$0.00	$0.00	$0.00	$0.00	0%	$0.00
Permit fees	6	$0.00	$0.00	$0.00	$0.00	0%	$0.00
Utility services	7	$0.00	$0.00	$0.00	$0.00	0%	$0.00
Bath acc.expense	8	$0.00	$0.00	$0.00	$0.00	0%	$0.00
Mirror expense	9	$0.00	$0.00	$0.00	$0.00	0%	$0.00
Appliance expense	10	$0.00	$0.00	$0.00	$0.00	0%	$0.00
Drape expense	11	$0.00	$0.00	$0.00	$0.00	0%	$0.00
Lighting expense	12	$0.00	$0.00	$0.00	$0.00	0%	$0.00
Mortar mix expense	13	$0.00	$0.00	$0.00	$0.00	0%	$0.00
Mortarsand expense	14	$0.00	$0.00	$0.00	$0.00	0%	$0.00
Brick labor	15	$0.00	$0.00	$0.00	$0.00	0%	$0.00
Concrete expense	16	$0.00	$0.00	$0.00	$0.00	0%	$0.00
Concrete labor	17	$0.00	$0.00	$0.00	$0.00	0%	$0.00
		$1,000.00	$1,250.00	$0.00	$1,250.00	125%	($250.00)

Figure 5-27(a) Top of Project Cost Template

113

Item Description	Item	Change order cost columns				
Land value	1	$0.00	$0.00	$0.00	$0.00	$0.00
Interest expense	2	$0.00	$0.00	$0.00	$0.00	$0.00
Site preparation	3	$0.00	$0.00	$0.00	$0.00	$0.00
Land scaping cost	4	$0.00	$0.00	$0.00	$0.00	$0.00
Plans	5	$0.00	$0.00	$0.00	$0.00	$0.00
Permit fees	6	$0.00	$0.00	$0.00	$0.00	$0.00
Utility services	7	$0.00	$0.00	$0.00	$0.00	$0.00
Bath acc.expense	8	$0.00	$0.00	$0.00	$0.00	$0.00
Mirror expense	9	$0.00	$0.00	$0.00	$0.00	$0.00
Appliance expense	10	$0.00	$0.00	$0.00	$0.00	$0.00
Drape expense	11	$0.00	$0.00	$0.00	$0.00	$0.00
Lighting expense	12	$0.00	$0.00	$0.00	$0.00	$0.00
Mortar mix expense	13	$0.00	$0.00	$0.00	$0.00	$0.00
Mortarsand expense	14	$0.00	$0.00	$0.00	$0.00	$0.00
Brick labor	15	$0.00	$0.00	$0.00	$0.00	$0.00
Concrete expense	16	$0.00	$0.00	$0.00	$0.00	$0.00
Concrete labor	17	$0.00	$0.00	$0.00	$0.00	$0.00
		$0.00	$0.00			

Instructions for the use of the template:

1. Change master header, if required.
2. Enter project identification in rows 10 through 12.
3. Enter original estimate for each item in rows 17 through 33, column C
4. Enter original cost for each item in rows 17 through 33, column D.
5. Enter the cost change orders in rows 41 through 57, columns C through F, as needed.
6. Column F, rows 17 through 33 automatically computes the Actual cost based upon Original cost column plus the Change order sum.
7. Percent complete is based upon the fraction of the Original Estimate divided by the Actual cost, expressed as a percentage.
8. The variance is computed as the difference between the Original Estimate minus the Actual cost.

Figure 5-27(b) Body of Project Cost Template

114

```
+------+-------+----------+--------------------------------------+
| Cell | Cell  | Cell     | Cell Contents                        |
|      | Width | Type **  | Label/Value/Formula                  |
+------+-------+----------+--------------------------------------+
| A17  | 18    | Label    | Land value                           |
| B17  | 6     | Value    | 1                                    |
| C17  | 12    | Value-D2 | 0                                    |
| D17  | 12    | Value-D2 | 0                                    |
| E17  | 12    | Value-D2 | @LOOKUP(B17,B41...B57)+(D41+E41+F41) |
| F17  | 12    | Value-D2 | +D17+E17                             |
| G17  | 10    | Value-P0 | @IF(F17>0,F17/C17,0)                 |
| H17  | 12    | Value-D2 | +C17-F17                             |
+------+-------+----------+--------------------------------------+
| A18  | 18    | Label    | Interest expense                     |
| B18  | 6     | Value    | +B17+1                               |
| C18  | 12    | Value-D2 | 0                                    |
| D18  | 12    | Value-D2 | 0                                    |
| E18  | 12    | Value-D2 | @LOOKUP(B18,B42...B57)+(D42+E42+F42) |
| F18  | 12    | Value-D2 | +D18+E18                             |
| G18  | 10    | Value-P0 | @IF(F18>0,F18/C18,0)                 |
| H18  | 12    | Value-D2 | +C18-F18                             |
+------+-------+----------+--------------------------------------+
| A19  | 18    | Label    | Site preparation                     |
| B19  | 6     | Value    | +B18+1                               |
| C19  | 12    | Value-D2 | 0                                    |
| D19  | 12    | Value-D2 | 0                                    |
| E19  | 12    | Value-D2 | @LOOKUP(B19,B43...B57)+(D43+E43+F43) |
| F19  | 12    | Value-D2 | +D19+E19                             |
| G19  | 10    | Value-P0 | @IF(F19>0,F19/C19,0)                 |
| H19  | 12    | Value-D2 | +C19-F19                             |
+------+-------+----------+--------------------------------------+
```

Note: ** Label means a text character string entry.
      Value means a numeric entry.
      D2 means dollar format with two decimal places.
      P0 means percent format with zero decimal places.

Figure 5-27(c)   *Cell Contents of Project Cost Template*

Fig. 5-27c for the E column formula entry. There are other modifications you might want to implement. Experiment a little.

The Actual Cost column is the addition of the Original Cost incurred plus the sum of all Change Orders entered: +D17+E17 for row 17.

The Percent Complete column uses the @IF function. Cell G17 has the following function/formula combination entered: @IF(F17>0,F17/C17,0). This function/formula says if the value in cell F17 is greater than zero, then divide the value in cell F17 by the value in cell C17 and place the result in cell G17. If, however, the value in cell F17 is zero or less, then place the value zero in cell G17. This prevents a division-by-zero error from occurring.

The last column, H, calculates the difference between the originally estimated cost for the item and the final actual cost to complete that item, including all change orders. The formula used is =C17−F17 for row 17.

```
+------+-------+----------+--------------------------------------+
I Cell I Cell  I Cell     I Cell Contents                        I
I      I Width I Type **  I Label/Value/Formula                  I
+------+-------+----------+--------------------------------------+
I A35  I 18    I Label    I Blank cell                           I
I B35  I 6     I Value    I Blank cell                           I
I C35  I 12    I Value-D2 I @SUM(C16...C34)                      I
I D35  I 12    I Value-D2 I @SUM(D16...D34)                      I
I E35  I 12    I Value-D2 I @SUM(E16...E34)                      I
I F35  I 12    I Value-D2 I @SUM(F16...F34)                      I
I G35  I 10    I Value-P0 I @IF(F35>0,F35/C35,0)                 I
I H35  I 12    I Value-D2 I @SUM(H16...H34)                      I
+------+-------+----------+--------------------------------------+
```

```
Note: ** Label means a text character string entry.
         Value means a numeric entry.
         D2 means dollar format with two decimal places.
         P0 means percent format with zero decimal places.
```

Figure 5-27(d)   *Totals Row of Project Cost Template*

All of the above formulas are replicated from row 17 through 33. The only difference is that each row's formula and function cell references are modified relative to its new row location.

The Total row, 35, sums the entries in rows 17 through 33. The cell entries are shown in Fig. 5-27d. The only exception is cell G35. This cell calculates the percentage completion for the entire project.

The bottom half of the template is a replication of columns A and B in rows 17 through 33 duplicated into rows 41 through 57. Columns C, D, E, and F are for values that represent the dollar amounts incurred for change orders.

Template instructions are placed in rows 63 through 76 and shown in Fig. 5-27e.

```
63IInstructions for the use of the template:
64I
65I1. Change master header, if required.
66I2. Enter project identification in rows 10 throught 12.
67I3. Enter original estimate for each item in rows 17 through 33, column C.
68I4. Enter original cost for each item in rows 17 through 33, column D.
69I5. Enter the cost change orders in rows 41 through 57, columns C through
70I   F, as needed.
71I6. Column F, rows 17 through 33 automatically computes the Actual cost
72I   based upon Original cost column plus the Change order sum.
73I7. Percent complete is based upon the fraction of the Original
74I   Estimate divided by the Actual cost, expressed as a percentage.
75I8. The variance is computed as the difference between the Original
76I   Estimate minus the Actual cost.
```

Figure 5-27(e)   *Instructions for Project Cost Template*

5.9.6 Personal Budget Example

The last template in this chapter is a personal budget. This template accomplishes two things: it helps create a personal budget spending plan and it tracks actual expenditures. The complete template is shown in Fig. 5-28.

At first glance, this template may seem very long and complicated. However, the entry and operation of this template is very easy. We will start with the first third of the template. This is shown in Fig. 5-28a.

This template is broken into three four-month segments: Jan–Apr, May–Aug, and Sep–Dec, plus a total column on each page. Each four-month segment is on a single page. The instructions for the use of the template are on the fourth page.

Figure 5-28a shows page 1 of the template. The first seven rows are the template header. All of these entries are labels. Row 9 is the column headers. The month labels are right-justified in a cell. The total column label is also right-justified. Rows 12 through 18 are for the entry of all income sources. These entries and formulas are shown in Fig. 5-28b.

Rows 21 through 56 are for the entry of the first four months' expenses and total column. Column F totals the entries in the rows containing value entry expenses with the function @SUM(B23 . . . E23) for row 23. This function is replicated relatively in all of the other rows requiring row totals. Row 56 totals the individual column expense entries. The formulas for row 56 are shown in Fig. 5-28c.

Rows 59 through 63 are for the totaling of all expenses; entry of the cash placed in savings accounts, IRA's, etc; and the totaling of the monthly cash remaining. Column F keeps a running total of the remaining cash. The entries are shown in Fig. 5-28d.

Notice there is a double dashed line in row 65, the bottom of a letter-size paper for page 1. The same is true in rows 131 and 197 for pages 2 and 3, respectively.

The second page of entries are in rows 67 through 132. The entry in A79 = First 4mo cash. Cell B79 = +F63 = 3000.00. The third page of entries go into rows 133 through 198. The entry in A145 = Second 4mo cash. Cell B145 = +F129 = 4046.40. By formatting your budget in this way you account for page breaks and format each page on a separate sheet of paper.

Once you have entered all of page 1 into the budget template, use the copy feature to replicate heading information rows and expense rows into page 2 and then into page 3. Relatively replicate the formulas. Then add the required blank rows, modify the required labels in column A, change a couple of formulas in column B, and your budget template is completed.

Finally, the fourth page entries are the instructions for the operation of the budget template. These rows are shown in Figure 5-28e.

5.10 DATA INTERCHANGE FORMAT (DIF)

The Data Interchange Format (DIF) is a file format for exchanging data between computer programs. It was developed by Robert M. Frankston, the ex-president of Software Arts, Inc., and now with Lotus Development, the creators of VisiCalc, as a method of

```
=======================================================================
```
For spreadsheet template instructions, press OPEN-APPLE 9.
```
=======================================================================
```

Date: 05/01   Year 1984
                                                     Page 1

                        PERSONAL BUDGET

Description	Jan	Feb	Mar	Apr	Total
Incomes:					
Beginning cash	2449.76				
First - source	2732.48	2732.48	2732.48	2732.48	$10,929.92
Second - source	0.00	0.00	2500.00	0.00	$2,500.00
Third - source	0.00	0.00	0.00	0.00	$0.00
Total Incomes	5182.24	2732.48	5232.48	2732.48	$15,879.68
Expenses:					
House:					
Mortgage	745.88	745.88	745.88	745.88	$2,983.52
Insurance	40.00	40.00	40.00	40.00	$160.00
Property taxes	50.00	50.00	50.00	50.00	$200.00
Life Insurance:					
Husband	15.00	15.00	15.00	15.00	$60.00
Wife	15.00	15.00	15.00	15.00	$60.00
Children	10.00	10.00	10.00	10.00	$40.00
Transportation:					
Car #1 gas/oil	56.00	44.00	53.42	46.58	$200.00
Car #1 payment	325.00	325.00	325.00	325.00	$1,300.00
Car #1 repair	0.00	0.00	123.76	0.00	$123.76
Car #2 gas/oil	48.32	55.44	46.24	50.00	$200.00
Car #2 payment	295.00	295.00	295.00	295.00	$1,180.00
Car #3 repair	0.00	0.00	101.45	0.00	$101.45
Household:					
Groceries	425.55	462.56	466.08	444.21	$1,798.40
Gas & Electric	274.43	288.09	266.67	272.66	$1,101.85
Telephone	44.02	46.23	52.88	43.55	$186.68
Water	22.00	23.05	22.98	35.99	$104.02
Garbage	5.00	5.00	5.00	5.00	$20.00
Miscellaneous	0.00	18.96	32.32	65.00	$116.28
Personal:					
Clothing	42.47	0.00	0.00	163.55	$206.02
Medical	148.68	0.00	162.50	0.00	$311.18
Babysitting	0.00	0.00	0.00	0.00	$0.00
Pocket money	225.44	212.00	225.00	250.00	$912.44
Gifts	0.00	0.00	37.22	72.44	$109.66
Entertainment	48.32	52.55	49.88	53.67	$204.42
Total Expenses	2836.11	2703.76	3141.28	2998.53	$11,679.68
Cash remaining	2346.13	28.72	2091.20	-266.05	$4,200.00
Cash to savings	500.00	100.00	500.00	100.00	$1,200.00
Ending cash	1846.13	-71.28	1591.20	-366.05	$3,000.00

PERSONAL BUDGET

Description	May	Jun	Jul	Aug	Total
Incomes:					
First 4mo cash	3000.00				
First - source	2732.48	2732.48	2732.48	2732.48	$10,929.92
Second - source	0.00	2500.00	0.00	0.00	$2,500.00
Third - source	0.00	0.00	0.00	0.00	$0.00
Total Incomes	5732.48	5232.48	2732.48	2732.48	$16,429.92
Expenses:					
House:					
Mortgage	745.88	745.88	745.88	745.88	$2,983.52
Insurance	40.00	40.00	40.00	40.00	$160.00
Property taxes	50.00	50.00	50.00	50.00	$200.00
Life Insurance:					
Husband	15.00	15.00	15.00	15.00	$60.00
Wife	15.00	15.00	15.00	15.00	$60.00
Children	10.00	10.00	10.00	10.00	$40.00
Transportation:					
Car #1 gas/oil	50.00	50.00	50.00	50.00	$200.00
Car #1 payment	325.00	325.00	325.00	325.00	$1,300.00
Car #1 repair	0.00	0.00	100.00	0.00	$100.00
Car #2 gas/oil	50.00	50.00	50.00	50.00	$200.00
Car #2 payment	295.00	295.00	295.00	295.00	$1,180.00
Car #3 repair	0.00	0.00	100.00	0.00	$100.00
Household:					
Groceries	450.00	450.00	450.00	450.00	$1,800.00
Gas & Electric	275.00	275.00	275.00	275.00	$1,100.00
Telephone	45.00	45.00	45.00	45.00	$180.00
Water	25.00	25.00	25.00	25.00	$100.00
Garbage	5.00	5.00	5.00	5.00	$20.00
Miscellaneous	25.00	25.00	25.00	25.00	$100.00
Personal:					
Clothing	0.00	0.00	0.00	0.00	$0.00
Medical	150.00	0.00	150.00	0.00	$300.00
Babysitting	0.00	0.00	0.00	0.00	$0.00
Pocket money	200.00	200.00	200.00	200.00	$800.00
Gifts	0.00	0.00	0.00	0.00	$0.00
Entertainment	50.00	50.00	50.00	50.00	$200.00
Total Expenses	2820.88	2670.88	3020.88	2670.88	$11,183.52
Cash remaining	2911.60	2561.60	-288.40	61.60	$5,246.40
Cash to savings	500.00	100.00	500.00	100.00	$1,200.00
Ending cash	2411.60	2461.60	-788.40	-38.40	$4,046.40

```
==================================================================
```

PERSONAL BUDGET

Description	Sep	Oct	Nov	Dec	Total
Incomes:					
Second 4mo cash	4046.40				
First - source	2732.48	2732.48	2732.48	2732.48	$10,929.92
Second - source	2500.00	0.00	0.00	2500.00	$5,000.00
Third - source	0.00	0.00	0.00	0.00	$0.00
Total Incomes	9278.88	2732.48	2732.48	5232.48	$19,976.32
Expenses:					
House:					
Mortgage	745.88	745.88	745.88	745.88	$2,983.52
Insurance	40.00	40.00	40.00	40.00	$160.00
Property taxes	50.00	50.00	50.00	50.00	$200.00
Life Insurance:					
Husband	15.00	15.00	15.00	15.00	$60.00
Wife	15.00	15.00	15.00	15.00	$60.00
Children	10.00	10.00	10.00	10.00	$40.00
Transportation:					
Car #1 gas/oil	50.00	50.00	50.00	50.00	$200.00
Car #1 payment	325.00	325.00	325.00	325.00	$1,300.00
Car #1 repair	0.00	0.00	100.00	0.00	$100.00
Car #2 gas/oil	50.00	50.00	50.00	50.00	$200.00
Car #2 payment	295.00	295.00	295.00	295.00	$1,180.00
Car #3 repair	0.00	0.00	100.00	0.00	$100.00
Household:					
Groceries	450.00	450.00	450.00	450.00	$1,800.00
Gas & Electric	275.00	275.00	275.00	275.00	$1,100.00
Telephone	45.00	45.00	45.00	45.00	$180.00
Water	25.00	25.00	25.00	25.00	$100.00
Garbage	5.00	5.00	5.00	5.00	$20.00
Miscellaneous	25.00	25.00	25.00	25.00	$100.00
Personal:					
Clothing	0.00	0.00	0.00	0.00	$0.00
Medical	150.00	0.00	150.00	0.00	$300.00
Babysitting	0.00	0.00	0.00	0.00	$0.00
Pocket money	200.00	200.00	200.00	200.00	$800.00
Gifts	0.00	0.00	0.00	0.00	$0.00
Entertainment	50.00	50.00	50.00	50.00	$200.00
Total Expenses	2820.88	2670.88	3020.88	2670.88	$11,183.52
Cash remaining	6458.00	61.60	-288.40	2561.60	$8,792.80
Cash to savings	500.00	100.00	500.00	100.00	$1,200.00
Ending cash	5958.00	-38.40	-788.40	2461.60	$7,592.80

```
==================================================================
```

```
=======================================================================
                                            Page 4
          PERSONAL BURGET INSTRUCTIONS
          Copyright (C) 1984 by Mesa Research, Inc.
```

```
Instructions for the use of the template:

1. Enter the date, month and day, in cell A4.
2. Enter the year for the budget in cell F4.
3. Enter the beginning cash at start of the year in cell B13.
4. Enter sources of income for current month in appropriate cells.
5. Enter expenses incurred for current month in appropriate cells.
6. Enter the cash to be placed into savings.in appropriate cells.
7. All other mathematics is done automatically.
8. The calculated entry in cell F195 is next year's starting cash.
9. Return to the top of the template using OPEN-APPLE 1.
=======================================================================
                                            jlc - srr
```

Figure 5-28 *Budget Template*

communicating and transferring data between a VisiCalc template and other computer spreadsheet templates. Software Arts, Inc., is actively encouraging the use of the DIF format as the standard format for data interchange. The DIF format is actually a concept, a method of organizing data, and not a stand-alone software product that can be purchased.

To date, the DIF concept has been used primarily on personal computers, but it could be an important bridge for the data exchange between personal computers and the larger multi-user mainframe computers. At least it could provide one way to transfer data between spreadsheets of different sizes and manufacturers.

The DIF concept is important because:

- The extraordinary popularity of VisiCalc over the past few years, along with other spreadsheet programs, has created a need for software developers to provide software that is compatible with some type of data transfer.

- The recognized need for a standard format for data interchange becomes more important as spreadsheet programs proliferate.

As a result, Software Arts, Inc., has established The DIF Clearinghouse to coordinate and distribute information about the DIF format. This nonprofit clearinghouse distributes written technical specifications of the DIF format, and publishes a list of products that support the DIF file format. The clearinghouse can be reached at:

The DIF Clearinghouse
P.O. Box 638
Newton Lower Falls, MA 02162

As a file format, DIF is essentially unrelated to computer hardware, and can be used to organize data on any storage device. The DIF format allows files from one computer to

```
=========A==========B=========C=========D=========E==========F=========G=
  1|========================================================================
  2|For spreadsheet template instructions, press OPEN-APPLE 9.
  3|========================================================================
  4| Date: 05/01                                              Year 1984
  5|                                                          Page 1
  6|                        PERSONAL BUDGET
  7|_____
  8|
  9|Description         Jan        Feb        Mar        Apr        Total
 10|_____
 11|
 12|Incomes:
 13|Beginning cash    2449.76
 14|First  - source   2732.48    2732.48    2732.48    2732.48  $10,929.92
 15|Second - source      0.00       0.00    2500.00       0.00   $2,500.00
 16|Third  - source      0.00       0.00       0.00       0.00       $0.00
 17|                  ---------  ---------  ---------  ---------  -----------
 18|Total Incomes     5182.24    2732.48    5232.48    2732.48  $15,879.68
 19|_____
 20|
 21|Expenses:
 22|House:
 23|     Mortgage      745.88     745.88     745.88     745.88   $2,983.52
 24|    Insurance       40.00      40.00      40.00      40.00     $160.00
 25|Property taxes      50.00      50.00      50.00      50.00     $200.00
 26|
 27|Life Insurance:
 28|      Husband       15.00      15.00      15.00      15.00      $60.00
 29|         Wife       15.00      15.00      15.00      15.00      $60.00
 30|     Children       10.00      10.00      10.00      10.00      $40.00
 31|
 32|Transportation:
 33|Car #1 gas/oil      56.00      44.00      53.42      46.58     $200.00
 34|Car #1 payment     325.00     325.00     325.00     325.00   $1,300.00
 35|Car #1  repair       0.00       0.00     123.76       0.00     $123.76
 36|Car #2 gas/oil      48.32      55.44      46.24      50.00     $200.00
 37|Car #2 payment     295.00     295.00     295.00     295.00   $1,180.00
 38|Car #2  repair       0.00       0.00     101.45       0.00     $101.45
 39|
 40|Household:
 41|     Groceries     425.55     462.56     466.08     444.21   $1,798.40
 42|Gas & Electric     274.43     288.09     266.67     272.66   $1,101.85
 43|     Telephone      44.02      46.23      52.88      43.55     $186.68
 44|         Water      22.00      23.05      22.98      35.99     $104.02
 45|       Garbage       5.00       5.00       5.00       5.00      $20.00
 46| Miscellaneous       0.00      18.96      32.32      65.00     $116.28
 47|
 48|Personal:
 49|      Clothing      42.47       0.00       0.00     163.55     $206.02
 50|       Medical     148.68       0.00     162.50       0.00     $311.18
 51|    Babysitting      0.00       0.00       0.00       0.00       $0.00
 52|  Pocket money     225.44     212.00     225.00     250.00     $912.44
 53|         Gifts       0.00       0.00      37.22      72.44     $109.66
```

```
54I Entertainment        48.32       52.55       49.88       53.67       $204.42
55I                     --------    --------    --------    --------    ----------
56ITotal Expenses       2836.11     2703.76     3141.28     2998.53    $11,679.68
57I_____
58I
59ICash remaining       2346.13       28.72     2091.20     -266.05     $4,200.00
60I
61ICash to savings       500.00      100.00      500.00      100.00     $1,200.00
62I
63IEnding cash          1846.13      -71.28     1591.20     -366.05     $3,000.00
64I
65I==========================================================================
66I
67I
68I
69I==========================================================================
70I
71I                                                              Page 2
72I                          PERSONAL BUDGET
```

Figure 5-28(a) *Partial Budget Template*

be used on another, assuming that a hardware connection, or some other type of communication link, exists between the two computers.

AppleWorks can write to a disk file the DIF format from either the spreadsheet or the data base. This allows you to save a file that could then be used in other application programs. AppleWorks can also read from a disk file a DIF-formatted file created by other programs into the applications. Reports from either the spreadsheet template or the data base can be exchanged using the DIF method.

Tip: To use the DIF files in AppleWorks, you must be in ProDOS. If the disk is in DOS 3.3, use the ProDOS User's Disk to convert the disk into a ProDOS disk.

If you are starting a spreadsheet template file from a DIF-created file, follow the steps below for loading a DIF file.

1. Choose *From a DIF file* on the spreadsheet menu. Type the complete pathname of the file. See Appendix F. A pathname is the complete series of names for the file, starting from the volume directory to the file. This includes the / character before the volume directory name and the / character used to separate the intermediary directory names and the file name. The directory name does not allow blank spaces. For example, a pathname for the file VALUES could be /BLANK00/VALUES. Once the pathname has been entered, press the RETURN key.

```
+------+------+----------+-------------------------------------------+
| Cell | Cell | Cell     | Cell Contents                             |
|      | Width| Type **  | Label/Value/Formula                       |
+------+------+----------+-------------------------------------------+
| A12  |  15  | Label    | Incomes:                                  |
+------+------+----------+-------------------------------------------+
| A13  |  15  | Label    | Beginning cash                            |
| B13  |  10  | Value-F2 | 2449.76                                   |
+------+------+----------+-------------------------------------------+
| A14  |  15  | Label    | First  - source                           |
| B14  |  10  | Value-F2 | 2732.48                                   |
| C14  |  10  | Value-F2 | 2732.48                                   |
| D14  |  10  | Value-F2 | 2732.48                                   |
| E14  |  10  | Value-F2 | 2732.48                                   |
| F14  |  13  | Value-D2 | @SUM(B14...E14) = $10,929.92              |
+------+------+----------+-------------------------------------------+
| A15  |  15  | Label    | Second - source                           |
| B15  |  10  | Value-F2 | 0                                         |
| C15  |  10  | Value-F2 | 0                                         |
| D15  |  10  | Value-F2 | 2500.00                                   |
| E15  |  10  | Value-F2 | 0                                         |
| F15  |  13  | Value-D2 | @SUM(B15...E15) = $2,500.00               |
+------+------+----------+-------------------------------------------+
| A16  |  15  | Label    | Third  - source                           |
| B16  |  10  | Value-F2 | 0                                         |
| C16  |  10  | Value-F2 | 0                                         |
| D16  |  10  | Value-F2 | 0                                         |
| E16  |  10  | Value-F2 | 0                                         |
| F16  |  13  | Value-D2 | @SUM(B16...E16) = $0.00                    |
+------+------+----------+-------------------------------------------+
| A18  |  15  | Label    | Total Incomes                             |
| B18  |  10  | Value-F2 | @SUM(B13...B17) = 5182.24                  |
| C18  |  10  | Value-F2 | @SUM(C14...C17) = 2732.48                  |
| D18  |  10  | Value-F2 | @SUM(D14...D17) = 5232.48                  |
| E18  |  10  | Value-F2 | @SUM(E14...E17) = 2732.48                  |
| F18  |  13  | Value-D2 | @SUM(B18...E18) = $15,879.68               |
+------+------+----------+-------------------------------------------+
```

Note: ** Label means a text character string entry.
         Value means a numeric entry.
         D2 means dollar format with two decimal places.
         F2 means fixed number format with two decimal places.

Figure 5-28(b)   *Cell Contents of Budget Template*

2. AppleWorks will load the specified file name and ask you to type a new name for the file. Do not use the same name; change the name to something else.

To create a DIF file from the spreadsheet that is to be used in the data base or other program, use the OPEN-APPLE P, print keystroke combination command for that application program. This will allow you to place a DIF file in either row or column order to the disk.

```
+------+-------+----------+-------------------------------------------+
| Cell | Cell  | Cell     | Cell Contents                             |
|      | Width | Type **  | Label/Value/Formula                       |
+------+-------+----------+-------------------------------------------+
| A56  |  15   | Label    | Total Expenses                            |
| B56  |  10   | Value-F2 | ?SUM(B22...B55) = 2836.11                  |
| C56  |  10   | Value-F2 | ?SUM(C22...C55) = 2703.76                  |
| D56  |  10   | Value-F2 | ?SUM(D22...D55) = 3141.28                  |
| E56  |  10   | Value-F2 | ?SUM(E22...E55) = 2998.53                  |
| F56  |  13   | Value-D2 | ?SUM(B56...E56) = $11,679.68              |
+------+-------+----------+-------------------------------------------+
```

Note: ** Label means a text character string entry.
      Value means a numeric entry.
      D2 means dollar format with two decimal places.
      F2 means fixed number format with two decimal places.

Figure 5-28(c)   *Cell Contents Row 56*

```
+------+-------+----------+-------------------------------------------+
| Cell | Cell  | Cell     | Cell Contents                             |
|      | Width | Type **  | Label/Value/Formula                       |
+------+-------+----------+-------------------------------------------+
| A59  |  15   | Label    | Cash remaining                            |
| B59  |  10   | Value-F2 | +B18-B56        = 2346.13                  |
| C59  |  10   | Value-F2 | +C18-C56        =   28.72                  |
| D59  |  10   | Value-F2 | +D18-D56        = 2091.20                  |
| E59  |  10   | Value-F2 | +E18-E56        = -266.05                  |
| F59  |  13   | Value-D2 | ?SUM(B59...E59) = $4,200.00               |
+------+-------+----------+-------------------------------------------+
| A61  |  15   | Label    | Cash to savings                           |
| B61  |  10   | Value-F2 | 500.00                                    |
| C61  |  10   | Value-F2 | 100.00                                    |
| D61  |  10   | Value-F2 | 500.00                                    |
| E61  |  10   | Value-F2 | 100.00                                    |
| F61  |  13   | Value-D2 | ?SUM(B61...E61) = $1,200.00               |
+------+-------+----------+-------------------------------------------+
| A63  |  15   | Label    | Ending cash                               |
| B63  |  10   | Value-F2 | +B59-B61        = 1846.13                  |
| C63  |  10   | Value-F2 | +C59-C61        =  -71.28                  |
| D63  |  10   | Value-F2 | +D59-D61        = 1591.20                  |
| E63  |  10   | Value-F2 | +E59-E61        = -366.05                  |
| F63  |  13   | Value-D2 | +F59-F61        = $3,000.00               |
+------+-------+----------+-------------------------------------------+
```

Note: ** Label means a text character string entry.
      Value means a numeric entry.
      D2 means dollar format with two decimal places.
      F2 means fixed number format with two decimal places.

Figure 5-28(d)   *Cell Contents Row 56*

```
200|
201|==================================================================
202|
203|                                                    Page  4
204|          PERSONAL BURGET INSTRUCTIONS
205|          Copyright (C) 1984 by Mesa Research, Inc.
206|_____
207|
208|Instructions for the use of the template:
209|
210|1. Enter the date, month and day, in cell A4.
211|2. Enter the year for the budget in cell F4.
212|3. Enter the beginning cash at start of the year in cell B13.
213|4. Enter sources of income for current month in appropriate cells.
214|5. Enter expenses incurred for current month in appropriate cells.
215|6. Enter the cash to be placed into savings in appropriate cells.
216|7. All other mathematics is done automatically.
217|8. The calculated entry in cell F195 is next year's starting cash.
218|9. Return to the top of the template using OPEN-APPLE 1.
219|==================================================================
220|                                                    jlc - srr
```

Figure 5-28(e)   *Budget Template Instructions*

5.11 SUMMARY

This chapter explored the built-in functions within the spreadsheet, including @IF, @LOOKUP, @CHOOSE, and @NPV.

Master forms were given that could be used as is or modified. The functions and formulas within the templates were examined.

The last section of this chapter discussed the DIF capability of AppleWorks.

PART FOUR

*It is best to do things systematically . . . since we are only human,
and disorder is our worst enemy.*
HESIOD, 8TH CENTURY B.C.

Systematically organizing things makes it easier for you to work with information and understand the contents. This part discusses how to arrange and organize data using the data base portion of AppleWorks.

CHAPTER SIX

The Data Base

It is a capital mistake to theorize before one has data.
Sir Arthur Conan Doyle, 1891

6.0 OVERVIEW

The AppleWorks data base makes it easy to create and keep lists of things, from names and addresses to schedules and stamp collections. Any set of information that can be organized logically can be made into a list and kept on the data base.

There are really only three major activities involved in working with lists: creating and entering information into a list, rearranging the order of the list, and printing a report from the list. This chapter discusses these skills and the information needed to successfully use the data base.

Section 6.1 examines a number of housekeeping capabilities and features that are embedded in the data base, including copying, moving, and deleting records.

Section 6.2 compares table- and label-style reports.

Section 6.3 gives a summary of the information discussed in this chapter.

6.1 HOUSEKEEPING CAPABILITIES

Every software package, regardless of its simplicity or complexity, requires that you have some knowledge or set of skills in order to effectively use it. The data base is no different. There are certain keystrokes and keystroke combinations that you need to know before you can effectivly use this application. The following subsections discuss these skills.

6.1.1 Planning a Data Base

Generally, the information you intend to keep in a list will determine the composition of the data base. For example, you really would not keep inventory items in a list of names and addresses. At least, we hope not. That's only done in the filing cabinets in the back room. However, you will have to arrange the logical order of presentation of the information.

The first step is to define the categories and category names of the information to be kept in the data base file. For example, if you are keeping a record of all the Christmas cards you send and receive each year, you probably would want the following categories: name, address, city, state, ZIP code, and possibly the individual years you sent and received cards. Each of these can become the category names of columnar headings for the Christmas card list.

Each set of items entered into this list is called a record. For example, if you sent and received a Christmas card from Aunt Harriet this year, that entry becomes an individual record in the list. Each item in the set of items for an individual record is called an entry.

For example, Aunt Harriet's full name is an entry. Aunt Harriet's name is made up of characters. A character may be any printable symbol in the alphabet, numbers 0 through 9, and special symbols such as $, #, @, &, *.

After deciding upon all of the categories and their names you need to decide on the number of characters each category entry will accommodate. For example, you might allow fifteen characters for the name of an individual and only two characters for a state abbreviation. Finally, you will need to allow for blank spaces between entries.

If any of the numeric column entries need to be summed, allowance must be made for the largest total number allowed in that column. This may necessitate widening a column.

After deciding upon the contents of your data base file, you must decide how your file is to be printed. If your file extends beyond the 80-column Desktop screen presentation, you probably will only be able to print all of the file's information in one printing if you change the character size or use wider paper. You may need to rearrange categories within the file in order to print selected categories. These considerations are covered in a later section.

We cannot stress strongly enough that you analyze and design a data base as thoroughly as possible before you actually start entering information.

6.1.2 Creating a Data Base

After planning a data base, it is time to actually create your new file:

1. Choose option 1, "Add files to the Desktop" from the Main Menu.
2. Choose option 4, "Make a new file for the data base."
3. Select the "From scratch" option to create a new file.

6.1.2.1 *From Scratch*

There are a number of additional items that must be defined before you can enter records into a new file. First, type the name of the new file. When you have completed entering the file name, press the RETURN Key.

Next, define each category or column heading for the new data base file. Before you start typing category names, give some thought to just how each of these column headings should be entered. Each column heading should be descriptive, reasonably short, and easily understood. Each column heading may be up to twenty characters long.

> **Tip:** It is recommended that you use the overstrike cursor to type over the default Category 1 entered automatically by the data base. Remember, OPEN-APPLE E does this for you. See Section 9.1.5.

After entering the category names, press the ESCape key to exit. You can then begin entering records into the file by pressing the SPACEBAR.

There are always times when you make typographic errors. When this happens, use the following procedures to make corrections.

To correct file names:

- Press the up-arrow key to return to the file name. Then retype the name and press the RETURN key.

To correct category names:

- Press the up-arrow key to go to the previous category name.
- Press the down-arrow key to go to the next category name.
- Press OPEN-APPLE I to insert a category name ahead of the one the cursor is positioned over.
- Press OPEN-APPLE D to delete a category name. Then correct the name and press the RETURN Key.

> **Tip:** The Data Base scans category names for the keywords "date" and "time" embedded in them. When a keyword is found, the entries into those categories will automatically be converted into standard date and time formats. See Chapter 7.

The other sources for an already planned data base file are explained in the next few sections.

6.1.2.2 *From a Text (ASCII) File*

You can use text (ASCII) files from a number of sources as your AppleWorks data base files. Text files are created by such systems as PASCAL, Apple Writer II/IIe, and other data bases. Appendix F and Chapter 9 discuss the required procedures. Text files have the following general characteristics:

- Each entry in a file is recorded on a separate line and followed by the RETURN key. This is the general characteristic of a sequential text file.
- Entries must be grouped by record and in the same order throughout the file.

> **Caution:** You *must* convert text files located on DOS 3.3 diskettes to the ProDOS operating system. Then use this option to acquire the file as an AppleWorks file.

To create AppleWorks files from ASCII files:

1. Choose option 1, "Add files to the Desktop" from the Main Menu.
2. Choose option 4, "Make a new file for the data base."
3. Choose "From a text (ASCII) file" option. The data base then asks you to enter the text file's complete pathname. Type the pathname and press the RETURN key.
4. Enter the name of the data base file.

> **Tip:** When you first enter a text file into the data base, the category names are Category 1, Category 2, etc. You can change the category names by using OPEN-APPLE N. See Section 9.1.14.

6.1.2.3 *From a Quick File*

Quick File is a data base program. The file structure of AppleWorks and Quick File are compatible.

To create AppleWorks files from Quick File:

1. Choose option 1, "Add files to the Desktop" from the Main Menu.
2. Choose option 4, "Make a new file for the data base."
3. Choose "From a Quick File" option. The data base gets the Quick File catalog from the disk in the current disk drive. After selecting the Quick File you want, the data base adds it to the Desktop.
4. Enter the name of the data base file.

6.1.2.4 *From a DIF File*

You can use a DIF file created by the spreadsheet portion of AppleWorks, the spreadsheet program VisiCalc, and other programs that support the DIF structure to move information into a data base file. There is one caution, however: when you create the DIF file you *must* use the column-wide option. This will cause all information to be grouped correctly.

Caution: You *must* convert text files located on DOS 3.3 diskettes to the ProDOS operating system. Then, you can use this option to acquire the file as an AppleWorks file.

To create AppleWorks files from a DIF file:

1. Choose option 1, "Add files to the Desktop" from the Main Menu.
2. Choose option 4, "Make a new file for the data base."
3. Choose "From a DIF file" option. The data base asks you to enter the DIF file's complete pathname. Type the pathname and press the RETURN key.
4. Enter the name of the data base file.

Tip: When you first get the DIF file into AppleWorks, all categories are named generically, Category 1, Category 2, etc. Change the name of the categories using the OPEN-APPLE N, Section 9.1.14.

6.1.3 Data Base Record Layout

When working with the data base, you may present information in either of two formats: single record and multiple record. You can move back and forth between these formats.

The single-record layout gives one record at a time. Information is listed vertically by category on the screen. Use this format to enter and check new records.

The multiple-record layout gives all of the records in a data base at once. This format, however, does not necessarily present all of the categories that have been defined, but only those that you choose to display. In the multiple-record format you can scroll around on the screen, change and rearrange the categories in the file, and change a number of entries within categories. If you want to look at an entire record, just zoom-in, using OPEN-APPLE Z.

6.1.4 Entering Information into Records

It is very easy to enter information into record entries and then edit any information that may be incorrectly entered. The next few paragraphs summarize the various editing and typing features available in the AppleWorks data base.

1. You can use either the insert cursor or the overstrike cursor when you are entering or editing entries in a record. The overstrike cursor replaces the characters that are typed at the cursor position. The insert cursor inserts characters, moving everything else to the right of the cursor. Cursors can be changed by using OPEN-APPLE E.

2. Use the DELETE key to delete one character at a time immediately to the left of the cursor.

3. Press the ESCape key to restore a former entry, and place the cursor at the first character of that entry.

4. Use the right/left and up/down arrow keys to move the cursor. This will not erase or otherwise change anything that is already typed in.

5. Press the CONTROL-Y-RETURN combination to erase characters from the cursor position to the end of that record entry.

6. Use the insert cursor to add characters into entries in the multiple-record lay-out. If the current entry becomes too large for the available space in that category, the information to the right of the cursor is placed "under" the entry for the next column. In order to see the entire entry, you will need to zoom-in to the single-record format.

Tip: Pressing the RETURN key in the middle of entry when all editing is complete does *not* truncate or disturb the remainder of an entry's characters.

When entering information into a record in the multiple-record layout, you can make multiple copies of an entry directly above the cursor by pressing the OPEN-APPLE QUOTATION MARK. Do not use the SHIFT key.

6.1.5 Inserting Records

After you have created a new data base file, you will need to enter new records.
    To enter the first record into a file:

1. Press ESCape key after you have set up the file and category names. The data base will tell you if there are records in the file.

2. Press the SPACEBAR. The data base presents the first blank record in the file.

3. Enter the entry information into each category of the numbered record; press the RETURN key after each entry. If the entry is a blank, then simply press the RETURN key.

4. After entering all the information for a record, press the RETURN key to present the next entry screen.

5. Press the ESCape key after you are finished creating new records. The data base then presents the newly entered records in the multiple-record layout.

Tip: You can enter information, up to 76 permissible characters, so that it fits into the space next to the next category. You will probably not be able to see all of the information except when you view individual records in the single-record format. This can be done by zooming-in, OPEN-APPLE Z.

You are able to enter new records into an existing file from the Review/Add/Change screen in either a single- or multiple-record layout.

To insert records in the single-record layout:

1. Press OPEN-APPLE I (insert command). The data base then presents a blank record in the single-record layout. Type in the information entries, pressing the RETURN key after each entry. The new record for insertion goes just before the record position of the cursor.

2. Enter information into each category and press the RETURN key after each entry. If the entry is a blank, then simply press the RETURN key.

3. Press the RETURN key after you type the information required by the last entry in the record. The data base then presents the next blank record.

4. Press the ESCape key after you are finished creating new records. The data base presents the newly entered records in the multiple-record layout along with the other records in the file.

5. Press OPEN-APPLE Z to return to the single-record layout.

Tip: If you are going to enter information into individual entries when in the multiple-record layout, you may want to set the cursor so that it will move to the right instead of down when you press the RETURN key. Type OPEN-APPLE L, press the ESCape key, and choose "Right" for the cursor direction.

6.1.6 Deleting Records

As your data base file changes, you will probably want to delete a record or groups of records.

To delete records from the multiple-record layout:

1. Place the cursor anywhere on the record that you want to delete.
2. Press OPEN-APPLE D (delete command). The data base will highlight that record to be deleted.
3. Use the up/down arrow keys to highlight additional records.
4. When all records to be deleted have been highlighted, press the RETURN key.

To delete records from the single-record layout:

1. Press OPEN-APPLE Z to zoom in to the record you want to delete. This will put you in the single-record layout.
2. Press OPEN-APPLE D (delete command).
3. Choose either "No" or "Yes," depending on whether you want to delete the displayed record. The data base will display the next record.
4. Continue to choose either "No" or "Yes" as the data base displays additional records. All selected records will be deleted.
5. Press the ESCape key when you are finished deleting records.

Tip: If you want to delete all of the information in a file while keeping the file's structure, use the following procedure:

1. In the single-record layout, create a blank record as the first record in the file.
2. Move the cursor to the second record.
3. Zoom out to the multiple-record layout.
4. Press OPEN-APPLE D (delete command).
5. Press OPEN-APPLE 9 and the RETURN key to place the cursor at the end of the file.

All records in the file, except the first record, will be deleted.

6.1.7 Moving Records

The AppleWorks data base allows you to rearrange the order of records. Actually, the following procedure moves a record to the Clipboard first and then back to the file in another location. Chapter 8 gives further information on moving records.

To move records from the multiple-record layout:

1. Make sure you are in the multiple-record format.
2. Place the cursor anywhere on the record that you want to move.
3. Press OPEN-APPLE M (move command).
4. Choose "To Clipboard (cut)" option.
5. Use the arrow keys to highlight the records you want to move.
6. Press the RETURN key. The highlighted records are then moved to the Clipboard.
7. Move the cursor, using the arrow keys, to the place in the file where you want the Clipboard records to be relocated.
8. Press OPEN-APPLE M (move command).
9. Choose "From clipboard (paste)" option. The records are then immediately relocated into the file.

6.1.8 Copying Records

The AppleWorks data base allows you to replicate, or make copies, of a record in a data base file. This feature is very handy when more than one record has information in common. This then reduces the amount of time required to enter new information.

To copy records in either the single or multiple-record layout:

1. Make sure you are in the multiple-record format.
2. Place the cursor anywhere on the record tht you want to copy.
3. Press OPEN-APPLE C (copy command).
4. Choose "Current record" option.
5. Type the number of copies you want and press the RETURN key.

6.1.9 Rearranging Records

The AppleWorks data base lets you arrange, or sort, records by the values of entries within a category. You can arrange records alphabetically in ascending or descending order, numerically in ascending or descending order, or with dates and times in chronological or reverse chronological order.

> **Tip:** When you want to arrange records by several categories, arrange values in reverse order of importance. First arrange the least important category, then the next most important category, etc.

When you arrange or sort categories, the data base arranges values in accordance with the collating sequence of the hexadecimal and/or decimal values that represent characters in the ASCII character set. This means numeric values are assigned to the individual characters. See Appendix G for the ASCII character set and corresponding hexadecimal and decimal values.

6.1.10 Changing Record Layouts

The AppleWorks data base allows you to change the layout of a record. This is a very powerful feature which lets you change your mind on how you want to have records presented.

To change a record layout in the single- or multiple-record layout use the outlined procedure in Section 6.3.4.

In the single-record layout you may use the following keystrokes to move within the active Desktop file.

What you want to do	**What you should use**
Move the cursor	Press any of the arrow keys or press the RETURN key
To move categories	Press OPEN-APPLE arrow key to move in direction of next category

In the multiple-record layout you may use the following keystrokes to move within the active Desktop file.

What you want to do	**What you should use**
Move the cursor to the next category	Right arrow or TAB key
Move the cursor to the previous category	Left arrow or OPEN-APPLE-TAB key
Switch the position of the category the cursor is on with the one to its right	OPEN-APPLE->. You do not need to use the SHIFT key for the > key
Switch the position of the category the cursor is on with the one to its left	OPEN-APPLE-<. You do not need to use the SHIFT key for the < key
Increase the width of the column the cursor is on	OPEN-APPLE right arrow key
Decrease the width of the column the cursor is on	OPEN-APPLE left arrow key
Delete the category the cursor is on. The information in this category stays in the record	OPEN-APPLE D
Insert the category previously deleted just to the left of the category the cursor is on	OPEN-APPLE I. After you type the keystrokes, previously deleted categories are displayed. Type the number of the category you want inserted and then press the RETURN key

6.1.11 Displaying Specific Records

You can change record selection rules to display only certain records in a file. For example, you may want to display the names of all employees in the personnel file who were hired before 1974.

When you first create a new file, the selection rule is "Selection: All records." The use of this rule in the early stages of entering information is satisfactory because your file does not contain many records. But with the addition of records to the file, you may want to limit the number records displayed to make them easier to read. You will have to change the selection rule.

To change a record selection rule:

1. Press OPEN-APPLE R (selection rule command).

2. Choose the category you want to use as a basis for the selection. You can use any category, even one that is not displayed in the multiple-record layout.

3. Choose a comparison. Using either the up/down arrow keys or number keys, select a comparison option from the following list of connectors:

equals	contains
is greater than	begins with
is less than	ends with
is not equal to	does not contain
is blank	does not begin with
is not blank	does not end with

4. Type the value for the selected category the specific category value to be compared with. Then press the RETURN key.

5. Continue making category comparison selections, comparisons, and values for a total of three.

6. Press the ESCape key when your record selection is complete. The data base displays all records that comply with the new selection rule. You may also use such connectors as AND, OR, and THROUGH.

Tip: You can define record selection rules that contain up to three connectors. This means that you may define an initial condition plus two additional selection conditions. For example, you can display all employees who have been with your company for over ten years and make over $20,000.00. Or you could display all stamps in your collection that were issued between 1939 and 1946.

Once you have specified a rule for the selection of records, you can then ask the data base to go back to selecting all records.

To change the record selection rule to "All" again:

1. Press OPEN-APPLE R.
2. Choose "Yes" to indicate that you want to display all records.

Once you have specified a rule for the selection of records, the data base will find and display all records that contain the rule information. The information may be in any category in a record and anywhere within an entry. For example, you may be looking for a specific date, time, age, etc.

To find a specific record:

1. Press OPEN-APPLE F (find command).
2. Type the value you want to find. The data base then displays those records that contain the value you have requested.
3. Press the ESCape key to return to the Review/Add/Change screen.

The Find feature gives you the flexibility of locating records that contain values regardless of where that particular value is located. This allows you to globally find and correct typographical errors, spelling changes, changes of any kind in the file, or common information spread throughout the file.

6.2 REPORT STYLES

The AppleWorks data base lets you create two different styles of reports: table and label.

A table-style report lists records in rows and columns. An example of this style is a stock market report. See Section 6.2.2.

A label-style report lists records with the category names printed vertically. An example of this style is a mailing list. See Section 6.2.3.

When deciding what style of report to produce, try to envision the way the information should look for it to be most readable and effective. See Chapter 7 for examples of table- and label-style reports.

6.2.1 Report Formats and Menu

Anytime the contents of a data base file are to be printed, the report format needs to be specified. For a table-style format, the arrangement of categories needs to be specified. For example, you may want only a few categories printed in one report and all categories printed in another. Or you may want to rearrange the order of some of the categories. Further, you may want to calculate numeric totals by groups and then have a grand total calculated and presented in the report.

Once all of the report identification items have been specified and the categories have been presented, the data base saves this information. Any one data base may have up to eight separate report formats saved. This allows you to produce a number of different reports from a data base file.

When in the Review/Add/Change screen with a data base loaded, you may want to print a report. You can do so by using OPEN-APPLE P. (See Section 9.1.16.) Once you have used this keystroke combination, the data base displays the Report Menu. This menu presents six available report options:

- The "Get a report format" option will display a report catalog, which lists all the stored reports. After you have selected a format, the report is presented so that you may make any changes and then print it.
- The "Create a new tables format" option first asks for the name of the new report and then displays the format display for a table-style report.
- The "Create a new labels format" option first asks for the name of the new report and then displays the format display for a label-style report.
- The "Duplicate an existing format" option allows you to copy an existing report format. The report catalog is first presented so that you can select the report format for duplication. After selecting the format, you *must* give the report a new name. The data base then displays the new report.
- The "Erase a format" option presents the report catalog for the data base file. You then select the format to be deleted. Remember, you can save no more than eight report formats at one time.
- The "Keep working with current format" option returns the data base to the format you have just used.

Now that you know the options available from the Reports Menu, you are ready to actually create report formats.

6.2.2 Table-style Reports

To create a table-style report:

1. Start in the Review/Add/Change screen display of the file for which you want to create a report.
2. Press OPEN-APPLE P. The data base then presents the Reports Menu.
3. Choose "Create a new tables format" option. The data base then prompts you for the report name.
4. Type the name of the report. The name may contain up to nineteen letters, numbers, or special characters. This name can be the same as the file name. Press the RETURN key.
5. The report format is presented.

6.2.3 Label-style Reports

To create a label-style report:

1. Start in the Review/Add/Change screen display of the file for which you want to create a report.
2. Press OPEN-APPLE P. The data base then presents the Reports Menu.
3. Choose "Create a new labels format" option. The data base then prompts for the name of the report.
4. Type the name of the report. The name may contain up to nineteen letters, numbers, or special characters. This name can be the same as the file name. Press the RETURN key.
5. The report format is presented.

Now that you know the two report formats, you have all of the basic knowledge necessary to actually work with a data base file. Chapter 7 continues the discussion of working with the data base by creating files and adding a number of useful capabilities.

6.3 SUMMARY

This chapter discussed two major facets of the data base: housekeeping features and report styles.

Housekeeping features include all of the capabilities of the data base that allow you to create and delete files and records; enter and edit information into those records; copy, move, and rearrange records within a file; and search and display only selected records from a data base file.

Report styles available through AppleWorks are table and label. The discussion in this chapter centered on the Report Menu and its options and the actual creation of these types of reports.

C H A P T E R S E V E N

Additional Data Base Features

*It takes a certain courage and a certain greatness even to be
truly base.*
Jean Anouilh, 1948

7.0 OVERVIEW

This chapter continues the discussion of the capabilities of the data base.

Section 7.1 examines the creation of a typical mailing list.

Section 7.2 describes an extension to the mailing list, a Christmas card list that keeps track of Christmas cards sent and received each year and the addresses of all recipients. Two different styles are shown for this list.

Section 7.3 shows how to create a job-costing list. Once this list is created you are shown how to develop a number of different reports from this one list.

Section 7.4 creates a classroom gradebook to keep track of student grades and to compute grade averages.

Section 7.5 summarizes the chapter.

After you have gone through this chapter, you should be confident enough with the operation of the data base to create lists, enter information, edit lists, change records, and create reports.

7.1 MAILING LIST

A mailing list is probably the easiest list to create and understand, and in which to enter information.

The next subsection shows you how to create a list from scratch and to enter information into it after all of the category names have been defined. You will also be shown how to customize screen presentations.

Section 7.1.2 shows how to create label-style reports for the mailing list. Then, finally, you will be ready to print the final product, mailing labels.

7.1.1 Creating and Editing the List

This section shows a step-by-step approach to developing a sample mailing list. You may want to power up your system now, get the data base, and start the file that is going to be created.

The general procedure for creating a mailing list from a report is as follows:

1. Press the ESCape key, more than once if necessary, to return to the Main Menu.

2. Select option 1, "Add files to the Desktop," using the up/down arrow keys or the number 1 key. This is the first option in the Main Menu. See Section 1.4.1 and Fig. 1-3.

3. Select option 4, "Data Base." This will activate the data base for your Desktop. See Fig. 1-4.

4. Select the "From scratch" option. This tells the data base to start a new list from the beginning.

5. Define the file name for the new list.

6. Define all of the category names needed for the list. See Figs. 7-3a and 7-3b.

7. Enter the data into the list as individual records. See Figs. 7-5 and 7-6.

8. Define a report format for the list. See Section 6.2 and Figs. 7-13 through 7-16.

9. Print mailing labels using a report format for the list.

10. Name this new file MAIL.LIST.

Tip: Before you start a new list, carefully plan both the contents of the list, with their category names, and at least one of the report formats that you want. This will help to prevent a lot of possible errors and to reduce much wasted time.

Figure 7-2 shows the screen used to enter category names into a list and later to edit or change names. Remember that all of the information in a category is related. For example, a category called ZIP will only have zip codes in that column. The data base enters the first generic category, Category 1, as a starting point. If that is not going to be the name of your category, change it to what you want.

If you change the first generic category name, you need to erase it and replace it with the new category name. There are three ways you can erase the default entry:

1. Use the insert cursor. Use the right arrow key to move the cursor just beyond the 1 in Category 1. Now, press the DELETE key ten times to erase the entry. This should leave the cursor at the left edge of the screen.

```
Disk: Drive 2                    DATA BASE              Escape: Erase entry

 |_____|
 |     Main Menu          |_____
 |   _____ |                                              |
 |   |   Add Files        |_____|__   |
 |   |  _____|                                          |   |
 |   |  |   Data Base      |_____|_  |
 |   |  |                                                             |  |
 |   |  |                                                             |  |
 |   |  |   Make a new file:                                          |  |
 |   |  |                                                             |  |
 |   |  |   --> From scratch                                          |  |
 |   |  |                                                             |  |
 |   |  |   2.  From a text (ASCII) file                              |  |
 |   |  |                                                             |  |
 |   |  |   3.  From a Quick File (TM) file                           |  |
 |   |  |                                                             |  |
 |___|  |   4.  From a DIF (TM) file                                  |  |
 |   |  |                                                             |  |
 |   |__|                                                             |  |
 |   |                                                                |  |
 |   |_____|

Type a name for this new file:  MAIL.LIST                      55K Avail.
```

Figure 7-1   *Name New File Screen*

```
File: MAIL.LIST              CHANGE NAME/CATEGORY    Escape: Review/Add/Change




Category names
==============================================================================
Category 1
                                |
                                | Options:
                                |
                                | Change category name
                                | Up arrow   Go to filename
                                | Down arrow Go to next category
                                | ?-I        Insert new category
                                |
                                |
                                |
                                |
                                |
                                |
                                |
--------------------------------|---------------------------------------------
Type entry or use ? commands                                  55K Avail.
```

Figure 7-2   *Enter Categories Screen*

2. Use the CONTROL-Y keys. Press this keystroke combination to erase characters from the cursor position to the end of the entry.

3. Use the overstrike cursor. Enter the new category name over the first generic category name. Erase any remaining characters present beyond the new category name.

If you make a mistake or want to change a category name, you can scroll through the list of category names, using the arrow keys, and/or delete any category entries. All of the entering, correcting, scrolling, and deleting is done in the same way that it is done in the word processor. The category names screen is shown in Figs. 7-3a and 7-3b.

#	Category name	Category description
1.	Last name	= Last name, first name, middle initial.
2.	First	
3.	I	
4.	St Address	= Street, city, state, and zip code.
5.	City	
6.	State	
7.	Zip	
8.	C	= Comma used to separate city and state or last name from first name, depending upon the report form specified.
9.	P	= Period used after the middle initial or state entry.

The category names to be used in the MAIL.LIST file are defined in the table below.

The only difference in the above two screens is in the prompt messages on the right-hand side of each. Figure 7-3a tells you that you can type a new category or use the up arrow key to go to another category. Figure 7-3b gives you additional options:

Type/Change a category name.

Use the up arrow key to go to the previous entry.

Use the down arrow key to go to the next entry.

Use OPEN-APPLE I to insert a new category in the middle of the list.

Use OPEN-APPLE D to delete the category at the cursor position.

When you have completed entering the category names, press the ESCape key to exit from this screen. Before you can proceed to entering record information into the list, the data base will tell you there is no record information in the file. This is shown in Fig. 7-4.

This screen tells you to "Press space bar to continue." When this is done, you will be presented with the screen shown in Fig. 7-5. The screen of Fig. 7-5 is Record 1 of 1, with all of the categories listed vertically but without any other record information entered. This is the "Insert New Records" screen and is used whenever entering a new record.

Figure 7-6 shows the first information record entered. After entering each record

```
File: MAIL.LIST              CHANGE NAME/CATEGORY      Escape: Review/Add/Change




Category names
====================================================================
Last name                         |
First                             | Options:
I                                 |
St Address                        | Type category name
City                              | Up arrow   Go to previous category
St                                |
ZIP                               |
C                                 |
P                                 |
                                  |
                                  |
                                  |
                                  |
                                  |
--------------------------------------------------------------------
Type entry or use ∂ commands                            55K Avail.
```

Figure 7-3(a)   *First Categories Screen*

```
File: MAIL.LIST              CHANGE NAME/CATEGORY      Escape: Review/Add/Change




Category names
====================================================================
Last name                         |
First                             | Options:
I                                 |
St Address                        | Change category name
City                              | Up arrow   Go to previous category
St                                | Down arrow Go to next category
ZIP                               | ∂-I        Insert new category
C                                 | ∂-D        Delete this category
P                                 |
                                  |
                                  |
                                  |
                                  |
                                  |
--------------------------------------------------------------------
Type entry or use ∂ commands                            55K Avail.
```

Figure 7-3(b)   *Second Categories Screen*

```
File: MAIL.LIST                REVIEW/ADD/CHANGE              Escape: Main Menu



Category names
================================================================================



                    This file does not yet contain
                    any information.  Therefore, you
                    will automatically go into the
                    Insert New Records feature.






--------------------------------------------------------------------------------
Press Space Bar to continue                                        55K Avail.
```

Figure 7-4   *No Records Screen*

```
MAIL.LIST                  INSERT NEW RECORDS      Escape: Review/Add/Change



Record 1 of 1
================================================================================
Last name: -
First: -
I: -
St Address: -
City: -
St: -
ZIP: -
C: -
P: -




--------------------------------------------------------------------------------
Type entry or use ⌘ commands                                       55K Avail.
```

Figure 7-5   *Insert New Records Screen*

```
File: MAIL.LIST              INSERT NEW RECORDS              Escape: Erase entry



Record 1 of 1
===============================================================================
Last name: Campbell
First: John
I: L
St Address: Rt #12 Box 480
City: Waco
St: Texas
ZIP: 76710
C: ,
P: .




--------------------------------------------------------------------------------
Type entry or use ⌂ commands                                        55K Avail.
```

Figure 7-6   *Record 1 Entered Screen*

entry, press the RETURN key to signal entry completion. The cursor is then placed at the first character of the next entry.

The Fig. 7-6 screen shows that you are working with record 1 of a 1-record file and that all information has been entered. Go ahead and enter the first record into your list at this time.

After entering the first record into the MAIL.LIST list, it would be a good idea to format the presentation of this and all subsequent record information on the screen. Then when you want the list information presented in the table-style format, the information will be presented in such a way that you can see as much as possible on one screen. First press the ESCape key and then use OPEN-APPLE Z to present the file in the table-style format.

When that is done, the MAIL.LIST file will be presented with the first record presented on one line of the screen, as shown in Fig. 7-7. Notice that only the first five categories are shown. This needs to be changed so that more of the categories and entries can be presented.

Now is the time to customize the record layout for the file. The default entry size is 15 characters for all category entries. Obviously, you do not need that many characters for such fields as the zip code, middle initial, comma, and period. In order to start customizing, use the OPEN-APPLE L keystroke combination from the table-style screen. The screen then changes to the "Change record layout" screen.

From this screen you can modify the record layout in a number of ways:

#	Keystroke				Keystroke description
1.	→ or ←			=	Use arrow keys to move the cursor from category to category, left and right.
2.	> @ <			=	Use OPEN-APPLE > or OPEN-APPLE < to switch category positions. It is not necessary to use the shift key.
3.	→ @ ←			=	Use OPEN-APPLE arrow keys to lengthen or shorten column widths.
4.	@-D			=	Use OPEN-APPLE D to delete a category.
5.	@-I			=	Use OPEN-APPLE I to insert a previously deleted category.

By using the arrow keys and the OPEN-APPLE key, you can move to each category and change the character length values. Do this now to conform to the length values shown in the table below. Since the length values for categories are not shown explicitly, it is necessary that you count the dashed-line spaces.

#	Category name		Length value
1.	Last name	=	15
2.	First	=	13
3.	I	=	1
4.	St Address	=	15
5.	City	=	15
6.	State	=	2
7.	ZIP	=	5
8.	C	=	1
9.	P	=	1
10.	Blank spaces	=	9
			77 characters

As you shorten the categories, the word "margin" will appear along the right edge of the screen. This signifies the present end of the screen file presentation. Figure 7-9 shows the first record as it will appear on the screen in the modified table-style format. All records will be presented in this format. When you are finished customizing the record layout, press the ESCape key.

The screen in Fig. 7-10 asks you to select the direction the cursor should move when you press the RETURN key. This is a very interesting and helpful capability. If you intend to enter record information in the label-style format, you may want to select option 1, "Down (standard)." This means that, when you press the RETURN key, the cursor will move down the screen. However, if you are planning to enter record information in the table-style format, you may want to select option 2, "Right." This means that, when you press the RETURN key, the cursor will move horizontally to the right on the screen. For now, select the standard cursor movement.

After selecting the cursor movement, you will be returned to the Review/Add/Change screen. This is shown in Fig. 7-11.

Now you have completed everything necessary except entering additional records into the list. This must seem like a long procedure; however, after you have done it once or twice, it becomes very easy.

```
File: MAIL.LIST              REVIEW/ADD/CHANGE              Escape: Main Menu

Selection: All records


Last name        First          I            St Address      City
======================================================================
Campbell         John           L            Rt #12 Box 480  Waco








---------------------------------------------------------------------------
Type entry or use ∂ commands                                   ∂-? for Help
```

Figure 7-7   *Table-Style Screen*

```
MAIL.LIST                 CHANGE RECORD LAYOUT    Escape: Review/Add/Change




=============================================================================
              --> or <--  Move cursor
               >  ∂  <    Switch category positions
              --> ∂ <--   Change column width
              ∂-D         Delete this category
              ∂-I         Insert a previously deleted category


---------------------------------------------------------------------------
Last name        First          I            St Address      City
---------------  -------------  ------------  --------------  ----------
Campbell         John           L            Rt #12 Box 480  Waco



------------------------------------------------------------- More --->
Use options shown above to change record layout              55K Avail.
```

Figure 7-8   *Change Record Layout Screen*

```
File: MAIL.LIST              CHANGE RECORD LAYOUT    Escape: Review/Add/Change




================================================================================

            --) or <--   Move cursor
              )  2   <    Switch category positions
            --) 2  <--    Change column width
            2-D           Delete this category
            2-I           Insert a previously deleted category

--------------------------------------------------------------------------------

Last name        First        I St Address     City           St ZIP   C P M
--------------   -----------   -  -----------   ------------   -- ----- - - A
Campbell         John         L Rt #12 Box 480  Waco           Tx 76710 , . R
                                                                           G
                                                                           I
                                                                           N
--------------------------------------------------------------------------------
Use options shown above to change record layout                 55K Avail.
```

Figure 7-9   *Customized Record Layout Screen*

```
File: MAIL.LIST              CHANGE RECORD LAYOUT    Escape: Review/Add/Change




================================================================================

            What direction should the cursor
            go when you press Return?

                 1.  Down (standard)
                 2.  Right

--------------------------------------------------------------------------------

Last name        First        I St Address     City           St ZIP   C P M
--------------   -----------   -  -----------   ------------   -- ----- - - A
Campbell         John         L Rt #12 Box 480  Waco           Tx 76710 , . R
                                                                           G
                                                                           I
                                                                           N
--------------------------------------------------------------------------------
Type number, or use arrows, then press Return                   55K Avail.
```

Figure 7-10   *RETURN Key Direction Screen*

```
File: MAIL.LIST              REVIEW/ADD/CHANGE              Escape: Main Menu

Selection: All records


Last name        First        I St Address      City           St ZIP   C P
==============================================================================
Campbell         John         L Rt #12 Box 480  Waco           Tx 76710 , .




----------------------------------------------------------------------------
Type entry or use ∂ commands                                   ∂-? for Help
```

Figure 7-11 *Modified Record Layout Screen*

7.1.2 Printing Labels

Before you can print a report it is necessary to define a report format. This format is then adhered to when each record in the list is printed.

The report format to be defined is a mailing label for each record in the MAIL.LIST file. However, before doing that, it might be a good idea to understand the physical characteristics of those stick-on mailing labels that seem to appear on so many letters nowadays.

Blank adhesive mailing labels can usually be purchased from office supply stores, stationers, office supply mail order catalogs, business form manufacturers, and some computer stores. Normally, the smallest number of labels that can be purchased at a time is a box of 1000 or 5000. Blank labels come in many sizes; the most widely used sizes are 15/16″ by 3″, 3.5″, or 4″.

In the data base, you can choose either 6 or 8 lines per inch to be printed vertically. The default value of 6 lines per inch for vertical spacing seems to work out very nicely. A blank label of 15/16″ with a 1/16″ spacing between labels means that the start of each label is 1″ apart and that there are 11 labels possible on each 11″ sheet of labels. Further a three- or four-line label fits very nicely on a blank label with that 15/16″ vertical label size.

There is a little planning required for deciding the horizontal size of a label. In the last section, each category width value was specified. For example, if you put the last name (15), C (1), First (13), I (1), P (1), and four blank spaces together on the first line of a label, the line will occupy 35 spaces (3.5″) if the print size is 10 characters per inch. The label-line will only occupy 3″ if the print size is set to 12 characters per inch. This is shown in the tables below.

At 10 characters per inch:

Category name		Category width
Last name	=	15
C	=	1
First	=	13
I	=	1
P	=	1
Blanks	=	4 (1 between each entry)
		35 = 3.5″

At 12 characters per inch:

Category name		Category width
Last name	=	15
C	=	1
First	=	13
I	=	1
P	=	1
Blanks	=	4 (1 between each entry)
		35 = 3.0″

Now, look at the second and third lines of the printed label.
At 10 characters per inch:

Category name		Category width
The second line:		
St Address	=	15
		15 = 1.5″
The third line:		
City	=	15
State	=	2
ZIP	=	5
Blanks	=	2 (between entries)
		24 = 2.4″

In order to create a report format, press the OPEN-APPLE P print keystroke combination. This is the same keystroke combination you will use to print a report, discussed later.

The screen presented to you is shown in Fig. 7-12. This screen tells you that you are using the MAIL.LIST file, that there are no reports specified, that the ESCape key will

```
MAIL.LIST                    REPORT MENU           Escape: Review/Add/Change
Report: None


=============================================================================


              1.  Get a report format
              2.  Create a new "tables" format
              3.  .Create a new "labels" format
              4.  Duplicate an existing format
              5.  Erase a format




-----------------------------------------------------------------------------
Type number, or use arrows, then press Return                    55K Avail.
```

Figure 7-12 REPORT MENU *Options Screen*

return you to the Review/Add/Change screen, and that you have five options available. The options are:

#	Report option available	Option description
1.	Get a report format	= Retrieve a previously defined report format
2.	Create a new "tables" format	= Define a new table-style report format
3.	Create a new "labels" format	= Define a new label-style report format
4.	Duplicate an existing format	= Make an exact copy of an existing report format
5.	Erase a format	= Delete an existing report format

Choose option 3, "Create a new labels format" by using the up/down arrow keys or the number 3 key. When you have made the selection, press the RETURN key.

After making the selection, name the report format MAIL.LIST since this is the first format created for the MAIL.LIST. Follow the file-naming conventions discussed in the Section 1.4.1.

After specifying the report format name, the Report Format screen, shown in Fig. 7-13, is presented. What you need to do now is to reformat the default report format so that you can print your MAIL.LIST records on blank mailing labels.

There are a number of formatting steps that need to be taken in order to define a label-style report. These include:

1. Delete all of the unnecessary category names for the report being formatted.
2. Place all of the remaining category names in the report into their appropriate positions.

```
File: MAIL.LIST              NAME THE NEW REPORT          Escape: Erase entry
Report: None




===============================================================================







-------------------------------------------------------------------------------
Type a name for the report:  MAIL.LIST.1                         55K Avail.
```

Figure 7-13   First REPORT FORMAT Screen

```
File: MAIL.LIST              REPORT FORMAT               Escape: Report Menu
Report: MAIL.LIST.1
Selection: All records



===============================================================================
Last name
First
I
St Address
City
St
ZIP
C
P
------------------------Each record will print  9 lines-----------------------




-------------------------------------------------------------------------------
Use options shown on Help Screen                                ?-? for Help
```

Figure 7-14   Second REPORT FORMAT Screen

3. Specify the spacing between the category names in one line of the report.

4. Left-justify those category names in the report that need to be printed at the left edge of the entry.

5. Specify the record selection rules. This step will be discussed in a later section.

Each of these steps will be discussed as needed.

For the first report format, MAIL.LIST.1, none of the category names will be deleted. Figure 7-14 shows you the first cut at formatting the MAIL.LIST.1 report. Refer to this figure for the discussion that follows.

The "Last name" category will be the pivotal point for this report and left in its initial position. Next, the comma category name entry, "C," will be placed in the report. The last two category names that will be placed on the first line of the report format will be "First" and "I." The procedure for doing all of this is as follows:

1. Place the cursor on the first character of the "C" category by using the arrow keys.

Keystroke	= Symbol	= Description
right arrow	= →	= Move cursor to the right
left arrow	= ←	= Move cursor to the left
up arrow	= ∧	= Move cursor up one line
down arrow	= ∨	= Move cursor down one line

2. Move "C" up to the first line and to the right of the "Last name" category. Use the OPEN-APPLE arrow keystroke combinations.

Keystroke combination	= Symbol	= Description
OPEN-APPLE right arrow	= @ →	= Move category to the right
OPEN APPLE left arrow	= @ ←	= Move category to the left
OPEN APPLE up arrow	= @ ∧	= Move category up one line
OPEN APPLE down arrow	= @ ∨	= Move category down one line

3. Move the "First" category name to the right of "C" with the OPEN-APPLE arrow keys.

4. Move the "I" category name to the right of the "First" category with the OPEN-APPLE arrow keys. The first line of the mailing label report is now formatted.

5. The "St Address" category name does not need to be moved. The second line of the mailing label report is now formatted.

6. The "City" category name does not need to be moved.

7. Move the "State" category name to the right of the "City" category with the OPEN-APPLE arrow keys.

8. Move the "P" category name to the right of the "State" category with the OPEN-APPLE arrow keys.

9. Move the "ZIP" category name to the right of "P" with the OPEN-APPLE arrow keys.

10. Left-justify the following category names:

C	State
First	P
I	ZIP

Use OPEN-APPLE J (left-justify command). Place the cursor at the first character of the category name to be left-justified and then type the OPEN-APPLE J command.

11. Continue justifying the remaining category names until each one shown in Fig. 7-14 is left-justified.

After completing all of the above steps, your screen should look like the one in Fig. 7-14. The next thing to do is to finish formatting the MAIL.LIST.1 REPORT FORMAT.

Place the cursor at the starting character of the "Last name" category name. Then use the OPEN-APPLE I keystroke combination. This command will let you insert a blank line either before or after the cursor position or insert previously deleted category names. Since you have not deleted any category names, the only option given is to insert a blank line. This is shown in Fig. 7-15.

There is only one more thing that needs to be done before the MAIL.LIST.1 report format is finished. Figure 7-16 shows the report format with the additional line added at the beginning of the report. However, the report is now 10 lines long. What is wanted is a report that is only 6 lines long so that it will fit nicely on a 15/16" deep mailing label.

Place the cursor anywhere on the line just above the one that tells you the length of the report. Then type the OPEN-APPLE D keystroke combination enough times to have the report length line show that the report is 6 lines deep. This is shown in Fig. 7-17.

You have now completed formatting the first report, MAIL.LIST, for the MAIL.LIST data base file. Of course, there are still a few more things left to do before actually printing a report. There always seem to be a few more things to do. However, the hard part is over.

Figure 7-18 shows a number of printer options that may be changed before printing a report. The Printer Options screen is reached using the OPEN-APPLE O (options command).

The values for all of the margins and the printer options are shown in this figure. They are the default values used in all of the other applications in AppleWorks and will be used when printing the report.

Making selections on this screen is very simple and straightforward. Just enter the two-character code followed by the RETURN key. If there is additional information needed, you will be prompted for it. Enter this additional information and press the RETURN key again. For the MAIL.LIST.1 report form, use a platen width (PW) of 3.5", a left margin (LM) and right margin (RM) of zero, and a characters per inch (CI) print

```
File: MAIL.LIST                 REPORT FORMAT              Escape: Report Menu
Report: MAIL.LIST.1
Selection: All records


================================================================================
Last name <C <First <I


St Address
City <St <P <ZIP




-----------------------Each record will print  9 lines-----------------------




--------------------------------------------------------------------------------
Use options shown on Help Screen                                   ?-? for Help
```

Figure 7-15 *Third REPORT FORMAT Screen*

```
File: MAIL.LIST                 INSERT A CATEGORY          Escape: Report Format
Report: MAIL.LIST.1
Selection: All records



================================================================================
  1.  A spacing line above cursor position
  2.  A spacing line below cursor position













--------------------------------------------------------------------------------
Type number, or use arrows, then press Return                     55K Avail.
```

Figure 7-16 *Fourth REPORT FORMAT Screen*

```
File: MAIL.LIST              REPORT FORMAT          Escape: Report Menu
Report: MAIL.LIST.1
Selection: All records


========================================================================

Last name <C <First <I
St Address
City <St <P <ZIP



------------------------Each record will print  6 lines-------------------------




-------------------------------------------------------------------------
Use options shown on Help Screen                          ?-? for Help
```

Figure 7-17 *Fifth REPORT FORMAT Screen*

```
File: MAIL.LIST              PRINTER OPTIONS       Escape: Report Format
Report: MAIL.LIST.1
========================================================================

-------Left and right margins--------        ------Top and bottom margins-------
PW: Platen Width        8.5 inches     PL: Paper Length        11.0 inches
LM: Left Margin         0.0 inches     TM: Top Margin           0.0 inches
RM: Right Margin        0.0 inches     BM: Bottom Margin        0.0 inches
CI: Chars per Inch      10             LI: Lines per Inch       6

    Line width          8.5 inches         Printing length     11.0 inches
    Char per line (est) 85                 Lines per page       66

          --------------------Formatting options--------------------
    SC:  Send Special Codes to printer                      No
    PD:  Print a Dash when an entry is blank                No
    PH:  Print report Header at top of each page            Yes
    OL:  Omit Line when all entries on line are blank        Yes
    KS:  Keep number of lines the Same within each record   Yes

    "Specify information about your printer" (on menu of Other
    Activities) gives you additional control over printers.
-------------------------------------------------------------------------
Type a two letter option code                             55K Avail.
```

Figure 7-18 *First PRINTER OPTIONS Screen*

size of 12. This allows 42 characters per label-line. The reason for using a left- and right-margin setting of zero is so that the mailing label will be as far to the left as possible and allow for a maximum label size. Both the top and bottom margins will remain at zero so that the printer will not have a skip distance of any kind between sheets of continuous paper and will fit neatly on a blank label. Figure 7-19 reflects the changes that have been suggested.

At the bottom of the screen shown in Fig. 7-19, you can specify a number of printer options that are unique to the data base.

#	Code	Report option available		Default
1.	SC	Send special codes to printer	= No	= This option is for the purpose of sending special codes to your printer not already supported by AppleWorks and your printer

Default = No. If you choose Yes, AppleWorks asks for the control or ESCape characters. Type the control or ESCape characters and type the caret ($\wedge$) when you finish

2.	PD	Print a dash when an entry is blank	= No	= If an entry is blank, then AppleWorks can print a single dash to mark the place

Default = No.

3.	PH	Print report header at top of each page	= Yes	= A report header contains the file name, report name, page number, date, and the record selection rule

Default = Yes. Always choose No for a labels report.

4.	OL	Omit line when all entries on line are blank	= Yes	= Yes means that AppleWorks will close up a blank line. No means that blank lines are left blank

Default = Yes. If you choose No, then the next option is eliminated since it is not needed. For a mailing list, this option should always be No.

5.	KS	Keep number of lines the same within each record	= Yes	= This option forces your report to occupy the same number of lines even though a line may be blank

Default = Yes.

For the MAIL.LIST.1 report, it is recommended that you use the following options: 1. = No, 2. = No, 3. = No, and 4. = No. The last option is eliminated. This is shown in Fig. 7-19. After you have made your selections, press the ESCape key to exit the printer options screen.

Finally, use the OPEN-APPLE P to print the mailing list. See Figure 7-20. The options on this screen are self-explanatory. For now, choose either the first or seond option. Actually, the second option will let you see your handiwork without using any paper. This is very handy because you may want to change or modify the report format.

At this point, it might be a good idea to look at a few of the other label-style reports that are possible from the MAIL.LIST data base file.

Figures 7-21 and 7-22 show two additional report formats. Notice in the

```
File: MAIL.LIST                    PRINTER OPTIONS            Escape: Report Format
Report: MAIL.LIST.1
=================================================================================

------Left and right margins--------       ------Top and bottom margins-------
PW: Platen Width              3.5 inches    PL: Paper Length         11.0 inches
LM: Left Margin               0.0 inches    TM: Top Margin            0.0 inches
RM: Right Margin              0.0 inches    BM: Bottom Margin         0.0 inches
CI: Chars per Inch            12            LI: Lines per Inch        6

    Line width                3.5 inches        Printing length      11.0 inches
    Char per line (est)       42                Lines per page       66

           --------------------Formatting options--------------------
      SC:  Send Special Codes to printer                          No
      PD:  Print a Dash when an entry is blank                    No
      PH:  Print report Header at top of each page                No
      OL:  Omit Line when all entries on line are blank           No


      "Specify information about your printer" (on menu of Other
      Activities) gives you additional control over printers.
---------------------------------------------------------------------------------
Type a two letter option code
                                                              55K Avail.
```

Figure 7-19 *Second PRINTER OPTIONS Screen*

```
File: MAIL.LIST                    REPORT FORMAT              Escape: Report Menu
Report: MAIL.LIST.2
Selection: All records



=================================================================================


First <I <P <Last name
St Address
City <C <State <ZIP


-----------------------Each record will print  6 lines-------------------------




-----------------------------------------------------------------------------
Use options shown on Help Screen
                                                              ∂-? for Help
```

Figure 7-20   *PRINT THE REPORT Screen*

```
File: MAIL.LIST              PRINT THE REPORT          Escape: Report Format
Report: MAIL.LIST.1
Selection: All records


================================================================================
                    Where do you want to print the report?

                    1.   ImageWriter

                    2.   The screen

                    3.   The clipboard (for the Word Processor)

                    4.   A text (ASCII) file on disk

                    5.   A DIF (TM) file on disk



--------------------------------------------------------------------------------
Type number, or use arrows, then press Return                       55K Avail.
```

Figure 7-21   *MAIL.LIST.2 Report Screen*

```
File: MAIL.LIST               REPORT FORMAT             Escape: Report Menu
Report: MAIL.LIST.3
Selection: All records


================================================================================
First <I <Last name
St Address
City <State <ZIP


-----------------------------Each record will print   6 lines-------------------



--------------------------------------------------------------------------------
Use options shown on Help Screen                                    ð-? for Help
```

Figure 7-22   *MAIL.LIST.3 Report Screen*

MAIL.LIST.2 format that the comma, C, and the period, P, category names have been used in different places within the report. Further, the first label-line has been changed.

The MAIL.LIST.3 report format has the category names C and P deleted. The rest of the report format is essentially the same as MAIL.LIST.2.

7.2 CHRISTMAS CARD LIST

This section creates a Christmas card data base list. The purpose of this list is to keep track of all of the Christmas cards sent and received each year from individuals or families. This list, XMAS.LIST, is an extension of the mailing label list, MAIL.LIST, created in the previous section.

Section 7.2.1 creates the list. Section 7.2.2 formats and prints two different reports for this list.

The discussion in this section will essentially follow the same format and steps as in the previous sections of this chapter.

7.2.1 Creating and Editing the List

The steps for creating a Chrismas card list are the same as for the mailing labels list. Power up your system and perform the first four steps outlined in Section 7.1.1. The discussion in this section starts with Step 5.

Name this new file XMAS.LIST. Then define all of the category names that are to be used as the column headings for the list. The category names, widths, and descriptions for the XMAS.LIST are shown in the table below. Remember that AppleWorks automatically uses "Category 1" as the first category name. Erase "Category 1" and replace it with "Name." Enter other new category names. Also remember to press the Return key after each entry.

#	Category name		Width	Category Description
1.	Name	=	20	= Full name for card recipient.
2.	St Address	=	19	= Street, city, state, and zip code.
3.	City	=	12	
4.	State	=	2	
5.	ZIP	=	5	
6.	84	=	2	= 1984 card sent and received.
7.	85	=	2	= 1985 card sent and received.
8.	86	=	2	= 1986 card sent and received.
9.	87	=	2	= 1987 card sent and received.
10.	88	=	2	= 1988 card sent and received.
11.	Blank spaces	=	10	= 1 blank space after each category name.
			78	characters

As you enter and edit category names, the right-hand portion of the screen gives you prompt message options. See the options listing on page 146.

> **Tip:** Before you start a new list, it is recommended that you carefully plan both the contents of the list, with their category names, and at least one of the report formats that you want. This will help to prevent a lot of possible errors, reduces much wasted time, and makes you more productive and effective. As a list gets larger, it usually will take more planning and analysis to produce a useful and meaningful list and set of reports.

The options are:

Type/Change a category name.

Use the UP arrow key to go to the previous entry.

Use the DOWN arrow key to go to the next entry.

Use the OPEN-APPLE I keystroke combination to insert a new category somewhere in the middle of the list of categories.

Use the OPEN-APPLE D to delete the category at the cursor position.

Category names 6 through 10 are for the purpose of keeping track of the Christmas cards sent/received to an individual/family for each year in that record of the list. To conserve space in the file and on the screen presentation, a coding scheme is used for each of the year entries. The coding scheme is shown below. You will have to remember the coding scheme since comments are not allowed in the data base.

Code RS	=	Meaning of Code		Alternate Code RS
00	=	No card received, no card sent	=	NN
01	=	No card received, card sent	=	NS
10	=	Card received, no card sent	=	RN
11	=	Card received, card sent	=	RS

Note that a zero (0) indicates that no card was sent/received, and a one (1) that a card was sent/received. The position of the numbers also has meaning: the left-column number is "received," the right-column number is "sent."

There is also an alternate coding scheme shown. The N represents "No card," S represents "Sent," and R represents "Received." You can use either coding scheme. Just make sure that your scheme is easily understood, shows all possible cases, is reasonably short, and is unique for each case.

After entering all category names and making all corrections, press the ESCape key to exit from the category name screen. See Fig. 7-23.

Figure 7-24 shows sample entries. Notice that the "Name" category contains the full

```
File: XMAS.LIST              INSERT NEW RECORDS      Escape: Review/Add/Change



Record 4 of 4
=================================================================================
Name: -
St. Address: -
City: -
ST: -
 ZIP: -
84: -
85: -
86: -
87: -
88: -




---------------------------------------------------------------------------------
Type entry or use a commands                                    53K Avail.
```

Figure 7-23   *XMAS. LIST Category Names*

```
File: XMAS.LIST              REVIEW/ADD/CHANGE          Escape: Main Menu



Record 3 of 4
=================================================================================
Name: Sam R. Redden
St. Address: 3101 Pioneer Ave
City: Waco,
ST: Tx
 ZIP: 76710
84: 11
85: -
86: -
87: -
88: -




---------------------------------------------------------------------------------
Type entry or use a commands                                 a-? for Help
```

Figure 7-24   *XMAS.LIST Entries*

name of the individual or family that is to receive a Christmas card. This is different from the mailing label list discussed earlier.

After entering the first record into XMAS.LIST, format the screen presentation for this record and all subsequent records. Use the width values in the table on page 164. Press the ESCape key and then the OPEN-APPLE Z zoom command to present the XMAS.LIST in the table-style format.

Now customize the record layout for the XMAS.LIST. The default entry size for all category name entries is 15 characters. Obviously, you do not need that many characters for such entries as ST, ZIP, or year.

From the Review/Add/Change screen, use the OPEN-APPLE L record layout command. The Change/Record/Layout screen allows you to modify the layout. The options available for modifying a record layout were given in Section 7.1.1.

The cursor is placed at the first character of a category. Use:

arrow keys to move between categories,

OPEN-APPLE right/left arrows to switch categories,

OPEN-APPLE arrow keys to widen/shorten categories,

OPEN-APPLE I to insert a previously deleted category, or

OPEN-APPLE D to delete a category.

As you shorten category widths, the word "Margin" appears along the right edge of the screen, showing the current end of a record. When you have finished modifying a record layout, all records will appear on the screen in the table-style format just specified. Press the ESCape key to exit this screen when finished. The modified record layout is shown in Fig. 7-25.

Now select the direction the cursor should move when you press the RETURN key. If you intend to enter record information in the label-style format, select option 1, "Down (standard)." This means that every time you press the RETURN key, the cursor will move vertically down the screen. However, if you are planning to enter record information in the table-style format, select option 2, "Right." This means that every time you press the RETURN key, the cursor will move horizontally to the right on the screen. For now, select the standard cursor movement. After selecting the cursor movement direction, you are returned to the Review/Add/Change screen.

Enter any additional record information into XMAS.LIST by using the procedure given in Section 7.1.4. Also, you may want to review how to insert records into the XMAS.LIST file.

7.2.2 Printing a Report

This section discusses the formatting of two different reports: a label-style report will be created in Section 7.2.2.1, and a table-style report in Section 7.2.2.2.

In order to create a report format, press the OPEN-APPLE P keystroke combination, the printing command. This keystroke combination is also used to print a report, discussed later in this section.

```
File: XMAS.LIST              CHANGE RECORD LAYOUT      Escape: Review/Add/Change



=================================================================================
          --> or <--   Move cursor
           >  ∂  <      Switch category positions
          --> ∂ <--     Change column width
          ∂-D           Delete this category
          ∂-I           Insert a previously deleted category

---------------------------------------------------------------------------------
Name                 St. Address          City        ST  ZIP  84 85 86 87 88 M
------------------   ------------------   ----------  --  ----- -- -- -- -- -- A
JL Campbell          Rt#1 Box 1456A       Waco,       Tx  76710 11              R
Mr. & Mrs. Smith     4422 Lakeview        Hewitt,     Tx  76710 01             G
Sam R. Redden        3101 Pioneer Ave     Waco,       Tx  76710 11              I
                                                                               N
---------------------------------------------------------------------------------
Use options shown above to change record layout                    53K Avail.
```

Figure **7-25** *Modified Record Layout Screen*

The screen presented was shown in Fig.7-12 in Section 7.1.2. This screen tells you that you are using the XMAS.LIST file, that there are no reports specified, that the ESCape key will return you to the Review/Add/Change screen, and that you have five options available. These options were also shown in Section 7.1.2.

7.2.2.1 Label-style Report

To create a new label-style report, choose option 3, "Create a new 'labels' format" from the Report Menu screen. This report format is for the purpose of creating mailing labels from the information in the XMAS.LIST. This is Step 8 of Section 7.1.1. See Fig. 7-12.

After making the selection, enter the name of the report format. Give this report format the name XMAS.LIST.LABELS, as shown in Fig. 7-26. Follow the file-naming conventions discussed in Section 1.4.1.

After specifying the name, the Report Format screen is presented. Reformat the default report format so that you can print blank mailing labels from the XMAS.LIST.

Follow the mailing label considerations and the required steps outlined in Section 7.1.2 needed to be taken in order to define a report format.

The Name category will be the pivotal point for this report and left in its initial position. This is the only category name on the first line of the report. The second line of the report is the St Address category name. This is the only category name on this line of the report.

Next, the City category name entry will also be left undisturbed on the third line of the mailing label. The last two category names placed on the third line of the report for-

```
File: XMAS.LIST              NAME THE NEW REPORT           Escape: Erase entry
Report: None




===============================================================================




-------------------------------------------------------------------------------
Type a name for the report:  XMAS.LIST.LABELS                        53K Avail.
```

Figure 7-26 *Name the New Report Screen*

mat are ST (state) and ZIP (zip code). The procedures and keystrokes for doing this were described in Section 7.1.2.

Do the following:

1. Place the cursor on the first character of the ST category name.

2. Move the ST category name up to the third line and to the right of the City category name.

3. Move the ZIP category name to the right of the ST category name.

4. Left-justify the ST and ZIP category names. Use the OPEN-APPLE J justify command. Place the cursor on the first character of the category name to be left-justified and then type OPEN-APPLE J. A left arrow character is placed just to the left of the category name to signify the category is left-justified.

5. Continue justifying category names until each one shown in Fig. 7-27 is left-justified.

6. Delete category names 84, 85, 86, 87, and 88. This is done by placing the cursor on the first character of the category name to be deleted. Use OPEN-APPLE D (delete command) to delete that category name.

After completing all of the above, your screen should look like the one in Fig. 7-27. The next thing is to finish with the formatting of the XMAS.LIST.LABELS REPORT FORMAT.

```
File: XMAS.LIST                 REPORT FORMAT                Escape: Report Menu
Report: XMAS.LIST.LABELS
Selection: All records



================================================================================

Name
St. Address
City <ST < ZIP



------------------------Each record will print  6 lines------------------------




--------------------------------------------------------------------------------
Use options shown on Help Screen                                    ?-? for Help
```

Figure 7-27   XMAS.LIST.LABELS Report Format Screen

Place the cursor at the starting character of the Name category name. Use the OPEN-APPLE I insert command. Since you have deleted a number of category names, the options you will be given to insert a blank line either before or after the cursor position or to insert any of the deleted category names, 84 through 88. Select to insert a blank line above the cursor position. These options are shown in Fig. 7-28.

Figure 7-29 shows the report format with a line added at the beginning of the report. However, the report is eleven lines long. You need a report that is six lines long so that it will fit nicely on a 15/16″ deep blank mailing label. (See the discussion on blank mailing labels in Section 7.1.1.) Place the cursor anywhere on the last line of the report. Use OPEN-APPLE D enough times to reduce the report length to six lines as shown in Fig. 7-30.

Formatting the report, XMAS.LIST.LABELS, for the XMAS.LIST file is complete. Figure 7-18 showed the printer options that may need to be changed before printing a report. The Printer Options screen may be reached by using OPEN-APPLE O from the Report Format screen.

Making change selections on the Printer Options screen is done by entering the two-character code followed by the Return key. Figure 7-19 reflected the changes that were previously suggested for the MAIL.LIST.1 report and are valid for this report format. At the bottom of the screen shown in Fig. 7-19, you can specify a number of printer options that are unique to the data base.

For the XMAS.LIST.LABELS report, it is recommended that all of these options be set to "No." After making selections, use the ESCape key to exit the Printer Options screen.

```
File: XMAS.LIST              INSERT A CATEGORY           Escape: Report Format
Report: XMAS.LIST.LABELS
Selection: All records



================================================●===============================
1.  84
2.  85
3.  86
4.  87
5.  88
6.  A spacing line above cursor position
7.  A spacing line below cursor position







---------------------------------------------------------------------------
Type number, or use arrows, then press Return                    53K Avail.
```

Figure 7-28   *XMAS.LIST.LABELS Insert Screen*

```
File: XMAS.LIST              REPORT FORMAT               Escape: Report Menu
Report: XMAS.LIST.LABELS
Selection: All records



================================================================================

Name
St. Address
City <ST < ZIP





----------------------Each record will print 11 lines---------------------



---------------------------------------------------------------------------
Use options shown on Help Screen                              ∂-? for Help
```

Figure 7-29   *Unmodified Report Length Screen*

```
File: XMAS.LIST              REPORT FORMAT              Escape: Report Menu
Report: XMAS.LIST.LABELS
Selection: All records



===================================================================

Name
St. Address
City <ST < ZIP


-----------------------Each record will print  6 lines-----------------------




----------------------------------------------------------------------
Use options shown on Help Screen                              a-? for Help
```

***Figure* 7-30** *Modified Report Length Screen*

Finally, print a report, Step 9. This is done by using the OPEN-APPLE P print command from the Report Format screen. The screen shown is the same as in Fig. 7-20. For now, choose either the first or second option. Actually, the second option lets you see your handiwork without using any paper. This is convenient because you may want to change or modify the format after you have seen your designed report. If you choose the first option, make sure your printer is powered up and ready.

You may want to leave your system powered up for the creation of a table-style report from the XMAS.LIST file.

7.2.2.2 *Christmas Card Table-style Report*

In this section, a table-style report format will be created from scratch. To create a new table-style report, choose option 2, "Create a new 'tables' format" from the Report Menu screen as shown in Fig. 7-12. This report format is for the purpose of creating a tabular list of the individuals and the sent/received card entries in XMAS.LIST.

After making the selection, name the report format XMAS.LIST.REPORT. The Name the New Report screen is shown in Fig. 7-31. Follow the same file-naming conventions discussed in Section 1.4.1.

After specifying the name, the Report Format screen is presented, as shown in Fig. 7-32. Each of the category entries has a default width size of twelve characters. Reformat this default report format for printing your XMAS.LIST record contents.

To define a table-style report:

```
File: XMAS.LIST              NAME THE NEW REPORT        Escape: Erase entry
Report: None
```

```
=======================================================================
```

```
-----------------------------------------------------------------------
Type a name for the report:  XMAS.LIST.REPORT                53K Avail.
```

Figure 7-31 *Name the Report Screen*

```
File: XMAS.LIST                 REPORT FORMAT          Escape: Report Menu
Report: XMAS.LIST.REPORT
Selection: All records
```

```
=======================================================================
--> or <--  Move cursor              @-J  Right justify this category
  >  @  <   Switch category positions @-K  Define a calculated category
--> @ <--  Change column width        @-N  Change report name and/or title
@-A  Arrange (sort) on this category  @-O  Printer options
@-D  Delete this category             @-P  Print the report
@-G  Add/remove group totals          @-R  Change record selection rules
@-I  Insert a prev. deleted category  @-T  Add/remove category totals
-----------------------------------------------------------------------

Name                 St. Address       City        ST ZIP  84 85 86 87 88 L
-A------------------ -B--------------- -C--------- -D -E--- -F -G -H -I -J e
JL Campbell          Rt#1 Box 1456A    Waco,       Tx 76710 11             n
Mr. & Mrs. Smith     4422 Lakeview     Hewitt,     Tx 76710 01             7
Sam R. Redden        3101 Pioneer Ave  Waco,       Tx 76710 11             8

-----------------------------------------------------------------------
Use options shown above to change report format             53K Avail.
```

Figure 7-32 *XMAS.LIST.REPORT FORMAT Screen*

1. Delete unnecessary category names for the report being formatted. No category names are to be deleted for this report format.

2. Place the remaining category names in the report in their appropriate positions. None of the category names are to be rearranged for this report.

3. Right-justify those category names in the report that need to be printed at the right edge of the entry. This is important for numeric entries. This step is not necessary for this report.

4. Define any calculated categories. There are no calculated categories in the report.

5. Specify the record selection rules, if necessary. This step is discussed in a later section.

The first step in reformatting a table-style report is to modify the default width size specifications for each entry. The width sizes to be used for the XMAS.LIST.REPORT table-style format will be the same as used for the record layout format. The information is repeated here for your convenience.

#	Category name	Width	Category Description
1.	Name	20	Full name for card recipient.
2.	St Address	19	Street address for card recipient.
3.	City	12	City location for card recipient.
4.	STATE	2	State location for card recipient.
5.	ZIP	5	U.S. Postal Service zip code. You may want to use 10 spaces for ZIP category.
6.	84	2	1984 card sent and received.
7.	85	2	1985 card sent and received.
8.	86	2	1986 card sent and received.
9.	87	2	1987 card sent and received.
10.	88	2	1988 card sent and received.
11.	Blank spaces	10	1 blank space after each category name.
		78	Characters long

Now, customize the report layout for the XMAS.LIST.REPORT. The default entry size for all category name entries is twelve characters. Obviously, you do not need that many characters for such entries as ST, ZIP, or the year.

The Report Format screen allows for the modification of the report record layout. The options available for modifying a report record layout were given in the table on page 150 and are shown on the screen.

The cursor is placed at the first character of a category name. There is a blank space between each category and a message at the bottom of the screen, at the right edge, that shows you there is "More" to the right of the Desktop screen.

The cursor is placed at the first character of a category.

Use:

Arrow keys to move between categories,

OPEN-APPLE right/left arrows to switch categories,

OPEN-APPLE arrow keys to widen/shorten categories,

OPEN-APPLE I to insert a previously deleted category, or

OPEN-APPLE D to delete a category.

As you adjust the width of category entries, you see the word "lenxx" appear along the right edge of the report record. The xx is the numeric width value of the report. This signifies the current end of a record. Modify the report record layout. After you have finished modifying a report record layout, all records are printed in the table-style format just specified. The modified record layout is shown in Fig. 7-33. Formatting the XMAS.LIST.REPORT for the XMAS.LIST file is now completed.

After customizing the report record layout, type OPEN-APPLE O (options command). Figure 7-34 shows the printer options for a table-style report format that may need to be changed before printing a report. The Printer Options screen may be reached by using OPEN-APPLE O from the Report Format screen.

Making selections on the Printer Options screen is done by entering the two-character code followed by the RETURN key. Figure 7-35 reflects the changes that are suggested for the XMAS.LIST.REPORT. The middle of the screen gives you the margin settings. At the bottom of the screen, shown in Fig. 7-35, you can specify printer options that are unique to a table-style report format.

A few words need to be said about the margin settings recommended for this report.

```
File: XMAS.LIST               REVIEW/ADD/CHANGE              Escape: Main Menu

Selection: All records


Name                St. Address          City          ST ZIP   84 85 86 87 88
================================================================================
JL Campbell         Rt#1 Box 1456A       Waco,         Tx 76710 11 -  -  -  -
Mr. & Mrs. Smith    4422 Lakeview        Hewitt,       Tx 76710 01 -  -  -  -
Sam R. Redden       3101 Pioneer Ave     Waco,         Tx 76710 11 -  -  -  -
  -                   -                    -              -  -  -  -  -  -


--------------------------------------------------------------------------------
Type entry or use ⌂ commands                                        ⌂-? for Help
```

Figure 7-33 *Modified Report Format for XMAS.LIST.REPORT Screen*

```
File: XMAS.LIST              PRINTER OPTIONS           Escape: Report Format
Report: XMAS.LIST.REPORT
================================================================================

-------Left and right margins--------        ------Top and bottom margins-------
PW: Platen Width           8.5 inches    PL: Paper Length         11.0 inches
LM: Left Margin            0.0 inches    TM: Top Margin            1.0 inches
RM: Right Margin           1.0 inches    BM: Bottom Margin         1.0 inches
CI: Chars per Inch         12            LI: Lines per Inch        6

    Line width             7.5 inches        Printing length       9.0 inches
    Char per line (est)    90                Lines per page        54

        ---------------------Formatting options--------------------
        SC:  Send Special Codes to printer                   No
        PD:  Print a Dash when an entry is blank             Yes
        PH:  Print report Header at top of each page         Yes
             Single, Double or Triple Spacing (SS/DS/TS)     SS


        "Specify information about your printer" (on menu of Other
        Activities) gives you additional control over printers.
--------------------------------------------------------------------------------
Type a two letter option code                                     53K Avail.
```

Figure 7-34   PRINTER OPTIONS Screen

```
File: JOBS.LIST           CHANGE NAME/CATEGORY     Escape: Review/Add/Change




Category names
================================================================================
Acct            |
S#              | Options:
Description     |
Est cost        | Change category name
Act cost        | Up arrow    Go to filename
Date pd.        | Down arrow  Go to next category
Contractor      | @-I         Insert new category
CK #            | @-D         Delete this category
                |
                |
                |
                |
                |
                |
                |
--------------------------------------------------------------------------------
Type entry or use @ commands                                      53K Avail.
```

Figure 7-35   JOBS.LIST Category Names

Since the report occupies 78 characters horizontally, an 8.5″ wide piece of paper will hold 85 characters for a print size of 10 characters per inch. This does not leave much room for the page number or the current date in the right margin at the top of a page. Therefore, it is recommended that you change the characters per inch print size to 12. It is futher recommended that the right margin be set to 1″. This will give you a line length of 7.5″ that will hold 90 characters on a line. Since the page number and date are printed at the right edge of the paper, one above the other, they will appear within the right margin setting above the report. Each report line will now fit within the 90 character line length.

A top and bottom margin of 1″ has been specified, so that the report will be placed in the middle of a page and will have sufficient space to be placed in a binder without covering up any of the report information.

For the XMAS.LIST.REPORT, it is recommended that the formatting options be set to "No," "Yes," "Yes," and "SS" respectively. This is shown in Figure 7-35. Use the ESCape key to exit the Printer Options screen.

Finally, print a report by using OPEN-APPLE P from the Report Format screen. The screen shown is the same as in Fig. 7-20.

7.3 SUBCONTRACTORS LIST

In this section, assume you are a general contractor engaged in constructing residential buildings. This section creates a subcontractors data base list. The purpose of this list is to keep basic payment information made to all subcontractors hired for a particular construction project.

You want to record:

- A general description of subcontract work item.
- The estimated dollar cost of subcontract item.
- The actual dollar cost of subcontract item.
- The date you paid subcontractor.
- The dollar amount you paid subcontractor.
- The subcontractor paid on a particular date.
- The cost differences between the estimated and actual cost for subcontracted work item.
- The account-subaccount number to which payment is posted by your bookkeeper.

The reports you may want to generate on demand and monthly are:

- The dollar amount and the date you paid a particular contractor.
- The total dollar amount paid to all subcontractors.
- The total dollar amount paid to individual subcontractors.

- The dollar amount to be posted to individual account-subaccount numbers.
- A list of all subcontractors used on a particular building.
- A report of all stored information.

This list, JOBS.LIST, is a good, simple, effective way to keep basic information on subcontractors hired by a general contractor.

Section 7.3.1 creates the list. Sections 7.3.2 through 7.3.4 format and print different reports for this list.

It is realized that not all readers of this section are general building contractors However, the examples shown could be used by a project manager who requires the services of consultants, outside engineers, or outside suppliers; a procurement officer who needs to track suppliers goods and services; or an accounts payable/receivable manager who needs to track those accounts requiring payment/collection.

7.3.1 Creating and Editing the List

This section creates the subcontractor data base list from scratch. Even though this list is targeted to the small business, the principles can be used for any list, regardless of the contents and form of the list.

The steps for the subcontractor list are essentially the same as for the mailing labels list and the Christmas card list except for the record contents and report formats.

Power up your system and perform the first four procedural steps as outlined at the beginning of Section 7.1.1. This section will start with Step 5.

Tip: Before you start a new list, it is recommended that you carefully plan both the contents of the list, with their category names, and at least one of the report formats that you want. This will help to prevent a lot of possible errors, reduce much wasted time, and make you more productive and effective. As a list gets larger, it usually will take more planning and analysis to produce a useful and meaningful list and set of reports.

When you start a new file from scratch, you are required to give the new file a name. Use JOBS.LIST.

Define all of the category names to be used as the columnar headings for the list. The category names, widths, and descriptions for the JOBS.LIST are shown in the table below. Remember, the data base uses "Category 1" as the first category name.

The category names and entry widths used in the JOBS.LIST file are defined as follows:

#	Category name	Width	Category Description
1.	Acct	4	Account number in general ledger.
2.	S#	2	Subaccount number in general ledger.
3.	Description	20	General account description.
4.	Est cost	8	Estimated cost of subcontract item.
5.	Act cost	8	Actual cost of subcontract item.
6.	Date pd.	9	Date payment is made to subcontractor.
7.	Contractor	13	Name of subcontractor.
8.	CK #	6	Check number written to subcontractor.
9.	Blank spaces	8	1 blank space after each category name.
		78	Screen format, characters long.
10.	COST DIF	8	Calculated category name entry.
			Difference between estimated and actual cost.
11.	Blank spaces	1	1 blank space after category name.
		87	Record length, characters long

The cursor is placed at the first character of the first category name. You will need to erase the first category name and replace it with the category name "Acct." After entering a category name, press the RETURN key to signal entry completion. The cursor is placed at the beginning of the next line for the entry of another category name.

If a mistake is made or a category name needs changing, edit the entry. As category names are entered, the right-hand portion of the screen gives you prompt message options. The options change depending upon the placement of the cursor. These options were shown in Sections 7.1.1 and 7.2.1.

Enter the category names at this time. After entering and correcting category names, press the ESCape key to exit. The category names are shown in Fig. 7-35. The data base tells you there is no record information in the file. The screen prompt message states, "Press Space Bar to Continue."

The screen presents "Record 1 of 1" with all of the category names listed vertically but without any other record information entered. Enter the first record information into the list. The "Acct" category should contain the general ledger account number 8501. Example entries are shown in Fig. 7-36.

After entering the first record into the JOBS.LIST, format the screen presentation for all record information. Use the width values given in the preceding table. First, press the ESCape key and then OPEN-APPLE Z to see the file in the table-style format.

Now, customize the record layout for JOBS.LIST. The default size for all category names is fifteen characters. You do not need that much space for the S# or Acct # entries. From the Review/Add/Change screen, use the OPEN-APPLE L record layout command to customize the record layout. The Change Record Layout screen allows you to modify the record layout. The options available for modifying a record layout were given in Section 7.1.1.

The cursor is placed at the first character of a category name. There is a blank space between each category and a message at the bottom of the screen, at the right edge, that shows you there is "More."

As you shorten category widths, the word "Margin" appears along the right edge of

```
File: JOBS.LIST              REVIEW/ADD/CHANGE         Escape: Main Menu

Selection: All records


Record 1 of 24
==================================================================================
Acct: 8501
S#: 01
Description: Land cost
Est cost: 7500.00
Act cost: 7500.00
Date pd.: Sep 13 84
Contractor: JL Campbell
CK #: 10300




----------------------------------------------------------------------------------
Type entry or use ] commands                              ]-? for Help
```

Figure 7-36   *Example JOBS.LIST Entries*

```
File: JOBS.LIST              REVIEW/ADD/CHANGE         Escape: Main Menu

Selection: All records


Acct S# Description        Est cost Act cost Date pd.  Contractor   CK #
==================================================================================
8501 01 Land cost          7500.00  7500.00  Sep 13 84 JL Campbell  10300
8501 02 Site preparation   1100     1000     Sep 14 84 Harry Hines  10308
8501 03 Permits and fees   450      450      Sep 22 84 AC Parsons   10309
8501 04 Utilities          155      160      Sep 27 84 Elec. Co.    10319
8501 05 Slab preparation   1832.50  1802.50  Sep 27 84 Gamble&Son   10320
8501 06 Concrete labor     650      650      Nov 22 84 Harry Hines  10390
8501 07 Framing labor      1455     1450     Oct  5 84 RT Gill      10351
8501 08 Roofing            1230     1225     Nov 10 84 Broadway     10382
8501 09 Masonry            -        -        -         -            -
8501 10 Painting           1230     1225     Nov 10 84 Trout Paints 10383
8501 11 Sheetrock          1455     1450     Oct  5 84 AC Parsons   10352
8501 12 Electrical         -        -        -         -            -
8501 13 Plumbing           2400     800      Sep 27 84 York Plumb.  10321
8501 13 Plumbing           -        800      Oct 10 84 York Plumb.  10358
8501 13 Plumbing           -        560      Nov 12 84 Ken Plumbing 10400
----------------------------------------------------------------------------------
Type entry or use ] commands                              ]-? for Help
```

Figure 7-37   *Modified Record Layout Screen*

the record showing the current end of a record. When you are finished modifying a record layout, press the ESCape key. Modify the record layout as shown in Fig. 7-37.

Select the direction the cursor should move when you press the RETURN key. If you intend to enter record information when you are in the label-style format, select option 1, "Down (standard)." However, if you are planning to enter record information in the table-style format, select option 2, "Right." For now, select the standard cursor movement. After you have selected the cursor movement direction, you are returned to the Review/Add/Change screen.

Enter all of the additional record information into JOBS.LIST. Also, you may want to review how to insert records into the JOBS.LIST file.

7.3.2 The First Report

To create a new table-style report, choose option 2, "Create a new 'tables' format" from the Report Menu screen. Figure 7-12 shows this screen. This report format lists all transactions and payments made to subcontractors on record in the JOBS.LIST. After making the selection, name the report SUBS.PYMT. The Name the New Report screen is shown in Fig. 7-38. Use the file-naming conventions of Section 1.4.1.

After specifying the name, the Report Format screen is presented, as shown in Fig. 7-39. Each of the categories has a default width size of twelve characters. Reformat this default report format for printing your JOBS.LIST record contents.

To define a table-style report:

```
File: JOBS.LIST               NAME THE NEW REPORT              Escape: Erase entry
Report: None



===================================================================================





-------------------------------------------------------------------------------
Type a name for the report:  SUBS.PYMT                         53K Avail.
```

Figure 7-38 *Name the Report Screen*

```
File: JOBS.LIST                REPORT FORMAT           Escape: Report Menu
Report: SUBS.PYMT
Selection: Acct equals 8001
   and      S# equals 13
   and      Contractor is not blank
Group totals on: S#
=============================================================================
--> or <--   Move cursor                    a-J  Right justify this category
 >  a   <    Switch category positions      a-K  Define a calculated category
-->  a  <--  Change column width            a-N  Change report name and/or title
a-A  Arrange (sort) on this category        a-O  Printer options
a-D  Delete this category                   a-P  Print the report
a-G  Add/remove group totals                a-R  Change record selection rules
a-I  Insert a prev. deleted category        a-T  Add/remove category totals
-----------------------------------------------------------------------------

Acct S# Description          Est cost Act cost COST DIF Date pd.  Contractor
-A-- -B -C------------------ -D------ -E------ -F------ -G------- -H---------
8501 01 Land cost            99999.99 99999.99 99999.99 Sep 13 84 JL Campbell
8501 02 Site preparation     99999.99 99999.99 99999.99 Sep 14 84 Harry Hines
8501 03 Permits and fees     99999.99 99999.99 99999.99 Sep 22 84 AC Parsons
                             ======== ======== ========
--------------------------------------------------------------- More --->
Use options shown above to change report format             53K Avail.
```

Figure 7-39 *SUB.PYMT REPORT FORMAT Screen*

1. Delete unnecessary category names for the report being formatted. NO category names are to be deleted for this report.

2. Place the remaining category names in the report in their appropriate positions. None of the category names are to be rearranged for this report.

3. Specify the calculated entries to be added to the report. This allows for horizontal mathematics within a record.

4. Right-justify those category names in the report that need to be printed at the right edge of the entry.

5. Specify group totals used in the report. This allows for vertical mathematics in a category.

6. Specify record selection rules, if necessary. Changing selection rules and multiple reports are created using the same report format.

The first step in reformatting a table-style report format is to modify the category name width sizes. The width sizes used for the SUBS.PYMT table-style report will be the same as used for the record layout format.

Modify the report format for the SUBS.PYMT report from the REPORT FORMAT screen.

The cursor is placed at the first character of a category name. There is a blank space between each category and a message at the bottom of the screen, at the right edge, that shows you there is "More" to the right of the Desktop screen.

Before completing the SUBS.PYMT report, it is necessary to discuss creating a calcu-

#	Category name	Length	Category Description
1.	Acct	4	General ledger account number.
2.	S#	2	General ledger subaccount number.
3.	Description	20	General ledger account description.
4.	Est cost	8	Estimated cost of subcontract item. Grand totaled column.
5.	Act cost	8	Actual cost of subcontract item. Grand totaled column.
6.	COST DIF	8	Cost difference between items 4 and 5. This is a calculated entry. Grand totaled column.
7.	Date pd.	9	Date payment is made to subcontractor.
8.	Contractor	13	Name of subcontractor.
9.	CK #	6	Check number written to subcontractor.
10.	Blank spaces	9	1 blank space after each category name.
		87	Record length, characters long

lated category name, right-justifying category entries, specifying category totals, specifying group totals, and dislaying dates and times. Please remember that all of these are done from the Report Format screen. This screen is reached when you use the OPEN-APPLE P print command.

We will digress now for the next four subsections to discuss these new capabilities and skills. The discussion will return to the report being formatted and use these new capabilities.

7.3.2.1 *Calculated Category*

A calculated category is a new category name inserted somewhere in a report format and created from the numeric information contained in other categories already in the report. This is newly generated information.

To create a calculated category:

1. Place the cursor one column to the right of the location of the calculated category.
2. Type OPEN-APPLE K (calculated category command). A new column is inserted into the report format to the left of the cursor. This is the new calculated category name. The symbol 9 is inserted into all twelve spaces for the new category.
3. Replace the predefined category name with one of your own and press the RETURN key. The new name appears as a category name in the report.

Tip: It is recommended that you enter your new category name in all CAPITAL letters. In that way you will be able to easily recognize the calculated categories.

---

4. Enter the calculation rules for the new category. The data base allows you to perform the following mathematics.

Math	Symbol	Note
Plus	+	1. All math is performed from left to right. Don't use the = symbol.
Minus	−	
Multiply	*	2. The entered calculation rule will appear above the double line at the top of the display.
Divide	/	

5. Enter the number of decimal places the resulting number should contain. Press the RETURN key. You may also accept the default number 0 by pressing the RETURN key.

6. Enter the number of blank spaces that should appear to the right of the calculated category. Press the RETURN key. You may also accept the default number 0 by pressing the RETURN key.

Examples of the mathematics that can be performed are:

Mathematics example	Description
$D - E$	Subtract column E from column D.
2.5 * D + F	Multiply column D by 2.5 and add column F to the result.
C / 10 − D	Divide column C by 10 and subtract column D from the result.
B + (3.0 * C + D) / 25	Column B is added to the result of multilying 3 times column C plus column D divided by 25.

Tips:
1. Make sure that there are enough 9's in a number to handle the largest possible number you expect in that record entry.
2. If a series of # # # # # appear in a column when it is printed, the column width is too small to display the number.
3. The actual contents of columns cannot be seen until you print a report either to the screen or to the printer.
4. All mathematics is carried out left to right.

In addition to performing horizontal mathematics, the data base performs columnar or category mathematics by allowing grand totals.

To add category grand totals:

1. Place the cursor on the column you want totaled.

2. Type OPEN-APPLE T (total command). The symbol 9 is inserted into all twelve spaces for the new category.

3. Enter the number of decimal places for the total and press the RETURN key.

4. Enter the number of blank spaces to appear to the right of the totaled category.

Tips:
1. The data base inserts 9's in the category with the number of decimal places shown. When you print the report, the correct value replaces the 9's.
2. Blanks replace entries when no entry is present. A double dashed line is placed below the totaled category name on the Report Format screen.

To remove category totals:

1. Place the cursor on the column totaled.

2. Type OPEN-APPLE T. The sample records replace the 9's.

Tips:
1. Follow the above procedure to get group totals or subtotals for a category. In addition, use the OPEN-APPLE G function on the category that should control the group totals.
2. You can use OPEN-APPLE T to get a group and a grand total for the numbers in a calculated category.
3. You cannot use OPEN-APPLE G on a calculated category to control group totals in other categories.
4. You cannot arrange records by the value in a calculated category.
5. Only three calculated categories are allowed in each data base report.

7.3.2.2 Group Totals

Group totals or subtotals are for the purpose of totaling common category values within a list of values having multiple common group values within the same category. Whenever a change in the category value occurs in the controlling category, a group total is calculated and printed for the categories specified with the OPEN-APPLE T command.

To specify the controlling category for group totals:

1. Place the cursor on the controlling category column.

2. Type OPEN-APPLE G (group total command).

3. Choose either "No" or "Yes," depending on whether you want to print group totals only, or whether you want to print all of the record information.

4. Choose either "No" or "Yes," depending on whether you want to go to a new page after each group total. The answer will depend on the number of category values in a group when that group total is printed.

Tips:

1. The data base displays group total information above the double-dashed line on the Report Format screen.

2. You may want to rearrange records in your report to reflect the controlling categories.

7.3.2.3 Dates and Times

Dates and times are presented in predefined standard formats, provided specific keywords are used in the category names.

Dates will be converted automatically if the word "date," "Date," or "DATE" appears anywhere within a category name. All dates will appear as a three-letter month name followed by a one-digit or two-digit day value plus a two-digit year value. Examples are shown in the table below.

What you enter	What is displayed
Legal Entries:	
Jul 4	Jul 4
09/05/86	Sep 5 86
04.05.86	Apr 5 86
06-06-86	June 6 86
3 83	Mar 83
August 18, 1986	Aug 18 86
1 January 1985	Jan 1 85
February 1985	Feb 85
Illegal entries:	
040586	Not converted. 04/05/86 is legal.
32882	Not converted. 3.28.82 is legal.
John	Not converted. Totally illegal.

If you use category names that contain the word "date" in any form, the data base converts any entry that can be converted to one of the formats shown in the table above. For example, use category names such as Date, date, Hire Date, Date Group, Birthdate, Expiration Date, or DATE.

What you enter	What is displayed
Legal Entries:	
630	6:30 AM
2	2:00 PM
6	6:00 AM
12	12:00 PM
435	4:35 PM
6 p or 6p	6:00 PM
12 a or 12a	12:00 AM
1400	2:00 PM
0800	8:00 AM
0002	12:02 AM

If you use category names that contain the word "time" in any form, the data base converts any entry that can be converted to a format shown in the table above. The data base assumes a normal business day and therefore, the A.M. or P.M. suffix normally will not have to be entered. For example, use category names such as Time, time, Hire Time, Time Sold, Expiration Time, or TIME.

The date and time conversions will not be done automatically if the words "date" and/or "time" are not used in a category name.

7.3.2.4 Justifying Entries

In the label-style report format, you are able to left-justify category name entries. In a table-style report, you can right-justify entries in a category. This is done from the Report Format screen.

To right-justify a column:

1. Place the cursor on the column to be right-justified.
2. Type OPEN-APPLE J (justify command).
3. Type the number of decimal places to be included in the entry for the specified column. Press the RETURN key.
4. Type the number of blank spaces you want used after the entry. Press the RETURN key.

Now we will return to the problem at hand, report record formatting for the SUBS.PYMT report. You now have all of the tools, skills, and capabilities necessary to complete the job.

> **Tips:**
> 1. The data base automatically right-justifies columns with grand totals specified. See Section 7.3.2.1.
> 2. The data base fills a column with 9's to show you how information will be aligned when it is printed.

From the Report Format screen and the table on page 179, columns D and E are set to a width of eight characters. Once you have done that, place the cursor at column D. Use the OPEN-APPLE T total command. This will place a double-dashed line under the column and set all entries in that column to 9's. This column will now be totaled.

Now place the cursor at column E. Use OPEN-APPLE T. This will place a double-dashed line under the column and set all entries in that column to 9's. This column will now be totaled.

A calculated column will now be inserted into the SUBS.PYMT report. Place the cursor at the F column, "Date pd." Use OPEN-APPLE K (calculated category command). This will insert a column, the new F column, into the report between "Act cost" and "Date pd." Name the new column "COST DIF." The "Date pd." column is now column G. The mathematics for this column is D − E. This new calculated column will contain the difference in the cost between the estimated cost (D) of an item and the actual cost (E) of the same item. The difference is placed in the calculated column, F, COST DIF. All of these columns, D, E, and F, need to be right-justified.

When you are finished customizing the report record layout, type OPEN-APPLE O (options command). The modified record layout is shown in Fig. 7-40. Formatting the SUBS.PYMT report for the JOBS.LIST file is complete.

Figure 7-41 shows the printer options for a table-style report format that may need to be changed before printing a report. The Printer Options screen may be reached by using OPEN-APPLE O from the Report Format screen. The values for the margins and other printer options are shown in Fig. 7-41. The defaults shown will be used for this report if you do not change them.

Making selections on the Printer Options screen is done by entering the two-character code followed by the RETURN key. Figure 7-42 reflects the changes suggested for the SUBS.PYMT report.

Since the report occupies 87 characters horizontally, an 8.5″ wide paper will hold only 85 characters at a print size of 10 characters per inch. This does not leave enough room for the page number or the current date at the top of the page. It is recommended that the characters per inch print size be 12. It is further recommended that the right margin be set to 1″. This will give you a line length of 7.5″ that will hold 90 characters on a line. Each report line fits within the 90 character line length. Since the page number and date are printed at the right edge of the paper, they will appear within the right margin setting above the report.

A top and bottom margin of 1/2″ has been specified, so that the report will be placed in the middle of a page.

```
File: JOBS.LIST              REPORT FORMAT           Escape: Report Menu
Report: SUBS.PYMT
Selection: Acct equals 8001
   and      S# equals 13
   and      Contractor is not blank
Group totals on: S#
========================================================================
--> or <--  Move cursor               @-J  Right justify this category
  >  @  <    Switch category positions @-K  Define a calculated category
--> @ <--   Change column width        @-N  Change report name and/or title
@-A  Arrange (sort) on this category   @-O  Printer options
@-D  Delete this category              @-P  Print the report
@-G  Add/remove group totals           @-R  Change record selection rules
@-I  Insert a prev. deleted category   @-T  Add/remove category totals
------------------------------------------------------------------------

Description         Est cost Act cost COST DIF Date pd.  Contractor   CK #  L
-C----------------- -D------ -E------ -F------ -G------- -H---------- -I---- e
Land cost           99999.99 99999.99 99999.99 Sep 13 84 JL Campbell  999999 n
Site preparation    99999.99 99999.99 99999.99 Sep 14 84 Harry Hines  999999 8
Permits and fees    99999.99 99999.99 99999.99 Sep 22 84 AC Parsons   999999 6
                    ======== ======== ========
<--- More ---------------------------------------------------------------
Use options shown above to change report format           53K Avail.
```

Figure 7-40 *Modified Report Format for SUBS.PYMT Screen*

```
File: JOBS.LIST              PRINTER OPTIONS        Escape: Report Format
Report: SUBS.PYMT
========================================================================

-------Left and right margins--------      ------Top and bottom margins-------
PW: Platen Width          8.5 inches   PL: Paper Length         11.0 inches
LM: Left Margin           0.0 inches   TM: Top Margin            0.0 inches
RM: Right Margin          1.0 inches   BM: Bottom Margin         0.0 inches
CI: Chars per Inch        10           LI: Lines per Inch        6

    Line width            7.5 inches       Printing length      11.0 inches
    Char per line (est)   75               Lines per page       66

         --------------------Formatting options--------------------
    SC:  Send Special Codes to printer                    No
    PD:  Print a Dash when an entry is blank              Yes
    PH:  Print report Header at top of each page          Yes
         Single, Double or Triple Spacing (SS/DS/TS)      SS


    "Specify information about your printer" (on menu of Other
    Activities) gives you additional control over printers.
------------------------------------------------------------------------
Type a two letter option code                             53K Avail.
```

Figure 7-41 *SUBS. PYMT Printer Options Screen*

```
File: JOBS.LIST              PRINTER OPTIONS        Escape: Report Format
Report: SUBS.PYMT
=============================================================================

-------Left and right margins--------      ------Top and bottom margins-------
PW: Platen Width           8.5 inches    PL: Paper Length       11.0 inches
LM: Left Margin            0.0 inches    TM: Top Margin          0.5 inches
RM: Right Margin           1.0 inches    BM: Bottom Margin       0.5 inches
CI: Chars per Inch         12            LI: Lines per Inch      6

    Line width             7.5 inches        Printing length    10.0 inches
    Char per line (est)    90                Lines per page      60

        --------------------Formatting options--------------------
        SC:  Send Special Codes to printer                 No
        PD:  Print a Dash when an entry is blank           Yes
        PH:  Print report Header at top of each page       Yes
             Single, Double or Triple Spacing (SS/DS/TS)   SS


        "Specify information about your printer" (on menu of Other
        Activities) gives you additional control over printers.
-----------------------------------------------------------------------------
Type a two letter option code                              53K Avail.
```

Figure 7-42   *SUBS.PYMT Modified Printer Options Screen*

```
File: JOBS.LIST              PRINT THE REPORT       Escape: Report Format
Report: SUBS.PYMT
Selection: All records


Group totals on: S#
=============================================================================
                    Where do you want to print the report?

                    1.   ImageWriter

                    2.   The screen

                    3.   The clipboard (for the Word Processor)

                    4.   A text (ASCII) file on disk

                    5.   A DIF (TM) file on disk




-----------------------------------------------------------------------------
Type number, or use arrows, then press Return             17K Avail.
```

Figure 7-43   *Printing All Records of JOBS.LIST*

For the SUBS.PYMT report record format, it is recommended the formatting options be set to "No," "Yes," "Yes," and "SS" respectively, as shown in Fig. 7-42. After making selections, use the ESCape key to exit the Printer Options screen.

Finally, print a report using OPEN-APPLE P from the Report Format screen. The screen shown is the same as in Fig. 7-20. For now, choose either the first or second option. Actually, the second option lets you see your design without using any paper; however, there is not enough room horizontally to do this for this report.

If you choose the first option, make sure your printer is powered up and ready. A sample report is shown for all records in the list in Fig. 7-43. More will be said about the individual entries in this list in the next section.

7.3.3 The Second Report

At the beginning of this section the requirements for the JOBS.LIST were specified. Now is the time to determine if the report contents and format have fulfilled specified requirements.

The first two categories of the JOBS.LIST and the SUBS.PYMT report contain the account and subaccount numbers of an automated accounting system. Normally, every computer-based general ledger system requires that each account in the system be defined by an account-subaccount number.

There are many different account numbering schemes. Here's a standard set of account numbers:

Account type		Ranges of numbers		
Current Assets	=	1000–1499	or	100–149
Fixed Asserts	=	1500–1799	or	150–179
Other Assets	=	1800–1999	or	180–199
Current Liabilities	=	2000–2599	or	200–259
Long-term Liabilities	=	2600–2999	or	260–299
Capital	=	3000–3999	or	300–399
Income	=	4000–4999	or	400–499
Cost of Sales	=	5000–5999	or	500–599
Expenses	=	6000–7999	or	600–799
Other Incomes	=	8000–8499	or	800–849
Other Expenses	=	8500–8999	or	850–899

Of the fifteen or sixteen different accounting software packages surveyed, all vary somewhat in their numbering of accounts. The ones shown are only guidelines. Each of the account numbers may allow a number of subaccounts. For example, the account 8502.02 might be Site Preparation for the Campbell home, 8501, account. 8502.02 might be Site Preparation for the Redden home, 8502, account. The 8501 account then could handle 99 subaccounts. The 8502 account also could handle 99 subaccounts.

For each record entry, enter the account and subaccount numbers used in your accounting software system. This, then, links your accounting system, the JOBS.LIST, the

```
+---------+
| General |
| Ledger  |
+---------+        +-----------+     +-----------+     +-----------+
| 8501.01 |        | Checkbook |     | JOBS.LIST |     | SUBS.PYMT |
| 8501.02 |<---+   +-----------+     +-----------+     +-----------+
|   :     |    +--->| 8501.01   |     | 8501.01   |     | 8501.01   |
| 8501.16 |         | 8501.02   |--->| 8501.02   |  --->| 8501.02   |---+
|   :     |         |   :       |     |   :       |     |   :       |   |
| 8502.01 |    +--->| 8502.01   |     | 8502.01   |     | 8502.01   |   |
| 8502.02 |<---+    | 8502.02   |--->| 8502.02   |  --->| 8502.02   |---|
|   :     |         +-----------+     +-----------+     +-----------+   |
| 8502.16 |------------------------------------------>+               |
+---------+                                            |               |
   |                                                                   |
   +<------------------------------------------------------------------+
```

Figure 7-44 *Linking of Information between Items*

SUBS.PYMT reports, and your company checkbook. The last category name of the JOBS.PYMT list is CK #. This should help you track building expenses.

All of the other information in the JOBS.LIST is self-explanatory. The account numbers, subaccount numbers, description, and estimated cost can be entered ahead of time when creating a bid proposal for a new building. Then, as you make expenditures to subcontractors, enter those amounts and dates into the list.

In the last section, all records in the list were printed (Fig. 7-43). The selection rule was "All records." Now, from the Report Format screen, change the selection rule and group totals selection. Place the cursor over the S# category. Use the OPEN-APPLE G group total command. Group totals will now be taken every time the S# value changes. Use the OPEN-APPLE R selection rule command to select Acct # equal to 8501. (See Section 7.1.11 for selection rules). These two changes are reflected when you print this revised report, as shown in Fig. 7-45.

You now know how to change a report's contents by changing group totals or selection rules.

7.4 GRADEBOOK LIST

In this section, assume you teach computer science and other courses. This section creates a student grade data base list. The purpose of this list is to keep track of three-semester student grades and a final grade made on examinations for a particular computer course.

You want to record:

Student names.

Student identification numbers.

Course being taken.

Individual examination grades.

Final examination grade.

```
File:   JOBS.LIST                                                    Page  1
Report: SUBS.PYMT
Acct S# Description          Est cost Act cost COST DIF Date pd.  Contractor   CK #
----  --  --------------------  --------  --------  --------  ---------  ------------  ------
8501 01 Land cost            7500.00  7500.00     0.00 Sep 13 84 JL Campbell  10300
                             7500.00  7500.00     0.00

8501 02 Site preparation     1100.00  1000.00   100.00 Sep 14 84 Harry Hines  10308
                             1100.00  1000.00   100.00

8501 03 Permits and fees      450.00   450.00     0.00 Sep 22 84 AC Parsons   10309
                              450.00   450.00     0.00

8501 04 Utilities             155.00   160.00    -5.00 Sep 27 84 Elec. Co.    10319
                              155.00   160.00    -5.00

8501 05 Slab preparation     1832.50  1802.50    30.00 Sep 27 84 Gamble&Son   10320
                             1832.50  1802.50    30.00

8501 06 Concrete labor        650.00   650.00     0.00 Nov 22 84 Harry Hines  10390
                              650.00   650.00     0.00

8501 07 Framing labor        1455.00  1450.00     5.00 Oct  5 84 RT Gill      10351
                             1455.00  1450.00     5.00

8501 08 Roofing              1230.00  1225.00     5.00 Nov 10 84 Broadway     10382
                             1230.00  1225.00     5.00

8501 09 Masonry                 0.00     0.00     0.00                             0
                                0.00     0.00     0.00

8501 10 Painting             1230.00  1225.00     5.00 Nov 10 84 Trout Paints 10383
                             1230.00  1225.00     5.00

8501 11 Sheetrock            1455.00  1450.00     5.00 Oct  5 84 AC Parsons   10352
                             1455.00  1450.00     5.00

8501 12 Electrical              0.00     0.00     0.00                             0
                                0.00     0.00     0.00

8501 13 Plumbing             2400.00   800.00  1600.00 Sep 27 84 York Plumb.  10321
8501 13 Plumbing                0.00   800.00  -800.00 Oct 10 84 York Plumb.  10358
8501 13 Plumbing                0.00   560.00  -560.00 Nov 12 84 Ken Plumbing  10400
                             2400.00  2160.00   240.00

8501 14 Heating & A/C           0.00     0.00     0.00                             0
                                0.00     0.00     0.00

8501 15 Cabinetry               0.00     0.00     0.00                             0
                                0.00     0.00     0.00

8501 16 Appliances              0.00     0.00     0.00                             0
                                0.00     0.00     0.00

8501 17 Interion Decor          0.00     0.00     0.00                             0
                                0.00     0.00     0.00

8501 18 Land site finish        0.00     0.00     0.00                             0
                                0.00     0.00     0.00
```

(Fig. 7-45 continued on next page)

```
File:   JOBS.LIST
Report: SUBS.PYMT                                                      Page  2
Acct S# Description        Est cost  Act cost  COST DIF  Date pd.  Contractor    CK #
---- -- -----------------  --------  --------  --------  --------- ------------  ------
8501 19 Misc. Expense        0.00      0.00      0.00
                             0.00      0.00      0.00                              0

8502 01 Land cost            0.00      0.00      0.00
                             0.00      0.00      0.00                              0

8502 02 Site preparation     0.00      0.00      0.00
                             0.00      0.00      0.00                              0

8502 03 Permits and fees     0.00      0.00      0.00
                             0.00      0.00      0.00                              0

                         19457.50*19072.50*  385.00*
```

Figure 7-45   *Revised SUBS.PYMT Report*

```
File:   JOBS.LIST
Report: SUBS.PYMT                                                      Page  1
Selection: Acct equals 8501                                           05/10/85
    and      S# equals 13
Acct S# Description        Est cost  Act cost  COST DIF  Date pd.  Contractor    CK #
---- -- -----------------  --------  --------  --------  --------- ------------  ------
8501 13 Plumbing           2400.00    800.00   1600.00  Sep 27 84  York Plumb.   10321
8501 13 Plumbing              0.00    800.00   -800.00  Oct 10 84  York Plumb.   10358
8501 13 Plumbing              0.00    560.00   -560.00  Nov 12 84  Ken Plumbing  10400
                           2400.00   2160.00    240.00

                          2400.00*  2160.00*   240.00*
```

Figure 7-46   *Plumbing Report*

The reports you may want to generate on demand and monthly are:

A list of all students.

A list of all grades per course taken.

A final course grade report.

A report of all stored information.

This list, GRADEBOOK, is a simple, effective way to keep basic information on students and their grades.

Section 7.4.1 creates the list. Sections 7.4.2 through 7.4.3 format and print reports for this list.

7.4.1 Creating and Editing the List

This section creates the data base list from scratch. Even though this list is targeted to the teacher, the principles can be used for any list.

The procedure for this list is essentially the same as for other lists except for the record contents and report formats.

Power up your system and perform the first four procedural steps outlined in Section 7.1.1. This section starts with Step 5.

First, name the new file, GRADEBOOK. Define all category names to be used as the columnar headings. The category names, widths, and descriptions for the GRADEBOOK are shown in the Table below. Remember, the data base predefines the first category name.

#	Category name	Width	Category Descriptions
Record entries			
1.	ID #	4	Student identification number.
2.	Student name	20	Student name.
3.	Course	6	Course number.
4.	1st	6	1st semester grade.
5.	2nd	6	2nd semester grade.
6.	3rd	6	3rd semester grade.
7.	Final	6	Final examination grade.
8.	Blank spaces	7	1 blank space after each category name.
		61	Screen format, characters long
Calculated columns:			
9.	G. AVG	6	Calculated category name entry.
			Average of individual semester grades
10.	GRADE	6	Calculated category name entry.
			Final course grade average.
11.	Blank spaces	2	1 blank space after category name.
		75	Record length, characters long

The cursor is placed at the first character of the first category name. Erase the first category name and replace it with the category name "ID #." After entering a category name, press the RETURN key. The cursor is placed at the beginning of the next line for the entry of another category name.

After entering and correcting category names, press the ESCape key to exit. The category names are shown in Fig. 7-47. The data base tells you there is no record information in the file. The screen prompt message states, "Press Space Bar to continue."

The screen presents "Record 1 of 1" with all of the category names listed vertically but without any record information. Enter the first record information. The "ID #" category should contain the first student identification, 0100. Example entries are shown in Fig. 7-48.

After entering the first record into GRADEBOOK, format the screen presentation for all record information. Use the width values of the table above. First, press the ESCape key and then OPEN-APPLE Z to present the file in the table-style format.

Now, customize the record layout for GRADEBOOK. The default size for all category names is fifteen characters. From the Review/Add/Change screen, use OPEN-APPLE L to customize the record layout from the Change Record Layout screen.

```
File: GRADEBOOK                 CHANGE NAME/CATEGORY      Escape: Review/Add/Change



Category names
===================================================================================
ID #                                    |
Student name                            | Options:
Course                                  |
1st                                     | Change category name
2nd                                     | Up arrow   Go to filename
3rd                                     | Down arrow Go to next category
Final                                   | @-I         Insert new category
                                        | @-D         Delete this category
                                        |
                                        |
                                        |
                                        |
                                        |
                                        |
                                        |
-----------------------------------------------------------------------------------
Type entry or use @ commands                                       54K Avail.
```

Figure 7-47   *GRADEBOOK Category Names*

```
File: GRADEBOOK                 REVIEW/ADD/CHANGE            Escape: Main Menu

Selection: All records


Record 1 of 15
===================================================================================
ID #: 0100
Student name: John Campbell
Course: CS101
1st: 86
2nd: 90
3rd: 94
Final: 94





-----------------------------------------------------------------------------------
Type entry or use @ commands                                      @-? for Help
```

Figure 7-48   *Example GRADEBOOK Entries*

The cursor is placed at the first character of a category name. There is a blank space between each category and a message at the bottom of the screen, at the right edge, that shows you there is "More."

As you shorten category widths, the word "Margin" appears along the right edge of the record showing the current end of a record. When you are finished modifying a record layout, press the ESCape key. The modified record layout is shown in Fig. 7-49.

Select the cursor direction movement. After selecting the cursor movement direction, you are returned to the Review/Add/Change screen. Enter all of the additional record information into GRADEBOOK.

7.4.2 The First Report

To create a new table-style report, choose option 2, "Create a new 'tables' format" from the Report Menu screen, as shown in Fig. 7-12. This report format lists all students and grades on record in the GRADEBOOK plus the grade average and a final course grade. After making the selection, name the report GRADES. The Name the New Report screen is shown in Fig. 7-50. Use the file-naming conventions of Section 1.4.1.

After specifying the name, the Report Format screen is presented, as shown in Fig. 7-51. Each of the categories has a default width size of twelve characters. Reformat this default report format for printing your GRADEBOOK record contents.

Follow the steps shown in Section 7.3.2 to define a table-style report.

The first step in reformatting a table-style report format is to modify the category name width sizes. The width sizes used for the GRADES table-style report will be the

```
File: GRADEBOOK              CHANGE RECORD LAYOUT     Escape: Review/Add/Change



===============================================================================

           --> or <--  Move cursor
            >  a  <    Switch category positions
           --> a <--   Change column width
           a-D         Delete this category
           a-I         Insert a previously deleted category


    ---------------------------------------------------------------------------
    ID #  Student name        Course 1st    2nd    3rd    Final  M
    ----- ------------------- ------ ------ ------ ------ ------  A
    0100  John Campbell       CS101  86     90     94     94     R
    0101  Sam Redden          CS101  90     92     94     94     G
    0102  Carolyn Hayes       CS101  100    90     95     98     I
                                                                 N
    ---------------------------------------------------------------------------
    Use options shown above to change record layout              54K Avail.
```

Figure 7-49   Modified Record Layout Screen

```
File: GRADEBOOK              NAME THE NEW REPORT         Escape: Erase entry
Report: GRADES
```

```
===============================================================================
```

```
-------------------------------------------------------------------------------
Type a name for the report:  GRADES                              54K Avail.
```

Figure 7-50 *Name the Report Screen*

```
File: GRADEBOOK                REPORT FORMAT            Escape: Report Menu
Report: Grades
Selection: All records
```

```
===============================================================================
--> or <--  Move cursor              ∂-J  Right justify this category
 >  ∂  <    Switch category positions ∂-K  Define a calculated category
--> ∂ <--   Change column width       ∂-N  Change report name and/or title
∂-A  Arrange <sort> on this category  ∂-O  Printer options
∂-D  Delete this category             ∂-P  Print the report
∂-G  Add/remove group totals          ∂-R  Change record selection rules
∂-I  Insert a prev. deleted category  ∂-T  Add/remove category totals
-------------------------------------------------------------------------------
```

```
ID #        Student name Course       1st          2nd          3rd        F
-A--------- -B---------- -C---------- -D---------- -E--- ------ -F--------- -
0100        John Campbel CS101        86           90           94         9
0101        Sam Redden   CS101        90           92           94         9
0102        Carolyn Haye CS101        100          90           95         9
-------------------------------------------------------------- More --->
Use options shown above to change report format              39K Avail.
```

Figure 7-51 *GRADES REPORT FORMAT Screen*

same as used in the table on page 000. Modify the report format for the GRADES report from the Report Format screen.

The cursor is placed at the first character of a category name. There is a blank space between each category name and a message at the bottom of the screen, at the right edge, that shows you there is "More" to the right of the Desktop screen.

A calculated column will now be inserted into the GRADES report. Place the cursor at column G, "Final." Use OPEN-APPLE K. Insert a column, the new G column, into the report between "3rd" and "Final." Name the new column G "AVG." The "Final" column is now column H. The mathematics for this column is D+E+F/3. This new calculated column will contain the average of the three semester grades, columns D, E, and F. The average is placed in the calculated column G. All numeric columns need to be right-justified.

A second calcualted column is placed to the right of the "Final" column. Use the right arrow key to move to the right of the Final column. Use OPEN-APPLE K to insert a column, the new I column. The "Final" column is still column H. The mathematics for this column is G+H/2. This new calculated column averages the G. AVG and Final grades. The average is placed in the calculated column I. This means that the three semester grades make up half of the final grade and the final exam grade makes up the other half.

Some interesting observations need to be made concerning the way mathematics is carried out in the data base. As you know, mathematics is carried out left to right. Therefore, you must be very careful in the way you organize formulas. For example:

Assume, column A = 20, B = 30, C = 40, D = ?, E = 60, F = ?, G = ? in a record. If the formula A+B+C/3 is entered into the calculated column D, the result is 30. All right, that was easy. Now enter the following into the calculated column: F = D.6+E*.4. The result is 31.4 not 42 as you might expect. This formula (F = D*.6+E*.4) says the semester grades account for 60% of the final grade and the final examination accounts for 40%. In order to implement this formula, it must be done in three steps, each placed into a calculated category. First is D*.6; second, E.4. Third is the sum of the two results. This will then give you the result 42.

The GRADEBOOK already has two calculated columns. Only one more calculated column is allowed.

When you are finished customizing the report record layout, type OPEN-APPLE O. See Fig. 7-52 for the modified report layout. Formatting the GRADES report for the GRADEBOOK file is now completed.

Figures 7-34 and 7-41 show the printer options for a table-style report format that may need to be changed before printing a report. The Printer Options screen may be reached by using OPEN-APPLE O from the Report Format screen. The defaults shown will be used for this report if you do not change them. Figure 7-53 reflects the changes suggested for the GRADES report.

Since the report occupies 75 characters horizontally, an 8.5" wide paper will hold 85 characters at a print size of 10 characters per inch. This leaves just enough room for the page number or the current date at the top of the page. It is still recommended that the characters per inch print size be 12. It is further recommended that the right margin be set

```
File: GRADEBOOK                REPORT FORMAT              Escape: Report Menu
Report: GRADES
Selection: All records



=============================================================================
--> or <--   Move cursor                     @-J  Right justify this category
  >  @  <     Switch category positions       @-K  Define a calculated category
-->  @  <--   Change column width             @-N  Change report name and/or title
@-A  Arrange (sort) on this category          @-O  Printer options
@-D  Delete this category                     @-P  Print the report
@-G  Add/remove group totals                  @-R  Change record selection rules
@-I  Insert a prev. deleted category          @-T  Add/remove category totals
-----------------------------------------------------------------------------

ID # Student name        Course 1st    2nd    3rd    G. AVG Final  GRADE L
-A-- -B-----------------  -C---- -D---- -E---- -F---- -G---- -H---- -I---- e
0100 John Campbell        CS101  999.99 999.99 999.99 999.99 999.99 999.99 n
0101 Sam Redden           CS101  999.99 999.99 999.99 999.99 999.99 999.99 7
0102 Carolyn Hayes        CS101  999.99 999.99 999.99 999.99 999.99 999.99 5


-----------------------------------------------------------------------------
Use options shown above to change report format              54K Avail.
```

Figure 7-52   *Modified Report Format for GRADES Screen*

```
File: GRADEBOOK                PRINTER OPTIONS           Escape: Report Format
Report: GRADES
=============================================================================

-------Left and right margins--------      ------Top and bottom margins-------
PW: Platen Width          8.0 inches      PL: Paper Length         11.0 inches
LM: Left Margin           0.0 inches      TM: Top Margin            1.0 inches
RM: Right Margin          1.0 inches      BM: Bottom Margin         1.0 inches
CI: Chars per Inch        12              LI: Lines per Inch        6

    Line width            7.0 inches          Printing length       9.0 inches
    Char per line (est)   84                  Lines per page        54

           --------------------Formatting options--------------------
       SC:  Send Special Codes to printer                 No
       PD:  Print a Dash when an entry is blank            Yes
       PH:  Print report Header at top of each page        Yes
            Single, Double or Triple Spacing (SS/DS/TS)    SS


       "Specify information about your printer" (on menu of Other
       Activities) gives you additional control over printers.
-----------------------------------------------------------------------------
Type a two letter option code                               54K Avail.
```

```
File: CH5.3                    PRINTER OPTIONS        Escape: Review/Add/Change
=====|====|====|====|====|====|====|====|====|====|====|====|====|====|====|===
```

Figure 7-53   *GRADES Modified Printer Options Screen*

```
File:   GRADEBOOK                                                    Page  1
Report: GRADES                                                       05/10/85
ID # Student name          Course    1st    2nd    3rd G. AVG  Final  GRADE
---- --------------------  ------  ------ ------ ------ ------ ------ ------
0100 John Campbell         CS101    86.00  90.00  94.00  90.00  94.00  92.00
0101 Sam Redden            CS101    90.00  92.00  94.00  92.00  94.00  93.00
0102 Carolyn Hayes         CS101   100.00  90.00  95.00  95.00  98.00  96.50
0103 Mitchell Wyatt        CS101    80.00  70.00  75.00  75.00  80.00  77.50
0104 Joyce DeWitt          CS101    85.00  82.00  88.00  85.00  89.00  87.00
0105 Dan Merrill           CS101    99.00 100.00 100.00  99.67 100.00  99.83
0106 Mark Oliver           CS101    91.00  84.00  90.00  88.33  93.00  90.67
0107 Mary Alice George     CS101    88.00  98.00  93.00  93.00  94.00  93.50
0108 Suzanne Winter        CS101    89.00  97.00  96.00  94.00  98.00  96.00
0109 Stanley Roper         CS101    75.00  70.00  74.00  73.00  82.00  77.50
0110                                 0.00   0.00   0.00   0.00   0.00   0.00
0111                                 0.00   0.00   0.00   0.00   0.00   0.00
0112                                 0.00   0.00   0.00   0.00   0.00   0.00
0113                                 0.00   0.00   0.00   0.00   0.00   0.00
0114                                 0.00   0.00   0.00   0.00   0.00   0.00
```

Figure 7-54   *Printing All Records of GRADEBOOK*

to 1″. This will give you a line length of 7.5″ that will hold 90 characters. Each report line fits within the 90 character line length. Since the page number and date are printed at the right edge of the paper, they will appear within the right margin setting above the report.

A top and bottom margin of 1″ has been specified, so that the report will be placed in the middle of a page.

For the GRADES report record format, it is recommended the formatting options be set to "No," "Yes," "Yes," and "SS" respectively, as shown in Fig. 7-42. After making selections, use the ESCape key to exit the Printer Options screen.

Finally, print a report using OPEN-APPLE P from the Report Format screen. The screen shown is the same as in Fig. 7-20. For now, choose either the first or second option. Actually, the second option lets you see your design without using any paper. If you choose the first option, make sure your printer is powered up and ready. A sample report is shown for all records in the list in Fig. 7-54.

7.4.3 Other Uses of the GRADEBOOK

In some schools, especially in high schools and junior highs, teachers also are home room monitors. These teachers may maintain grades and records for students in many courses. The GRADEBOOK data base could be used to track grades for students from many different courses. For example, you could group grades for the same student together. In this way you can keep a record for all students for which you are responsible.

Another modifiction you might want to make to the GRADEBOOK is to eliminate the G. AVG category and add two additional calculated columns in order to figure the final grade averages for the semester. This mathematics was discussed in the last section.

7.5 SUMMARY

This chapter discussed a number of practical lists:

- Mailing list
- Christmas card list
- Subcontractors payment list
- Gradebook

Each of these lists was followed from their creation to the final printing of a report.

The mailing list was for the purpose of showing how to create a general mailing labels report that could be used for any number of mailing label uses.

The second data base file created in this chapter was a specialized mailing labels list. Actually, this list, a Christmas card list, was a modification and extension of the mailing labels list. The purpose of doing a second mailing list was to show you that, with very little modification, one list could be used in a number of ways to create a number of reports. The Christmas card list showed you how to format both a label-style and table-style report.

The subcontractors payment list is for the purpose of keeping track of money expenditures to subcontractors. This list used a calculated category, group totals, and date conversions. This list provided many of the characteristics of a real situation that could be encountered in a business situation. This list also showed you how to link information in the list with information in other parts of a business.

The purpose of the gradebook was to keep track of semester grades, final exam grade, semester average, and final grade average.

This chapter discussed additional features in the data base portion of AppleWorks:

- Grand totals
- Group totals
- Right-justifying values
- Date conversion
- Time conversions
- Mathematical formulas

PART FIVE

I am a part of all that I have met.
ALFRED LORD TENNYSON, 1842

You have been introduced to all of the individual parts of AppleWorks. Now is the time to put these parts together and transfer information among them. This capability allows you to be more productive when working with AppleWorks.

Putting Things Together

*Most Americans don't, in a vital sense, get together; they only
do things together.*
LOUIS KRONENBERGER, 1954

8.0 OVERVIEW

This chapter discusses probably the most important and most exciting capabilities of AppleWorks—the ability to work with more than one file at a time in memory and the ability to cut and paste information from one document to another with only a few keystroke commands.

When you exercise the cut and paste capability, you transfer information from one file to another through a mechanism known as the Clipboard. This is the subject of Section 8.1.

Sections 8.2 through 8.4 discuss moving documents to and from each of the AppleWorks application levels.

Section 8.5 summarizes the chapter.

8.1 WHAT IS CUT AND PASTE?

The Clipboard is a term used with the Apple Lisa and Macintosh computers, as well as AppleWorks, to designate a temporary storage location in memory. *Cut* means to move information from one document to the Clipboard. *Paste* means to move information from the Clipboard to an active document on the Desktop.

The concept of cut and paste is very simple to visualize. Suppose you have a list of names and addresses you need to put into a letter. With a pair of scissors you could cut them up and paste them carefully into the text of the letter. This is the essential idea behind the cut and paste capability of AppleWorks. With AppleWorks, though, all of the cutting and pasting is done electronically.

Using this capability you are able to cut as little as one letter or as much as an entire document to the Clipboard. Then you can transfer the information from the Clipboard to another file. This section discusses in general how to cut and paste and provides specific instructions for using this capability in the word processor, the spreadsheet, and the data base.

When you transfer information, you can:

- Transfer only one block of information at a time.
- Move the information from a file on the Desktop to the Clipboard or from the Clipboard to a file.
- Copy the information from a file on the Desktop to the Clipboard or from the Clipboard to a file.
- Print data base or spreadsheet information to the Clipboard and then move or copy the information into a word processor file. If you move information from the Clipboard, the Clipboard information is gone. If you copy information from the Clipboard, another copy of the information is still on the Clipboard.

Tip: You can move data base files to a spreadsheet file or vice versa through the DIF procedure. Then you can read the DIF file into the other application.

8.1.1 Cut and Paste with the Word Processor

There are times when you need to move or copy information from one word processor file to another word processor file. The cut and paste capability allows you to move or copy a maximum of 250 lines of text.

To move/copy text in the word processor to/from the Clipboard:

1. Place the source document you want to move or copy information from on the Desktop memory.
2. Place the cursor at the first or last character of the information you want to move or copy.
3. Press OPEN-APPLE M (move command) or OPEN-APPLE C (copy command).
4. Choose the "To Clipboard (cut)" option from the prompt message at the bottom of the screen.
5. Using the arrow keys, move the cursor to highlight the information you want to move or copy. Press the RETURN key to signify the beginning or end of the information to be moved or copied.
6. Release the source document and activate (bring to the Desktop) the destination document for the information now in the Clipboard.

7. Place the cursor at the first character of the information you want to move from the Clipboard.

8. Press OPEN-APPLE M or OPEN-APPLE C.

9. Choose the "From Clipboard (paste)" option from the prompt message at the bottom of the screen.

10. AppleWorks will now move the information in the Clipboard to the new document.

Tips: • Use the move capability to delete information from the source document and insert that information into the destination document.
   • Use the copy capability to duplicate information from a source document to multiple-destination documents.
   • Once information has been cut to the Clipboard, use either the move or copy command from the Clipboard, depending on whether you need single or multiple copies of the Clipboard information pasted into Desktop documents.

8.1.2 Cut and Paste with the Spreadsheet

The cut and paste capability in the spreadsheet allows you to relocate up to a maximum of 250 rows within a file, between spreadsheet templates, or to the word processor.
   The following procedure describes how to:

   • Copy or move information from one Desktop template to another.
   • Print a template to the Clipboard and move it to another document.

To move/copy information in the spreadsheet to/from the Clipboard:

1. Place the source document you want to move or copy on the Desktop memory.

2. Place the cursor to the first or last cell of the row or section you want to move or copy.

3. Press OPEN-APPLE M or OPEN-APPLE C.

4. Choose the "To Clipboard (cut)" option from the prompt message at the bottom of the screen.

5. Using the arrow keys, move the cursor to highlight the rows you want to move or copy. Press the RETURN key to signify the end of the information cells to be moved or copied. The chosen cells are then moved to the Clipboard.

6. Release the source document and activate the destination document for the information now in the Clipboard.

7. Place the cursor at the first cell of the location for the information you want to move from the Clipboard.

8. Press OPEN-APPLE M or OPEN-APPLE C.

9. Choose the "From Clipboard (paste)" option from the prompt message at the bottom of the screen.

10. AppleWorks will now move the information in the Clipboard to the new document.

8.1.3 Cut and Paste with the Data Base

The cut and paste capability in the data base allows you to relocate up to a maximum of 250 records within a file, between data base files, or to a word processor file.

The following procedure describes how to:

• Copy or move information from one Desktop template to another.

• Print a template to the Clipboard and move it to another document.

To move/copy records in the data base to/from the Clipboard:

1. Place the source document you want to move or copy on the Desktop memory. Make sure you are in the multiple-record layout screen presentation.

2. Place the cursor in an entry on the top or bottom record of the group you want to move or copy.

3. Press OPEN-APPLE M or OPEN-APPLE C.

4. Choose the "To Clipboard (cut)" option from the prompt message at the bottom of the screen.

5. Using the arrow keys, move the cursor to highlight the records you want to move or copy. Press the RETURN key to signify the end of the records to be moved or copied.

6. Release the source document and activate the destination document for the records now in the Clipboard.

7. Make sure you are in the multiple-record layout screen presentation.

8. Place the cursor at the beginning of the record(s) you want to move from the Clipboard.

9. Press OPEN-APPLE M or OPEN-APPLE C.

10. Choose the "From Clipboard (paste)" option from the prompt message at the bottom of the screen.

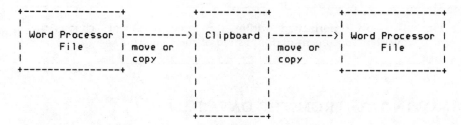

Figure 8-1 *Moving or Copying a Word Processor Document*

11. AppleWorks will now move the records(s) in the Clipboard to the new
document.

8.2 MOVING TO/FROM THE WORD PROCESSOR

In Section 8.1.1, the procedure for moving or copying word processor documents from
one file to another was given. This procedure is very straightforward and is shown in Fig.
8-1.

To print a document to the Clipboard:

1. Place the source document you want to move or copy on the Desktop
memory.

2. Place the cursor at the first or last character of the information you want to
move or copy.

3. Press OPEN-APPLE M or OPEN-APPLE C.

4. Choose the "To Clipboard (cut)" option from the prompt message at the
bottom of the screen.

5. Using the arrow keys, move the cursor to highlight the information you
want to move or copy. Press the RETURN key to signify the end of the
information to be moved or copied.

6. Release the source document and activate the destination document for the
information now in the Clipboard.

7. Place the cursor at the first character of the location for the information
you want to move from the Clipboard.

8. Press OPEN-APPLE M or OPEN-APPLE C.

9. Choose the "From Clipboard (paste)" option from the prompt message at
the bottom of the screen.

10. AppleWorks will now move the information in the Clipboard to the new
document.

> **Tip:** To move information within the same document, choose the "Within" document option instead of the Clipboard.

8.3 MOVING TO/FROM THE DATA BASE

In Section 8.1.3, the procedure for moving or copying data base documents from one file to another was given. This procedure is very straightforward and is shown in Fig. 8-2.

Before you add data base information to a word processor document, you must first format a data base report, then print the report format to the Clipboard. Finally, move the contents of the Clipboard to the word processor document.

To print information from a data base to/from the Clipboard:

1. Create the data base report format for the information you want to transfer to a word processor document by placing the source data base document you want to print on the Desktop memory.

2. Press OPEN-APPLE P (print command).

3. Choose the Clipboard option from the prompt message at the bottom of the screen.

4. Type the report date, when prompted, if your report requires a header. Press the RETURN key. If you do not want a date printed, then just press the RETURN key. AppleWorks will then tell you that the report has been placed into the Clipboard.

5. Press OPEN-APPLE Q (switch command) to have the Desktop index presented. Choose the word processor document you want to use and activate the document. If the document is not on the Desktop, then add it.

6. Place the cursor at the first character in the document where you want the information to be printed.

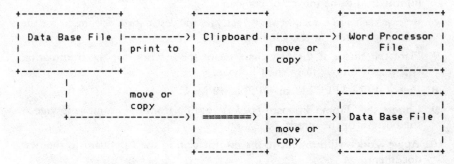

Figure 8-2 *Moving or Copying a Data Base Document*

7. Press OPEN-APPLE M if you want to move information into the document, or press OPEN-APPLE C if you want to copy the information into the document.

8. Choose the "From Clipboard (paste)" option from the prompt message at the bottom of the screen in response to the "Move?" or "Copy?" prompt.

9. AppleWorks will now move or copy the information in the Clipboard to the new document.

Tips:
1. AppleWorks will transfer all information to the new document, including formatting.
2. When designing the data base report format, particular attention should be given to the maximum number of characters to be printed horizontally. A maximum of about 75 per line will be printed when the characters per inch is set to 10. Otherwise, the move will change the formatting of the information in the word processor document.
3. You can edit the spreadsheet information after it is in the word processor document.

8.4 MOVING TO/FROM THE SPREADSHEET

In Section 8.1.2, the procedure for moving or copying spreadsheet documents from one file to another was given. This procedure is very straightforward and is shown in Fig. 8-3.

To print information from the spreadsheet template to/from the Clipboard:

1. Place the source document you want to print on the Desktop memory.

2. Press OPEN-APPLE P.

3. Choose "All," "Rows," "Columns," or "Block" option from the prompt message at the bottom of the screen. If you choose the "All" option, the entire template will be printed.

4. Highlight the rows, columns, or area you want to print. Press the RETURN key to signify the end of the information cells to be printed.

5. Choose the Clipboard as the printing destination for the document to be printed.

6. Enter the date for the report header if your report is to have a date shown. AppleWorks will then tell you that the report has been placed on the Clipboard.

7. Press OPEN-APPLE Q to have the Desktop index presented. Choose the word processor document you want to use, and activate the document. If the document is not on the Desktop, then add it.

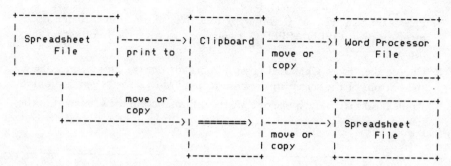

Figure 8-3 *Moving or Copying a Spreadsheet Document*

8. Place the cursor at the first character in the document where you want the information to be printed.

9. Press OPEN-APPLE M if you want to move information into the document, or press OPEN-APPLE C if you want to copy the information into the document.

10. Choose the "From Clipboard (paste)" option from the prompt message at the bottom of the screen.

11. AppleWorks will now move or copy the information in the Clipboard to the new document.

8.5 SUMMARY

This chapter gave you the tools needed to move or copy information from one type of document to another. You were also given the procedures for moving or copying information between documents of the same type.

This chapter discussed the most important and exciting capabilities of AppleWorks—the ability to work with more than one file in memory at a time on the Desktop and to be able to cut and paste information from one document to another with only a few keystroke commands.

Common Features

*That which is common to the greatest number has the least
care bestowed upon it.*
ARISTOTLE, 4TH CENTURY B.C.

9.0 OVERVIEW

This chapter discusses the common keystrokes that have been used throughout AppleWorks. By having keystrokes, functions, and menu presentations that are common and that perform common processing throughout an entire software package, learning, operating, and using that software package becomes much easier.

Because many of the special keystrokes and keystroke combinations you will be using to perform processing operations and functions are common to both the system and application levels, this software becomes very easy to learn and to use. The keystroke combinations, in most cases, have a relationship to the function performed. This is quite different from some other word processors, spreadsheets, and data bases, where keystroke combinations have very little relation to the operation being performed.

Section 9.2 discusses the common key functions performed when other keystroke combinations are used. These keystrokes allow you to move around within a document quickly or let you exit easily from one operation or application to another.

A summary of the entire chapter is presented in Section 9.5.

> **Note:** Since this chapter discusses keystrokes and keystroke combinations, you may want to skip it entirely and start using AppleWorks. If that is the case, use this chapter as a reference and review chapter. Come back to the information in this chapter as you need additional information while using other portions of this book.

9.1 COMMON KEYSTROKES

This section discusses those keystrokes that are common to the system and application levels in AppleWorks. Many of these keystrokes allow a shorter method of performing processing operations. If you have looked through the table of contents, you have probably already noticed that these common keystroke combinations combine OPEN-APPLE with a letter key. The OPEN-APPLE key is located just to the left of the space bar on the keyboard.

> **Tip:** The CLOSED-APPLE key, located to the right of the space bar, may also be used like the OPEN-APPLE key. However, we will talk only about using the OPEN-APPLE key when explaining keystroke combinations.

Press down and hold the OPEN-APPLE key and then press the second key. Hold down both keys together and then let up on both of the keys together.

When discussing each of the keystroke combinations, the specific explanation order is:

1. The word processor application
2. The spreadsheet application
3. The data base application

Even though the initial keystroke combinations to perform common processing features are similar, the remainder of the keystrokes and option choices may be different.

In this chapter, there may be terms used that are unfamiliar to you. Please don't get upset or discouraged. Each term will be explained as it is encountered.

9.1.1 OPEN-APPLE A (Arrange)

- OPEN-APPLE A is not active in the word processor.
- AppleWorks allows you to arrange or sort rows in a template by the values of their entries in a specified column in the spreadsheet. Rows may be arranged alphabetically or numerically.

To arrange rows in a spreadsheet:

1. Place the cursor to the column that contains the information for the rows you want arranged.
2. If you are arranging only specific rows, move the cursor to the top or bottom of the group of rows you want arranged.

3. Press OPEN-APPLE A keystroke combination.

4. Choose either "All rows" or "Specific rows" option.

5. If you choose "Specific rows," use the cursor up/down arrow keys to highlight the rows you want to arrange. Then press the RETURN key.

6. Choose the way you want rows arranged. You have four arrangement options as shown below:

   —From A to Z

   —From Z to A

   —From 0 to 9

   —From 9 to 0

• The data base lets you arrange, or sort, records by category values. Records can be arranged in alphabetical order, numeric order, and in order of dates and times.

To arrange data base records:

1. Place the cursor anywhere in the category entry you want your records arranged.

2. Press OPEN-APPLE A.

3. Choose the way you want records arranged by using the up/down arrow keys or the number keys. You have four arrangement options as shown below.

   —From A to Z

   —From Z to A

   —From 0 to 9

   —From 9 to 0

4. The data base will automatically redisplay your file rearranged.

Tip: When you want to arrange records by several categories, arrange by the values in reverse order of importance. First arrange the least important category, then the next most important category, etc.

9.1.2 OPEN-APPLE B (Blank)

• OPEN-APPLE B is not active in the word processor.

• Being able to blank an individual cell or groups of cells is very handy, since no column or row readjustment of the worksheet or template will take place like the delete keystroke command does.

To blank an individual cell or cells:

1. Place the cursor on the cell you want blanked.
2. Press OPEN-APPLE B (blank cell(s)) command.
3. Choose "Entry," "Rows," "Columns," or "Block" option. Use the right/left arrow keys to make a selection and then press the RETURN key.
4. If you have chosen to blank an entry, the chosen cell will be automatically blanked.
5. If you have chosen any of the other options, use the arrow keys to highlight the rows, columns, or blocks of cells you want blanked, then press the RE-TURN key.
6. You are then returned to the modified worksheet.

> **Tips:**
> 1. All blanked cells referred to by other cells are considered to contain a zero. Therefore, you should recheck all formula and pointer references.
> 2. Protected cells using the OPEN-APPLE L command cannot be blanked.
> 3. Protected cells for labels only or values only may be blanked; as a result, they lose their protection.

- OPEN-APPLE B is not active in the data base.

9.1.3 OPEN-APPLE C (Copy)

- This keystroke combination lets you copy text in a word processor document, records in a data base, or entries in a spreadsheet from one place to another either within a document or to/from the Clipboard.

> **Tip:** The copy feature in all applications is very similar to the move feature, except that copy leaves the original information in its original location in the application.

Copying text within a word processing document makes it easy to duplicate paragraphs or larger sections of a document. You can copy a maximum of 250 lines of text at one time. (A line of text is considered a single screen line as shown and computed at the bottom of the word processing screen.)

To copy text in a word processor document:

1. Move the cursor to either the first or last character of the information you want to copy.
2. Press OPEN-APPLE C.
3. Choose "Within document," "To clipboard (cut)," or "From clipboard (paste)" option from the highlighted prompt message presented at the bottom of the screen. Use the left/right arrow keys to highlight a selection, then press the RETURN key.
4. Using the arrow keys, move the cursor to either the end or the beginning of the information you want to copy, then press the RETURN key. The text to be copied will be highlighted.
5. If you have chosen "Within document":
   —Move the cursor to the place in the document where you want the copy to appear.
   —Press the RETURN key again.
   —The information is then copied and the presentation screen is adjusted appropriately.
6. If you have chosen "To clipboard (cut)":
   —The highlighted information is immediately copied to the Clipboard.
   —The cursor is left at its last position.
7. If you have chosen "From clipboard (paste)":
   —The information previously placed on the Clipboard is immediately copied to the active document on the Desktop.
   —The cursor is left at its last position.
8. You are now returned to the active document on the Desktop.

• You can also copy single or multiple cells within a spreadsheet template. This feature lets you quickly replicate similar information into any number of cells.

To copy information in a spreadsheet document:

1. Move the cursor to the cell you want to copy. If you are copying entire rows or columns, place the cursor either at the extreme left or right cell of a row or at the top or bottom cell of a column of cells. (A cell is an individual information item in an array of information items.)
2. Press OPEN-APPLE C.
3. Choose "Within worksheet," "To clipboard (cut)," or "From clipboard (paste)"option from the highlighted prompt message presented at the bot-

tom of the screen. Use the left/right arrow keys to highlight a selection, then press the RETURN key.

4. If you have chosen "Within worksheet":

—Use the arrow keys to highlight the copy-from cells, then press the RE-TURN key.

—Move the cursor to the cell in the worksheet where you want the copy to appear. If you are copying entire rows and columns, place the cursor either at the extreme left or right edge cell of a row or at the top or bottom cell of a column.

—If you are making only one copy, press the RETURN key in response to the prompt message. If you are making several copies of the same information, type the period (.) key. Then use the arrow keys to highlight the other copy-to cells, and press the RETURN key.

—AppleWorks then tells you the contents of each of the copy-from cells, if the cells contain formulas, and asks you if you want to make an exact copy of each reference to another cell. The referenced cells will be highlighted as you go along. Further, you will be required to choose either "No change" or "Relative" for each cell referenced.

Tip: Relative copying means that cell references are modified to reflect the new location of the copy. More will be said about this in later chapters.

---

5. If you have chosen "To clipboard (cut)":

—Move the cursor to highlight the rows you want to copy, then press the RETURN key.

—The highlighted information is immediately copied to the Clipboard.

—The cursor is left at its last position.

6. If you have chosen "From clipboard (paste)":

—The information previously placed on the Clipboard is immediately copied to the active worksheet on the Desktop.

—The cursor is left at its last position.

7. You are now returned to the active worksheet on the Desktop.

• You can make multiple copies of a record in a data base file. This capability is extremely helpful if your records have common information, such as city, state, zip code, etc.

To copy records in a data base document:

1. Move the cursor to the first record in the file you want to copy.

2. Press OPEN-APPLE C.

3. Choose either "Current record," "To clipboard (cut)," or "From clipboard (paste)" option from the highlighted prompt message presented at the bottom of the screen. Use the left/right arrow keys to highlight a selection, then press the RETURN key.

4. If you have chosen "Current record":

   —Type the number of copies you want and then press the RETURN key.

5. If you have chosen "To clipboard (cut)":

   —Move the cursor to highlight the records you want to copy, then press the RETURN key.

   —The highlighted information is immediately copied to the Clipboard.

   —The cursor is left at its last position.

6. If you have chosen "From clipboard (paste)":

   —The information previously placed on the Clipboard is immediately copied to the active data base file on the Desktop.

   —The cursor is left at its last position.

7. You are now returned to the active data base on the desktop.

9.1.4 OPEN-APPLE D (Delete)

- This keystroke combination lets you delete text in a word processor document, records in a data base, or entries in a spreadsheet. You can delete information in any application in two ways.

Caution: Once information is deleted, it is gone and not retrievable.

The first way to delete information in all application level programs, and probably the easiest to understand, is to use the DELETE key in the upper right hand corner of the keyboard. The DELETE key will delete only one character at a time, for example, with each press of the DELETE key. This key is used by placing the cursor just to the right of the character to be deleted. Then press the DELETE key. The character is then deleted.

The other way to delete information in a word processor document is to use the following procedure.

To delete text in a word processor document:

1. Move the cursor to either the first or last character of the information you want to delete.

2. Press OPEN-APPLE D.

3. Move the cursor to either the end or the beginning of the information you want to delete.

4. Press the RETURN key.

5. The information is then deleted and the presentation screen is adjusted appropriately. AppleWorks closes up the document where the text was deleted.

Tips:
1. This procedure is used to delete large amounts of information.
2. Use the OPEN-APPLE up/down arrow keys to delete complete screen lines of text.
3. To delete embedded text commands, place the cursor on that line and press OPEN-APPLE D, then press the RETURN key.
4. You can delete large information blocks by using the OPEN-APPLE 1 through 9 keys to move the cursor.

• To delete information in a spreadsheet template, use the following procedure.

To delete rows or columns in a spreadsheet worksheet:

1. Move the cursor to the first cell containing the information you want to delete.

2. Press OPEN-APPLE D.

3. Choose "Rows" or "Columns" from the prompting message.

4. Move the cursor to highlight the rows or columns you want to delete, then press the RETURN key.

Tips:
1. This procedure is used to delete entire rows or columns, not just the part displayed.
2. Before you start deleting anything, you may want to review the entire row or column, checking to make sure you do not delete anything you want.
3. When you delete a row or column, you might delete cell contents that are

needed elsewhere in your template. This will cause an ERROR message in the cell(s) affected.

4. When you delete rows or columns, the section of the worksheet to the right and below all of the deleted rows or columns is closed up. All closed up rows or columns are renumbered.

If you need only to blank out a single cell or a small group of cells, it is much faster to use the OPEN-APPLE B command.

• To delete information in a data base list, use the following procedure when in the table-style format.

To delete records in a data base document:

1. Make sure you are in the multiple-record layout.

2. Move the cursor to the first record in the file you want to delete.

3. Press OPEN-APPLE D. AppleWorks will highlight the first record to be deleted.

4. Move the cursor to highlight any other records you want to delete.

5. Press the RETURN key.

Tips:
1. This procedure is used to delete large amounts of information.
2. Use the OPEN-APPLE up/down arrow keys to delete complete records.

You can also delete records when in the single-record layout format.
To delete records in a data base document:

1. Make sure you are in the label-style layout.

2. Press OPEN-APPLE Z to zoom in to the label-style layout.

3. Press OPEN-APPLE D. AppleWorks will highlight the first record to be deleted.

4. Choose "No" or "Yes" depending on whether you want to delete the displayed record.

5. Continue to choose "No" or "Yes" as AppleWorks displays succeeding records.

6. Press the ESCape key after you are finished deleting records.

9.1.5 OPEN-APPLE E (Switch Cursor)

This keystroke combination lets you switch the cursor from an overstrike cursor to an insert cursor or vice versa. The cursor of choice, the default cursor, in AppleWorks is the insert cursor. When you want to change cursors, use the OPEN-APPLE E keystroke combination.

AppleWorks has two cursors:

- The blinking bar cursor is the insert cursor. When you see this cursor, any characters typed will be inserted at the cursor position. All characters to the right of the cursor will be moved to the right.
- The blinking rectangle cursor is the overstrike cursor. When you see this cursor, any characters typed will replace any character under the cursor. The only exception is the carriage return character, which is moved to the right. This cursor is useful for correcting typographical errors.

> **Tip:** You may find using the overstrike cursor helpful when you are entering new text material or correcting typographical errors.

In general, you may use these two cursors, along with the arrow keys, to edit typed information, regardless of the application level program of AppleWorks.

9.1.6 OPEN-APPLE F (Find)

- This keystroke combination lets you search, review, or find specific text in a word processor document, individual text and records in a data base, or cell entries in a spreadsheet. This keystroke combination only finds information; it does not change information. OPEN-APPLE R is used to find and change information.

> **Tip:** AppleWorks keeps a record of the last text you asked to be found.

The word processor lets you find five different types of information within any document These are:

Text—words, phrases, or characters.
Page—A specific page within a document.

Case-sensitive text—Finds text exactly as you type it, accounting for a mixture of uppercase and lowercase letters.

Printer options—These are the embedded text and printer commands within your document.

Marker—This could be any marker that identifies a specific place within a document. Markers are places within a document that you have previously set through the printer options menu.

When you want to find text within a document, AppleWorks starts at the current cursor position and looks forward in the document for the text you have specified. You may specify up to thirty characters to be found. After the first match has been found, you can ask for the next occurrence.

To find specific text within a word processor document:

1. Move the cursor to the place in a document where you want AppleWorks to start searching.

2. Press OPEN-APPLE F.

3. Choose the "Text" option to indicate you want to find any text that matches your text for comparison. AppleWorks will automatically supply any previously used Find character(s), text, sentence, phrase, etc.

4. Type the text you want found and then press the RETURN key, or just press the RETURN key to find the next occurrence of the last found or replaced text. Press the RETURN key after you have finished making a new entry. AppleWorks will move the cursor to the next occurrence of the found text.

5. Choose either "Yes" or "No," using the right/left arrow keys and the RETURN key, depending upon whether you want AppleWorks to find or not find the next occurrence of the text that is displayed.

When you are defining the text to be found, leading and trailing spaces become part of the phrase you want to find.

At any time, you may terminate the Find processing by pressing the ESCape key or by answering the "Find next occurrence?" prompt message with "No."

If AppleWorks cannot find a phrase after a search has been performed, you will be told that the phrase has not been found and asked to press the space bar to continue. The cursor is left at its last position in the document.

To find a specific page within a document:

1. Press OPEN-APPLE F.

2. Choose "Page."

3. Type the page number you want found and then press the RETURN key.

> **Tip:** AppleWorks always starts searching for a page from the beginning of a document. The cursor will be placed at the beginning character on the page that was requested. To get to any page other than the first page, you must have first calculated the page numbers by using the OPEN-APPLE K keystroke combination. These keystrokes will calculate and display the page breaks just as is done when you print any document.

When you want to find case-sensitive text, use the text procedure after you have chosen this option from the prompting message at the bottom of the screen.

In order to find any of the printer options embedded as text commands within a document, use the following procedure.

To find a printer option within a document:

1. Press OPEN-APPLE F.
2. Choose "Option".
3. Type the two-letter option code you want found (e.g., CI, UJ, etc.), and then press the RETURN key.

Markers are places within a document that you identify. These markers are for the purpose of identifying those places you may want to return to quickly. The marker number may be any number from 1 through 254.

To set a marker within a document:

1. Move the cursor to the place within a document where you want to set the marker.
2. Press the OPEN-APPLE O (printer options) command.
3. Choose the SM (set marker) option.
4. Type the number of the marker, for example, a 1, 2, or 3.
5. Press the ESCape key to escape from the printer options menu.

• AppleWorks lets you find a cell either by specifying a cell's coordinates or the contents of that cell. In addition, you can specify that AppleWorks is to find the next occurrence of the last information you defined.

After you have specified what it is you want AppleWorks to find, AppleWorks will move the cursor to the place in the template of the first occurrence of the matched value.

To find a cell or specific information in a spreadsheet:

1. Move the cursor to the place within a template where you want the search to begin.

2. Press OPEN-APPLE F.

3. Choose "Repeat last," "Coordinates," or "Text" option to indicate you want to find any text or value that matches your text or value for comparison.

4. If you have chosen "Repeat last," AppleWorks supplies any previously used Find character(s), text, or value(s).

5. If you have chosen "Coordinates," AppleWorks will ask you to provide the coordinates of the cell wanted. Type the coordinates and then press the RETURN key.

6. If you have chosen "Text," AppleWorks will ask you to provide the specific text you want to find. The text may be up to 25 characters long. Then press the RETURN key after you have finished the entry.

Tips:
1. AppleWorks searches for information across rows and then down columns of a worksheet.
2. AppleWorks does not differentiate between upper- and lowercase characters when "Text" is chosen.

- You can find records in a data base based upon the information that you specify. This information may be any category within any record(s) and anywhere within an entry.

To find specific records in a data base document:

1. Press OPEN-APPLE F.

2. Type the value you want AppleWorks to find. AppleWorks will then display those records that contain the value you provided. Value in this sense may be either numeric or alphabetic.

3. Press the ESCape key to return to the Review/Add/Change screen.

Tip: AppleWorks displays all of the records that contain the value specified.

9.1.7 OPEN-APPLE G (Group Totals)

- OPEN-APPLE G is not active in the word processor or the spreadsheet.

You can specify group totals or subtotals for any category. In addition you may specify which category will control the group total. Whenever the value in the control category changes, a new group total is calculated and printed for the category you have specified with OPEN-APPLE T.

To designate the controlling category for group totals:

1. Place the cursor on the controlling category.
2. Press OPEN-APPLE G.
3. Choose "No" or "Yes," depending on whether you want to print only group totals or all the records.
4. Choose "No" or "Yes," depending on whether you want to go to a new page after each group total.

9.1.8 OPEN-APPLE H (Print Screen)

This keystroke combination lets you print the current screen presentation in any of the three application level documents or reports without having to go through the set-up procedure before printing.

To print a copy of what is displayed on a screen, press the OPEN-APPLE H keystroke combination.

> **Caution:** You must make sure that you have previously set up your printer correctly, that the printer is powered up, that the printer is on-line, and that AppleWorks knows your printer characteristics. See option #7 in Other Activities Menu.

Since you can print a copy of the screen anytime, this is a very handy way to help you keep a running record of your work, to see entries you have made in a data base, to show the embedded text commands you have entered in a document, and to show cell formulas in a template.

9.1.9 OPEN-APPLE I (Insert)

- OPEN-APPLE I is not active in the word processor.
- This keystroke combination allows you to insert either new rows or columns into a worksheet or template. A maximum of nine new rows or columns may be inserted at a time.

To insert new rows or columns:

1. Place the cursor on the row below or on the column to the right of the row or column you want inserted.

2. Press OPEN-APPLE I.

3. Choose "Rows" or "Columns." Use the right/left arrow keys to make a selection and then press the RETURN key.

4. Type the number of blank rows or columns, up to nine, that you want to have inserted, and then press the RETURN key.

5. You are then returned to the modified worksheet.

Tips:
1. AppleWorks renumbers the rows below the inserted rows and reletters the columns to the right of the inserted columns.

2. Formulas are modified to account for inserted rows or columns, if necessary.

3. You are not allowed to insert rows or columns that would place worksheet information beyond the limits imposed by the spreadsheet portion of AppleWorks.

4. The spreadsheet does not allow you to insert new rows or columns beyond pre-existing information. This is different from adding new information at the end of a worksheet, which is allowed.

• The data base uses OPEN-APPLE I to insert previously deleted categories in either a label- or table-style format.

To reinsert a previously deleted category:

1. Decide where you want to reinsert the previously deleted category. Place the cursor on the category just to the right of that position.

2. Press OPEN-APPLE I.

3. You are asked to choose a category from the numbered list of deleted categories presented. Choose the category you want to insert.

You may insert spacing lines or previously deleted categories in the table-style format. To insert spacing or a previously deleted category:

1. Place the cursor where you want the category or spacing lines to be inserted.

2. Press OPEN-APPLE I. You are asked to choose a category from the numbered list of deleted categories presented. You are also given the option to

insert a spacing line above or below the cursor position. Just press the RE-TURN key to insert a line below the cursor.

3. Choose the option you require. It is then inserted into the report.

9.1.10 OPEN-APPLE J (Right Justify, Jump)

- OPEN-APPLE J is not active in the word processor.
- This keystroke combination works in conjunction with a split-window worksheet presentation. A split window is initiated using the OPEN-APPLE W command. This keystroke combination allows you to move directly to the corresponding cell in the other displayed window of a worksheet.

To jump to a specific cell:

1. Press OPEN-APPLE J, which jumps the cursor directly to the corresponding cell in the other window.

- Information within columnar categories can be right-justified. When you right-justify alphabetic information, the entries in that category line up right under each other with an even right margin. When you right-justify numeric information, the decimal points are aligned.

To right-justify a column entry:

1. Place the cursor on the column category you want to right-justify.
2. Press OPEN-APPLE G. You are asked to specify the number of decimal places that should be included in each entry in the specified column.
3. Type the number of decimal places and press the RETURN key. If you are right-justifying alphabetic information, enter 0 and press the RETURN key. You are then asked how many blank spaces should be placed after each entry. This is very important in spacing columns across a single line on a printed page.
4. Enter the number of blank spaces you want to be included and press the RETURN key.

9.1.11 OPEN-APPLE K (Calculate Page Numbers, Automatic Recalculation, Calculated Categories)

- There are times when creating a document that you want to know the location of page breaks. It may be that you want certain information on a single page and not broken between two pages.

There are a couple of ways that this may be done. First, you may want to force information to be placed on new pages. This is done by using the New Page (NP) printer option command placed somewhere within a document. The second way is to group information together using the printer options Group Begin (GB) and Group End (GE) commands. Grouping of information will be discussed later.

The way to see how page breaks will appear in your final document is done by using the OPEN-APPLE K keystroke combination.

To calculate page numbers:

1. Press OPEN-APPLE K. This keystroke calculates the page breaks in a typed document.

2. Choose the printer for which you want the pages calculated.

3. Scroll through your document, using the arrow keys, to review where the page breaks will be made.

Look at how the final page breaks will be made when the document is printed by scrolling around within the next material. You will see that the word processor identifies each page and page number by breaking the text material with a dashed line across the screen presentation.

- You have the capability to have a worksheet calculated automatically after every cell entry or manually when requested. When the standard value is set to manual, you are required to tell the spreadsheet when you want a worksheet recalculated.

To force recalculation:

1. Press OPEN-APPLE K.

Tips:
1. AppleWorks recalculates all formulas in a worksheet during recalculation. That means that the entire worksheet is recalculated even though you may have made only one new entry. Use the OPEN-APPLE V command to change the recalculation status.
2. It is recommended that you turn off the automatic recalculation feature when making changes to a worksheet. It will save you time because you will not have to wait for the recalculation.
3. If a recalculation cannot take place in a cell, the word ERROR is placed there.

- When you are creating calculated categories in the data base, use the following procedure.

To create a calculated category:

1. Place the cursor one coumn to the right of where you want the calculated category to appear.
2. Press OPEN-APPLE K. 9's will appear in the category and be right-justified.
3. Type the name of the category and press the RETURN key. This name may be up to 20 characters long. This is also the name that appears on the report.

9.1.12 OPEN-APPLE L (Underline, Cell Layout, Layout)

- OPEN-APPLE L is not active in the word processor.
- When you have specified all of the standard values for a worksheet, you have also specified how all cells in the worksheet are to be displayed. However, you can also override these display values for a cell, column, or row by using the cell layout keystroke combinations.

Cell layout specifications may be given for value formats, label formats, column widths, and protection.

When you specify a layout for a group of cells within a template, that formatting is active for only those cells. Values already in those cells are then redisplayed in the layout specifications. Blank cells and cells with labels do not get the specification unless you specify them with this command's entry or block option. Therefore, new value entries are displayed with the new layout, but according to the standard values.

To change cell layouts:

1. Press OPEN-APPLE L.
2. Choose "Entry," "Rows," "Columns," or "Block." Use the right/left arrow keys to make a selection, then press the RETURN key.
3. If you have chosen "Entry," then only an individual cell is affected.
4. If you have chosen "Rows," use the up/down arrow keys to select, or highlight, the rows, then press the RETURN key.
5. If you have chosen "Columns," use the right/left arrow keys to select the columns and then press the RETURN key.
6. If you have chosen "Block," use the arrow keys to select the block of cells, then press the RETURN key.
7. Choose "Value format," "Label format," or "Protection." Use the right/left arrow keys to make a selection and then press the RETURN key.

8. If you have chosen "Columns," you will be given an additional option, "Column widths." Use the OPEN-APPLE left/right arrow keys to decrease/increase the width of a column. Press the ESCape key when finished.

9. If you have chosen "Value format":

   —Choose "Fixed," "Dollars," "Commas," "Percent," "Appropriate," or "Standard." Use the right/left arrow keys to select the selection, then press the RETURN key. For all but the last two items, type the number of decimal places and press the RETURN key.

10. If you have chosen "Label format," use the right/left arrow keys to highlight the selection and then press the RETURN key.

    —Choose "Left justify," "Right justify," "Center," or "Standard." Use the right/left arrow keys to highlight the selection, then press the RETURN key.

11. If you have chosen "Protection," use the right/left arrow keys to highlight the selection and then press the RETURN key.

    —Choose "No changes," "Labels only," "Values only," "Allow changes," or "Anything." Use the right/left arrow keys to highlight the selection, then press the RETURN key.

The specific layout of a cell can be seen by placing the spreadsheet cursor on that cell and looking at the cursor line cell display near the bottom of the screen.

The OPEN-APPLE V keystroke combination also shows you another way to set these same items.

- It is possible to change the layout of a record. This capability is very powerful because you may change your mind on how you want to have records presented.

To change a multiple-record layout:

1. Make sure you are in the multiple-record layout.
2. Press OPEN-APPLE L. AppleWorks displays the options on the top and three sample records on the bottom of the screen.
3. Change the record layout by using the cursor movement options.
4. After you have made all of the changes you want in the layout of a record, press the ESCape key to exit this evolution.

The word MARGIN will appear on the right side edge of the screen when you have selected those categories that will fit on the Desktop video screen display.

To change a single-record layout:

1. Make sure you are in the single-record layout.

2. Press OPEN-APPLE L. AppleWorks displays the CHANGE RECORD LAYOUT screen.

3. Place the cursor on the first letter of the name of the category you want to change, then move the category.

4. After you have made all of the changes you want in the layout of a record, press the ESCape key to exit this evolution.

9.1.13 OPEN-APPLE M (Move)

- This keystroke combination lets you move text in a word processor document, records in a data base, or entries in a spreadsheet from one place to another either within a document or to/from the Clipboard.

Tips:

1. The move feature in all applications is very similar to the copy feature, except that copy leaves the information in its original location. Move deletes the original text and moves it to a new location.

2. AppleWorks closes up all empty space left open by the information that was moved.

3. AppleWorks makes room for the moved information and readjusts all succeeding information.

Moving text within a word processing document makes it easy to rearrange paragraphs or larger sections of a document. You are allowed to move a maximum of 250 screen lines of text at one time.

To move text in a word processor document:

1. Move the cursor to either the first or last character of the information you want to move.

2. Press OPEN-APPLE M.

3. Choose "Within document," "To clipboard (cut)," or "From clipboard (paste)" option from the highlighted prompt message presented at the bottom of the screen. Use the left/right arrow keys to highlight a selection, then press the RETURN key.

4. Move the cursor to either the end or the beginning of the information you want to move, then press the RETURN key. The text to be moved will be highlighted.

5. If you have chosen "Within document":

   —Move the cursor to the place in the document where you want the text to appear.

   —Press the RETURN key again.

   —The information is then moved and the presentation screen is adjusted appropriately.

6. If you have chosen "To clipboard (cut)":

   —The highlighted information is immediately moved to the Clipboard.

   —The cursor is left at its last position.

7. If you have chosen "From clipboard (paste)":

   —The information previously placed on the Clipboard is immediately moved to the active document on the Desktop.

   —The cursor is left at its last position.

8. You are now returned to the active document on the Desktop.

- AppleWorks allows you to move up to 250 rows or 125 columns from one place to another at one time within a spreadsheet.

Tip: It is recommended that you move an individual cell in two steps: first, copy the cell into the new location, and then blank the original cell using the OPEN-APPLE B command. In this way, no readjustment of the remainder of your worksheet will take place. You make all necessary adjustments. This should save you and the worksheet possible readjustment problems.

To move rows or columns in a spreadsheet:

1. Move the cursor to a cell in the row or column you want to move.

2. Press OPEN-APPLE M.

3. Choose "Within Worksheet," "To clipboard (cut)," or "From clipboard (paste)" option from the highlighted prompt message presented at the bottom of the screen.

4. If you have chosen "Within document":

   —Choose either "Columns" or "Rows" from the prompt message.

   —Move the cursor to highlight the rows or columns you want to move, then press the RETURN key.

—Move the cursor to the place in the template where you want to move the rows or columns, then press the RETURN key again.

5. If you have chosen "To clipboard (cut)":

—Move the cursor to highlight the rows you want to move, then press the RETURN key.

—The highlighted information is immediately moved to the Clipboard.

—The cursor is left at its last position.

6. If you have chosen "From clipboard (paste)":

—The information previously placed on the Clipboard is immediately moved to the active worksheet on the Desktop.

—The cursor is left at its last position.

7. You are now returned to the active worksheet on the Desktop.

Tips:
1. AppleWorks renumbers all rows and reletters all columns after all moves have been made.
2. Formulas are readjusted to take care of all changed references. It is recommended that you check all formulas to make sure they are still correct.

To move records in a data base document:

1. Make sure you are in the multiple-record layout. This is because you are not allowed to select an entire record when in the single-record layout.

2. Move the cursor to the first record of the group of records to be moved.

3. Press OPEN-APPLE M.

4. Choose "Current record," "To clipboard (cut)," or "From clipboard (paste)" option from the highlighted prompt message presented at the bottom of the screen. Use the left/right arrow keys to highlight a selection, then press the RETURN key.

5. If you have chosen "Current record":

—Use the arrow keys to highlight the records that you want to move, then press the RETURN key.

—Move the cursor to the position in the list where the records need to go, and press the RETURN key again.

6. If you have chosen "To clipboard (cut)":

—Move the cursor to highlight the records you want to move, then press the RETURN key.

—The highlighted information is immediately moved to the Clipboard.

—The cursor is left at its last position.

7. If you have chosen "From clipboard (paste)":

   —The information previously placed on the Clipboard is immediately moved to the active data base file on the Desktop.

   —The cursor is left at its last position.

8. You are now returned to the active data base on the Desktop.

9.1.14 OPEN-APPLE N (Change Name)

This keystroke combination lets you change the current name of a word processor document, a data base file, or a spreadsheet worksheet.

Remember that you can change the name of any file, regardless of the application you are using, when you save the file to its diskette storage location, provided a previous copy of that file has been stored.

The following procedure may be used for changing the name of a file, regardless of the application being used.

To change the name of an application file:

1. Press OPEN-APPLE N.

2. Type the name of the new file. The name may contain up to fifteen characters and must start with a letter of the alphabet. The name may contain both upper- and lowercase letters, numbers, and spaces. After typing the name of the file, press the RETURN key to signify the end of the entry. Entering the new file name may be done in either of two ways:

   —Using the insert cursor. Press the right arrow key to move the cursor to the end of the present file name. Press the DELETE key as many times as necessary to erase the present file name, then enter the new name.

   —Using the overstrike cursor. Type the new file name over the present one. Make sure that any remaining characters are deleted.

3. Just press the RETURN key if you do not want to change the name of the file after all.

Tips:

1. AppleWorks changes the name of the file on the Desktop.

2. When you save the newly named file, it is saved under this new name. The old name is still on the disk.

3. Using this procedure is one way of keeping several copies of a document with different names on the same diskette.

There is just one last caution before leaving this section.

> **Caution:**   It is always a good idea to have at least one backup copy of each file. Disasters do happen. Murphy told us that.

9.1.15 OPEN-APPLE O (Display Options)

This keystroke combination lets you display text-embedded options, or printer options, in any of the three application documents or reports. The options allow you to format pages, reports, sentences, records, etc.

To display the printer options within an application document:

1. Move the cursor to the place where you want the printer options to take effect within a document.
2. Press OPEN-APPLE O. AppleWorks then displays text in the zoomed-in format. All of the possible options will also be shown at either the top or the bottom of the screen, depending upon the active application.
3. Type the code sequence that stands for the option you want started at that point in the text, worksheet, or report, then press the RETURN key.
4. Type the new value for the printer option, if AppleWorks asks or requires one, then press the RETURN key. AppleWorks will change the screen, if necessary, and present the embedded text option just activated.
5. If you have more printer options to enter, repeat steps 3 and 4 until you have entered all of the options you require.
6. Press the ESCape key when you are finished entering options.

Printer options may be activated in:

—The word processor when in the Review/Add/Change display.
—The spreadsheet when in the Review/Add/Change display.
—The data base when in the Report Format display.

9.1.16 OPEN-APPLE P (Print File)

This keystroke combination lets you print any of the three application documents or reports without having to go through the set-up procedure before printing a document.
 • Activate your printer before printing a word processor document.

Tips:
1. AppleWorks lets you press the ESCape key to terminate the printing process.
2. You can interrupt printing by using the printer option Pause Here (PH), then use the ESCape key to quit. Pressing the space bar may also be used to interrupt the printing of any document. Pressing the space bar again will continue the printing of a document.
3. If you use multiple pitch and font sizes in an application, your printer *must* be able to support those sizes.

To print a word processor file:

1. Press OPEN-APPLE P.
2. Choose "Beginning" if you want to start printing the document from the beginning. Choose "This page" if you want to start printing from the beginning of the page the cursor is on. Choose "Cursor position" if you want to start printing the document beginning from the cursor position.
3. Choose the printer you want to use.
4. Enter the number of copies desired or accept the default number of one copy by pressing the RETURN key.

• Before you print a spreadsheet you need to set printer options for a spreadsheet report.

To print a spreadsheet file:

1. Be sure you are in the Review/Add/Change screen presentation.
2. If you are *not* printing the entire worksheet, place the cursor in the cell that marks a corner (the upper left-hand corner is recommended) of the area you are going to print.
3. Press OPEN-APPLE P.
4. Choose "All," "Rows," "Columns," or "Block." "All" refers to all information, not all cells. However, AppleWorks will print only as much information on each row as can fit on your printer.
5. If you choose "Rows," "Columns," or "Block," move the cursor to highlight the area you want to print, then press the RETURN key.
6. Make sure your report is not too wide for your printer's platen. If it is, go back and replan your report. For example, choose a larger characters per inch printer option, such as 12 or 15. If not, choose the printer device for the report.

7. When you choose a printer, AppleWorks will ask you for the number of copies you desire. Type the number of copies, then press the RETURN key.

8. If your report has a header, AppleWorks asks you to either type a new report date and press RETURN, or to accept the default report date by just pressing RETURN. The default date is the date used when the report was last printed.

9. If you indicate that you want to print to a text (ASCII) file or a DIF file, or you choose to print to a diskette, AppleWorks asks you for the pathname for the file you are printing. Enter the pathname and press RETURN.

• Before you print, you need to set printer options for a data base report.

To print a data base file:

1. Be sure you are in the Report Format screen presentation.

2. Press OPEN-APPLE P.

3. Choose the device with which you want to print the report.

4. If your report has a header, AppleWorks asks you either to type a new report date and press the RETURN key, or to accept the default report date by just pressing the RETURN key. The default report date is the last date you entered for printing a report.

5. If you chose a printer, AppleWorks asks the number of copies you want printed. Type the number and then press the RETURN key.

6. If you indicate that you want to print to a text (ASCII) file or a DIF file, or you choose to print to the diskette, AppleWorks asks you for the pathname for the file you are printing. Enter the pathname and press the RETURN key.

9.1.17 OPEN-APPLE Q (Switch Files)

This keystroke combination lets you switch quickly from one application document to another on the Desktop.

To select another file on the Desktop:

1. Press OPEN-APPLE Q.

2. AppleWorks presents the Desktop index box, from which you can choose the new file name you want to use. Select the file by highlighting the name using the arrow keys or number keys. When the file name is highlighted, press the RETURN key to select it as the active file.

Tip: AppleWorks lets you get to the Desktop index box anytime by using
OPEN-APPLE Q, regardless of the application.

9.1.18 OPEN-APPLE R (Replace Text)

- The word processor lets you replace one or several occurrences of a character, word, or phrase. Further, you are allowed to replace all occurrences at
once or just one at a time, depending upon the choices you make from the
prompting messages.

This keystroke combination lets you search for, find, and replace specific text. You
can find and replace either text or case-sensitive text.

The text option will find and replace text without regard to the mixture of the upper-
and lowercase characters within the word(s) or phrase to be replaced. For example, if you
want to replace the word "began" with "begin," all occurrences of began or Began will be
replaced with "begin." The case-sensitive text option will find and replace text that exactly
matches the word(s) or phrase to be replaced. For example, if you want to replace the
word "began" with "begin," all occurrences of "began," but not "Began" will be replaced
with "begin."

When you want to replace text, the word processor starts at the current cursor position and looks forward in the document for the text you have specified. You may specify
up to thirty characters to be found. After the first match has been found and replaced, you
can ask for the next occurrence and so on through the entire document.

To replace specific text:

1. Move the cursor to the place in the document where you want to start
searching.

2. Press OPEN-APPLE R.

3. Choose "Text" or "Case-sensitive text" option to indicate you want to find
and replace text that matches your entered text for comparison. AppleWorks will automatically supply the last found and replaced character(s),
text, sentence, phrase, etc., if you have previously used this capability.

4. Type the text you want found and replaced, then press the RETURN key.

5. Type the new text, then press the RETURN key. Simply press the RE-
TURN key to replace the next occurrence of the last replaced text.

6. Choose "One at a time" or "All" option.

7. If you have chosen "One at a time":

   —AppleWorks highlights the first occurrence of the old information.

—Choose either "Yes" or "No," using the right/left arrow keys and then the RETURN key, depending on whether you want to replace that occurrence.

—If you choose "Yes," the text is replaced. If you choose "No," the text is not replaced. You are then asked if you want to find the next occurrence. Again, choose either "Yes" or "No."

—If you choose the "No" option, the operation is terminated.

8. If you have chosen "All":

—All occurrences of the old information are automatically replaced with the new information.

9. You may stop the searching, finding, and replacing of text by answering "No" to prompting questions or by pressing the ESCape key.

When you are defining the text to be found, leading and trailing spaces become part of the phrase you want to find and replace.

If you want to change a name in your last will and testament, for example, it is very easy to find and replace the name "Emma" with "Roger." Place the cursor at the beginning of your will; select OPEN-APPLE R; enter the text you want to find and replace (Emma); enter the replacement text (Roger); and finally select the "All" option. Emma has now been written out of your will and Roger just got wealthy.

Be careful when you select to replace a word or phrase automatically. All occurrences are then replaced without giving you the opportunity to say no. For example, suppose you want to replace "sat" with "set." Every occurrence of "sat," "satisfy," "satan," etc., will be replaced with "set," "setisfy," "setan," etc. To prevent this disaster from happening, you will need to make the replacement much more unique, such as adding blank spaces before and/or after the word or phrase, adding more characters to the word or phrase, or replacing only one occurrence at a time.

Tip: One of the useful tricks you can perform using the replace feature is to use an abbreviation or shorthand notation for long words or phrases when entering a document. After you are finished, place the cursor at the top of the text and use the replace feature to automatically replace your shorthand notations with the expanded words or phrases. For example, you might want to use WISD to stand for Waco Independent School District.

Of course, there are a couple of cautions when using the above tip. The shorthand notation *must* be unique, and you *must* use the same shorthand notation each time to represent the phrase. Caution: remember what you use!

- OPEN-APPLE R is not active in the spreadsheet.
- When you first create a data base, the selection rule is "All records." To change this rule, use OPEN-APPLE R. The record selection rules then stay with the data base when it is saved.

9.1.19 OPEN-APPLE S (Save File)

This keystroke combination lets you save any of the three application documents or reports without having to go through the set-up procedure before saving a document. To do this, type OPEN-APPLE S. AppleWorks saves the file immediately to the current disk, replacing the original file of the same name.

As the file is being saved to the current disk, you will be given a number of messages as to the progress of the saving procedure. If you decide to terminate the saving procedure, you may do so by pressing the ESCape key.

9.1.20 OPEN-APPLE T (Tabbing, Titles, Total)

- The preset tab marks are shown by the vertical line markers in the dashed ruler marker at the top of each word processor screen. Tab settings let you control the horizontal movement of the cursor on any line of text. New documents have tabs already set every five spaces across the screen. You can set and clear tabs anywhere along a text line. You can also set or clear tab markers to meet your own needs.

To set and clear tabs:

1. Press OPEN-APPLE T. The screen cursor is placed in the double-dashed line at the top of the screen.
2. Use the left/right arrow keys to move the cursor to the position where you want to set, clear, or remove a tab.
3. Type S to set a tab, C to clear a tab, or R to remove all already set tabs in the cursor position.
4. Press the ESCape key when you are finished setting or clearing tabs.

- You can fix a title area at the top, at the left, or at both areas of a template. After you fix a title area, you can use the cursor to view the rest of a template. The title area identifies information in a template.

To set a fixed title area:

1. Place the cursor:
   —in a cell just below the bottom row of title area.
   —in a cell to the right of the title area.

—in a cell that marks the outside corner of the unfixed area if you are fixing title areas at the top and on the left.

2. Press OPEN-APPLE T.

3. Choose "Top," "Left side," or "Both." Use the right/left arrow keys to highlight the selection, then press the RETURN key.

Tip: You may use the normal cursor movement keystrokes to move the cursor in the unfixed area. You are not allowed to move the cursor within the fixed title area.

To remove a fixed title area:

1. Press OPEN-APPLE T.

2. Choose "None" to confirm your selection of removing the title area. Press the ESCape key if you change your mind.

• With this keystroke combination you can take grand totals of category columns in the data base.

To total a category:

1. Place the cursor on the column category you want to total.

2. Press OPEN-APPLE T. You are then asked for the number of decimal places that should be included in each entry in the specified column total.

3. Type the number of decimal places for the total and press the RETURN key. You may accept the default value (0) by pressing the RETURN key. You are also asked how many blank spaces should be placed after each entry. This is very important in spacing columns across a single line on a printed page.

4. Enter the number of blank spaces you want to be included, and press the RETURN key.

5. A series of 9's are placed in the category with the appropriate number of decimal places. These 9's will be replaced by the entries in the category when you print a report. If there is no information in an entry blanks are inserted in the report.

6. A double dashed line is inserted at the end of a totaled category just before the total amount is printed.

You can also remove a grand total from your file.
To remove a total from a category:

1. Place the cursor on the column category with the grand total.
2. Press OPEN-APPLE T. The sample records will replace the series of 9's.

9.1.21 OPEN-APPLE U (Edit Entries)

- OPEN-APPLE U is not active in the word processor or the data base.
- This command allows you to edit individual cells within a template.

To edit cell information:

1. Place the cursor on the cell you want to edit.
2. Press OPEN-APPLE U. AppleWorks will then display the contents of the cell on the entry line.
3. Use the cursor of your choice for editing.
4. Press the ESCape key to restore the former entry.
5. Press the RETURN key after you have finished editing an entry.

Once you are in the edit mode for a cell, you can use the DELETE key to remove the character to the left of the cursor, the insert and overstrike cursors to enter or overstrike cell information, the left/right arrow keys to move past characters, and the CONTROL-Y keystroke combination to erase from the cursor the remainder of the cell contents.

9.1.22 OPEN-APPLE V (Values, Print Category Names)

- OPEN-APPLE V is not active in the word processor.
- Standard values may be set and reset using this command. This command and OPEN-APPLE L can be used to set the values for a template. The keystrokes for both of these commands are essentially the same.

To set standard values for an entire template:

1. Use the ESCape or RETURN key to have the REVIEW/ADD/CHANGE spreadsheet screen display presented.
2. Press OPEN-APPLE V.
3. Choose from one of the following options, depending upon which of the standard values you want to change.

   —Value format—The formats that can be selected for value entries are "Fixed decimal," "Dollars," "Commas," "Percent," and "Appropriate."

After you have selected the value format, you are asked to enter the number of decimal places to be presented for the value numbers. The default is "Fixed decimal." "Appropriate" means that AppleWorks will try to present a number in exactly the format entered, even though the format of the number may not correspond to one of the predefined formats. Leading and trailing zeros are dropped and the number is right-justified.

—Label format—The formats that can be selected for label entries are "Left justify," "Right justify," or "Center." The default is "Left justify."

—Column width—OPEN-APPLE right or left arrow keystroke combinations to widen or narrow the width of columns. The default width is 9 characters.

—Protection—Choose either "No" or "Yes." "Yes" forces protection. "No" removes all protection. The default is "Yes."

—Recalculate—You will be required to choose both the order and frequency of calculation. For the order of calculation, specify either rows or columns. The default is columns. For the frequency of calculation, specify either automatic or manual. The default is automatic.

4. Return to the template and continue entering information.

• You can specify the category names that should be printed on a report, as well as the actual entries.

To print a category name:

1. Place the cursor on the first character of the category name you want to appear on the report.

2. Press OPEN-APPLE V. The entry from the first record in the file appears next to the category name to show how the printed information will look.

To remove a category name from a report:

1. Place the cursor on the first character of the category name you want to remove from the report.

2. Press OPEN-APPLE V.

9.1.23 OPEN-APPLE W (Window)

• OPEN-APPLE W is not active in the word processor or the data base.

• You have the option of three different screen presentations for the active worksheet: single, horizontally split, or vertically split.

To split the worksheet into two windows:

1. Place the cursor to the approximate location within the worksheet where you want to split the presentation into two windows.

2. If you are going to split the worksheet into vertical (side by side) windows, place the cursor in a cell in the column that will form the left boundary of the right-hand window.

3. If you are going to split the worksheet into horizontal (top and bottom) windows, place the cursor in a cell in the row that will form the top boundary of the bottom window.

4. Press OPEN-APPLE W.

5. Choose "Side by side" or "Top and bottom." Use the right/left arrow keys to make a selection, then press the RETURN key.

6. The Desktop display will change to reflect the split-window presentation.

7. The cursor stays in the cell where it was placed in step 1 above.

After you have split windows displayed, each window may be scrolled independently using the arrow keys, as is done with a single-window presentation. There may be times when you will want both windows to scroll together, synchronously. That is, they will move row for row or column for column in each window.

To synchronize windows or return to one window:

1. Make sure you have two windows displayed. If you do not, do so using the OPEN-APPLE W command.

2. Press OPEN-APPLE W a second time.

3. Choose "One" or "Synchronized." Use the right/left arrow keys to make a selection, then press the RETURN key.

4. If you have chosen "One," AppleWorks restores the Desktop presentation to a single window.

5. If you have chosen "Synchronized," the two windows will scroll together.

6. You are then returned to the active window.

Note: If both windows are already synchronized, you are asked, when you use the OPEN-APPLE W command, if you want to *un*synchronize the windows.

9.1.24 OPEN-APPLE Y (Line Delete)

- This keystroke combination is active in the word processor. It deletes from the cursor position on a screen line to the end of that line. The remaining text material beyond the deleted screen line to the next RETURN character is closed up to the cursor screen position.

Note: This is an undocumented feature of the word processor. Use this with caution! Side effects may result that we are not aware of at this time. Be careful!

- This keystroke combination is active in the spreadsheet. This keystroke combination deletes the contents of a cell when you are in the edit mode for that cell. You must press the RETURN key to complete the blanking of that cell.

Note: This is an undocumented feature of the spreadsheet. Use this with caution! Side effects may result that we are not aware of at this time. Be careful!

9.1.25 OPEN-APPLE Z (Zoom)

This keystroke combination lets you zoom in to see the printer option commands within a word processor document. This feature is very handy because it allows you to see and observe all of the printer options and text formatting commands embedded in a document.

The spreadsheet will present all of the mathematics, values, and formulas used in a template when you zoom in. However, only the number of characters that will fill a cell are presented. If you want to see all of the information, you may need to increase the size of that column of cells. This is a very handy way to review large blocks of information in a template. Remember to change the column width back to its original size when you are through.

The data base uses this command to toggle between the label-style and record-style formats.

Zooming in is somewhat analogous to looking at a file with a microscope.

9.2 COMMON KEY FUNCTIONS

This section discusses those additional keystrokes that are common to the system and application levels in AppleWorks. These keystrokes allow you to either quickly scroll or move the cursor leisurely through a document. If you have looked through the table of contents, you probably have noticed that these keystrokes combine OPEN-APPLE with some other letter or number key.

9.2.1 OPEN-APPLE Numbers 1–9 (Faster Scroll)

This keystroke combination allows you to move very quickly from one place to another in the same document. This is known as the Ruler. Each of these keystroke combinations will place the cursor in a relative location from the top of a document, depending upon the value of the number used. For example, OPEN-APPLE 1 is the top of the document, OPEN-APPLE 9 is the bottom. OPEN-APPLE 5 is the approximate middle of a document. The Ruler is active regardless of the application you are using.

9.2.2 OPEN-APPLE Left Arrow (Move Cursor Left)

This keystroke combination allows you to move very quickly from one place to another on the same line, a word, cell, or record. The cursor is then repositioned to the beginning of the preceding word, cell, or record in the same category.

9.2.3 OPEN-APPLE Right Arrow (Move Cursor Right)

This keystroke combination allows you to move very quickly on the same line, a word, cell, or record. The cursor is repositioned to the beginning of the succeeding word, cell, or record in the same category.

9.2.4 OPEN-APPLE Up Arrow (Scroll Up)

This keystroke combination allows you to move page by page in a document. The first time you use this keystroke combination, the cursor is placed at the first line of a page at the relative cursor position, at the cell at the top of the screen in the same relative cell position, or at the preceding record in the same category. By using this keystroke again, the cursor is then placed at the top of the preceding page, at the preceding page of cells, or at the preceding record page in the same category.

9.2.5 OPEN-APPLE Down Arrow (Scroll Down)

This keystroke combination allows you to move page by page in a document. The first time you use the keystroke combination, the cursor is placed at the last line of a page at the relative cursor position, at the cell at the bottom of the screen in the same relative cell position, or at the next record in the same category. By using this keystroke again, the cursor is then placed at the bottom of the next page, at the next page of cells, or at the next record page in the same category.

9.2.6 ESCape Key (Escape from Menu)

This keystroke lets you exit from your present place in a document or menu to the preceding operation or menu. when you use the ESCape key, located in the upper left-hand corner of the keyboard, you return to the previous display or remove your response to a prompt message.

When you have the Main Menu displayed on your Desktop, pressing the ESCape key will return you to the last file you were using, except if you have just used the Other Activities Menu. In this case, AppleWorks does not display the current active file on the Desktop.

All AppleWorks screens tell you where you will be returned if you press the ESCape key. This is shown in the upper right-hand corner of each screen presentation. If you ever want to get out of any part of AppleWorks, just press the ESCape key.

9.2.7 RETURN Key (Accept an Option)

The RETURN key is used to perform three general operational functions:

The first is to accept a highlighted option in a menu presentation. By pressing the RETURN key at this point, you are signifying that you accept that option for processing.

The second function is to signify the acceptance of a default value, number, or answer to a prompt message or question, for example, the acceptance of the date as presented when you are booting AppleWorks.

The third function that the RETURN key performs is to signify that you are finished with an entry. This could be the end of a line or paragraph in a word processor document, the end of a value or formula in a spreadsheet template, or the end of a field or record in a data base file.

9.3 SPECIAL FEATURES

Within AppleWorks, there are a few special features that need to be discussed. The special features in AppleWorks include:

- The Help key combination
- Moving between files
- Determining available file space

9.3.1 The Help Feature

Whenever you feel you need help understanding keystroke combinations, you can always get it. Help is available with the OPEN-APPLE ? keystroke combination.

You will find that this keystroke combination is always displayed in the lower right-hand corner of your Desktop screen. Once you have asked for help, you may use the up/down arrow keys to scroll through the information displayed on the Desktop screen.

The Help screen gives you all the OPEN-APPLE keystroke combinations and an abbreviated meaning for each.

At any time in the Help screen presentation, you may return to your previous position by pressing the ESCape key.

9.3.2 Moving Between Files

To move between files, use OPEN-APPLE Q (switch command), as described earlier. When you have more than one file in memory on your Desktop, an index box is presented that lists all of the files. You may then select, by using the up/down arrow keys, the file you want presented to the screen, then press the RETURN key to activate that file.

9.3.3 Determining Desktop Space

When you want to find out how much memory space you have left on your Desktop, use OPEN-APPLE ?. This command presents the Help screen with the memory space available on your Desktop in the lower right-hand corner.

OPEN-APPLE Q also shows the amount of memory space available on the Desktop when the index box is displayed.

9.4 COMMON MISTAKES

Listed below are a series of some common mistakes to avoid when working with any of the applications of AppleWorks.

Do not forget to:

1. Save all active files before you turn off the power on your computer.
2. Remove all diskettes from the disk drives when you are finished with them.
3. Initialize a new blank diskette before you try to save anything on it.
4. Press the OPEN-APPLE key before pressing the letter key, then holding both down.
5. Press the RETURN key to accept defaults, menu selections, prompting message values, etc.
6. Make backup copies of important files. This is insurance against the loss of the original file.
7. Store your AppleWorks diskettes in a safe place.
8. Save your files frequently as you are working on them.
9. Proofread a document from beginning to end before you print it.
10. Clear memory of extraneous files before loading any new files.

Do not try to:

1. Delete more than 250 lines of text at a time.
2. Save files on a full diskette.
3. Save a file to a diskette when the File is larger than the remaining space on the diskette.
4. Load a file into the Desktop when the File is larger than the space available in memory.
5. Insert or remove a diskette from a disk drive when the red light is on.
6. Save any files on the AppleWorks program diskette.

Do not:

1. Close the disk drive door when there is no diskette in the disk drive. This will cause an undo extension of the door spring for extended times.
2. Spill coffee, soda, or any other liquid on the keyboard.
3. Allow direct sunlight to fall on your diskettes.
4. Touch the magnetic surface of a diskette.
5. Allow any magnetic equipment near your diskettes or computer.

The list of things to remember *not* to do is long, but most of the items are really only common sense and are easy to remember.

9.5 SUMMARY

This chapter discussed the OPEN-APPLE keystroke combinations that are common to all of the AppleWorks application level programs. Since you will be using these keystroke combinations so often, it is necessary that you completely understand how to use them. The information about these keystrokes in this chapter may be used as reference and review material when working with AppleWorks.

The second major section of this chapter discussed the common features of AppleWorks, including arrow keys, the ESCape key, and the RETURN key.

The last section discussed the special features that are used throughout AppleWorks:

- The Help key combination
- Moving between files
- Determining available file space

Finally, the chapter listed a series of common mistakes to avoid. These were given, not to discourage you, but to try to help you avoid disaster.

All of the items discussed in this chapter will be used when working with AppleWorks.

Word Processor Commands

You don't write because you want to say something; you write
because you've got something to say.
F. Scott Fitzgerald, 1945

These are the OPEN-APPLE plus a letter character keystroke combination keys and the CONTROL key combinations used in the word processor portion of the AppleWorks software package.

Key Combination	Description
OPEN-APPLE A	N/A
OPEN-APPLE B	N/A
OPEN-APPLE C	Copy text either within a document or to/from the Clipboard.
OPEN-APPLE D	Delete text in a document.
OPEN-APPLE E	Switch between the insert and overstrike cursors.
OPEN-APPLE F	Find specified text, page, case-sensitive text, printer options, or set marker within a document.
OPEN-APPLE G	N/A
OPEN-APPLE H	Print an exact copy of the current Desktop video screen display on the printer.
OPEN-APPLE I	N/A
OPEN-APPLE J	N/A
OPEN-APPLE K	Calculate the page breaks in a document.
OPEN-APPLE L	N/A
OPEN-APPLE M	Move text either within a document or to/from the Clipboard.
OPEN-APPLE N	Change the name of the currently active file on the Desktop.
OPEN-APPLE O	Display the possible text-embedded printer options menu available in this application.
OPEN-APPLE P	Print the currently active Desktop file to the printer.
OPEN-APPLE Q	Switch to another file on the Desktop.
OPEN-APPLE R	Search for, find, and replace existing text with specified text.

PEN-APPLE S	Save the currently active file on the Desktop to the specified diskette storage.
OPEN-APPLE T	Set horizontal tabs within a line of text in a document.
OPEN-APPLE U	N/A
OPEN-APPLE V	N/A
OPEN-APPLE W	N/A
OPEN-APPLE X	N/A
OPEN-APPLE Y	N/A
OPEN-APPLE Z	Display all of the format and printer option settings within a document.
OPEN-APPLE ?	Display the Help information screen.
OPEN-APPLE 1 to OPEN-APPLE 9	Move within a file from the beginning (1) to the end (9) or proportionally (2–8) within any one document.
OPEN-APPLE Right arrow	Move the cursor to the right to the first character of the next word.
OPEN-APPLE Left arrow	Move the cursor to the left to the first character of the next word.
OPEN-APPLE Up arrow	Move the cursor to the top of the screen. Then move the cursor to the top of the next screen.
OPEN-APPLE Down arrow	Move the cursor to the bottom of the screen. Then move the cursor to the bottom of the next screen.
OPEN-APPLE TAB	Move the cursor to the previous tab stop.
CONTROL-B	Use this keystroke combination to begin and end boldfacing.
CONTROL-L	Use this keystroke combination to begin and end underlining.
CONTROL-Y	Delete text information from the cursor position to the end of a line or to a carriage RETURN, whichever occurs first.

The Data Base Commands

For table-talk, I prefer the pleasant and witty before the
learned and the grave; in bed, beauty before goodness.
MONTAIGNE, 1580

These are the OPEN-APPLE plus a letter character keystroke combination keys used in the data base portion of the AppleWorks software package.

Key Combination	Description
OPEN-APPLE A	Arrange or sort a category.
OPEN-APPLE B	N/A
OPEN-APPLE C	Copy records either within a document or to/from the Clipboard.
OPEN-APPLE D	Delete a record or a category within the file.
OPEN-APPLE E	Switch between the insert and overstrike cursors.
OPEN-APPLE F	Find a specified record within the file.
OPEN-APPLE G	Add or remove group totals in a report.
OPEN-APPLE H	Print an exact copy of the Desktop video display.
OPEN-APPLE I	Insert a record or reinsert a previously deleted report category.
OPEN-APPLE J	Justify a report category, left or centered.
OPEN-APPLE K	Define a calculated report category.
OPEN-APPLE L	Change the record layout. Also change the direction of the cursor movement when you press the RETURN key in the multiple-record layout.
OPEN-APPLE M	Move a record either within the file or to/from the Clipboard.
OPEN-APPLE N	Change the name of the currently active report or category name.
OPEN-APPLE O	Display the possible text-embedded printer options menu available in this application.
OPEN-APPLE P	Go to the report menu or print the report.
OPEN-APPLE Q	Switch to another file on the Desktop.
OPEN-APPLE R	Change the record selection rules.

OPEN-APPLE S	Save the currently active file on the Desktop to the current diskette storage.
OPEN-APPLE T	Add or remove report category totals.
OPEN-APPLE U	N/A
OPEN-APPLE V	Set standard values in a report.
OPEN-APPLE W	N/A
OPEN-APPLE X	N/A
OPEN-APPLE Y	N/A
OPEN-APPLE Z	Zoom to either a single- or multiple-record layout form.
OPEN-APPLE ?	Display the Help information screen.
OPEN-APPLE 1 to OPEN-APPLE 9	Move within a file from the beginning (1) to the end (9) or proportionally (2–8) within any one document.
OPEN-APPLE >	Switch the category with one on the right.
OPEN-APPLE <	Switch the category with one on the left.
OPEN-APPLE Right arrow	Increase the width of a column.
OPEN-APPLE Left arrow	Decrease the width of a column.
OPEN-APPLE Up arrow	Move the cursor to the top of the screen display. Then move to the top of the next screen display.
OPEN-APPLE Down arrow	Move the cursor to the bottom of the screen display. Then move to the bottom of the next screen display.
OPEN-APPLE TAB	Move the cursor to the previous entry when you are on the first character in an entry.
CONTROL-Y	Use this keystroke combination followed by a carriage RETURN key to erase from the cursor position to the end of the record entry.

Spreadsheet Commands and Functions

When [man] is happy, he takes his happiness as it comes and
doesn't analyse it, just as if happiness were his right.
LUIGI PIRANDELLO, 1921

C.1 COMMANDS

These are the OPEN-APPLE plus a letter character keystroke combination keys used in the spreadsheet portion of the AppleWorks software package.

Key Combination	Description
OPEN-APPLE A	Arrange or sort rows.
OPEN-APPLE B	Blank out cell(s).
OPEN-APPLE C	Copy entries either within a file or to/from the Clipboard.
OPEN-APPLE D	Delete columns or rows in a file.
OPEN-APPLE E	Switch between the insert and overstrike cursors.
OPEN-APPLE F	Find text within a file or specified coordinates.
OPEN-APPLE G	N/A
OPEN-APPLE H	Print an exact copy of the current Desktop video display.
OPEN-APPLE I	Insert rows or columns into the file.
OPEN-APPLE J	Jump to the other window when in split window mode.
OPEN-APPLE K	Recalculate all values.
OPEN-APPLE L	Change the cell layout.
OPEN-APPLE M	Move rows or columns either within a file or to/from the Clipboard.
OPEN-APPLE N	Change the name of the currently active file on the Desktop.
OPEN-APPLE O	Display the possible text-embedded printer options menu available in this application.
OPEN-APPLE P	Print the currently active file to the printer.
OPEN-APPLE Q	Switch to another file on the Desktop.
OPEN-APPLE R	N/A

OPEN-APPLE S	Save the currently active file on the Desktop to the diskette storage medium.
OPEN-APPLE T	Set titles in the currently active file.
OPEN-APPLE U	Edit the contents of a cell.
OPEN-APPLE V	Set standard values in a worksheet or template.
OPEN-APPLE W	Create windows within a worksheet or template.
OPEN-APPLE X	N/A
OPEN-APPLE Y	N/A
OPEN-APPLE Z	Display all of the formulas in a worksheet or template.
OPEN-APPLE ?	Display the Help information screen.
OPEN-APPLE 1 to OPEN-APPLE 9	Move within a file from the beginning (1) to the end (9) or proportionally (2–8) within any one document.
OPEN-APPLE Right arrow	Move the cursor to the right of the screen. Then move right a full screen at a time.
OPEN-APPLE Left arrow	Move the cursor to the left of the screen. Then move left a full screen at a time.
OPEN-APPLE Up arrow	Move the cursor to the top of the screen. Then move the cursor to the top of the next screen.
OPEN-APPLE Down arrow	Move te cursor to the bottom of the screen. Then move the cursor to the bottom of the next screen.
OPEN-APPLE TAB	Move the cursor to the next cell to the left.

C.2 FUNCTIONS

Functions are a form of evaluated expressions in the spreadsheet portion of AppleWorks. Actually, they are really code sequences that represent a common or complex set of calculations. When you enter a function into a cell, you are calling for a special built-in formula, embedded into the spreadsheet, that operates on the cell(s) or values that you have specified in the function. The functions are discussed in the next sections.

C.2.1 Arithmetic Functions

This section describes, defines, and gives examples of the arithmetic funtions available in the spreadsheet portion of Appleworks.

Funtions have three major component parts:

- @—the character symbol used to designate that a function call follows immediately.
- The specific characters that define the function.
- The argument(s) of the function enclosed in parentheses.

The argument definitions used below are as follows:

Argument word	Meaning
Value	A single numeric value, cell reference, number, or expression that evaluates to a number.
Range	A series of adjacent cells separated by three periods. For example, (B22 ... B27) or (C11 ... F11).
List	A list of single values or ranges separated by commas. For example, (D13,F22,222) or (A17 ... A22,B18 ... F18).
Rate	The interest rate, discount rate of money, or cost of money expressed as a decimal number.
Logical	Refers to the operator symbols that define specific logical operations.

Function Syntax	Description
@ABS(value)	Returns the absolute value of the argument. Examples: • G22 contains @ABS(−33.5). Places the absolute value of the argument (−33.5) in cell G22, 33.5. This numeric value will always be a positive number. • G22 contains @ABS(C22). Places the absolute value of the argument (C22) in cell G22. This numeric value will always be a positive number.
@AVG(list)	Returns the arithmetic mean of the values in the argument list. Examples: • F44 contains @AVG(22,44,66). Places the arithmetic mean of the values in the list in cell F44. There is no limit to the number of elements in the list. • F44 contains @AVG(C12,R55,B2,66). Places the arithmetic mean of the values in the list in cell F44. There is no limit to the number of elements in the list.
@CHOOSE(value,list)	Returns the value in the list pointed to by the value index. Example: • A2 contains @CHOOSE(A3,33,45,17,22). A2 will assume the values of 33, 45, 17, or 22, depending on the value contained in cell A3. If the value in cell A3 is evaluated in the range 1 through 4 then the corresponding value will be placed in cell A2. If the value in A2 is evaluated at 0 or less or greater than 4, then the characters NA appear in cell A2.
@COUNT(list)	Returns the number of non-blank entries in the argument list. Examples: • D23 contains @COUNT(B11,C11,D11,E11). Places the number of non-blank entries in cell D23. There is no limit to the number of elements in the list. • D23 contains @COUNT(B11 ... G11). Places the number of non-blank entries in cell D23. There is no limit to the number of elements in the list.
@ERROR	Displays the word ERROR in the cell. Example: • E33 contains @ERROR. Places the ERROR word in all cells in

which this function is entered. Used in conjunction with the @IF and @LOOKUP functions, as a good debugging function.

@INT(value)   Returns the integer portion of the argument. Examples:
- F22 contains @INT(125.36). Places the integer (125) in cell F22.
- F22 contains @INT(E15). Places the integer part of the value in cell E15 in cell F22.

@LOOKUP(value,range)   Searches successfully through range for the largest entry that is less than or equal to the value specified in the first table. Then the function returns the corresponding value in the second table. Example:
- F45 contains @LOOKUP(44,B11 ... E11). Returns the value 30 in cell F45.

```
Assume: columns =      A  |  B  |  C  |  D  |  E  |
                     - + --------------------- +
                     : :  : :  : :  : :  : :
                     - + --------------------- +
First table = row 11 =    | 30  | 35  | 40  | 45  |
                     - + --------------------- +
Second table = row 12 =   | 50  | 40  | 30  | 20  |
                     - + --------------------- +
```

The first table, B11 through E11 is specified in function call in cell F45. The @LOOKUP function will search through the row table until it finds the largest value in the table that is less than or equal to the specified search value. The function then returns the corresponding value in the second table.

This means that the search will find the value 40 in cell D11 as the largest value less than or equal to the search value of 44. The function then returns the value of 30, which is the corresponding value in the second table.

There are five additional things you need to know about the @LOOKUP function:

1. The values in the first table *must* be in ascending order.
2. A value of NA is returned if the search is unsuccessful because all values in the search table are larger than the search value.
3. The last value in the search table is returned if the search value is larger than any value in the search table.
4. Tables may be arranged in either a row or a column.
5. The second table may be either below, in the case of a row table, or to the right, in the case of a column table.

@MAX(list)   Returns the largest value in the argument list. Example:
- E15 contains @MAX(A3,144,A2*22). Places the maximum value between cells A3, 125, and A2 times 22 in cell E15.

@MIN(list)   Returns the smallest value in the argument list. Example:
- E15 contains @MIN(A3,144,A2*22). Places the minimum value between cells A3, 125, and A2 times 22 in cell E15.

@NA	Displays NA in the cell. Example:
	• D21 contains @NA. Places the characters NA in the specified cell. This function may be used in those cells where you know you will need a value, but the value is not yet available or entered.
@SQRT(value)	Returns the square root of the argument value. Example:
	• D4 contains @SQRT(4). Places the square root of the argument value (4) in cell D4.
	• D4 contains @SQRT(C5). Places the square root of the argument cell (C5) in cell D4.
@SUM(list)	Returns the sum of all the values in the argument list. Examples:
	• C8 contains @SUM(C5,C6,C7). Adds the values in cells C5, C6, and C7, and places the result in cell C8.
	• C8 contains @SUM(C5 . . . C7). Adds the values in cells C5 through C7, and places the result in cell C8.

C.2.2 Financial Function

This section describes, defines, and gives examples of the financial function available in the spreadsheet portion of AppleWorks.

@NPV(rate,range)	Calculates the net present value according to the interest rate and a range of even or uneven payments. Example:
	• G21 contains @NPV(.1,B20 . . . G20). Places the net present value based on the contents of cells B20 through G20, with a discount rate of money equal to 10%, in cell G21.

C.2.3 Logical Function

This section describes, defines, and gives examples of the logical function available in the spreadsheet portion of AppleWorks.

@IF(logical value,value1,value2)	If the logical value is TRUE, then this function returns a value of 1. If the logical value is FALSE, it returns a value of 2. The logical operators are:

$<$ less than
$>$ greater than
$=$ equal to
$<=$ less than or equal to
$>=$ greater than or equal to
$<>$ not equal to

- E17 contains @IF(B1$>$B2,13,0). If the value in cell B1 is greater than the contents of cell B2, a value of 13 is placed in cell E17; otherwise, 0 is placed in cell E17.
- E17 contains @IF(B2$>$B1,13,0). If the value in cell B2 is greater than the contents of cell B1, a value of 13 is placed in cell E17; otherwise 0 is placed in cell E17.

- E17 contains @IF(2=B1,23,5). If the value in cell B1 is equal to 2, then the contents of cell E17 takes on the value of 13. If B1 is not equal to 2, then 5 is placed in cell E17.

The @IF statement has the following evaluation rules.

Value of First Argument	Evaluation
TRUE	Value of the second argument returned.
FALSE	Value of the third argument returned.
NA	NA.
Not logical or ERROR	ERROR message returned.

APPENDIX D

Printer Options

*We pick out a text here and there to make it serve our
turn....*
JOHN SELDEN, 1689

This appendix discusses the text printer options available in the word processor portion of
AppleWorks. These options are made available through the use of the OPEN-APPLE O
keystroke combination.

The word processor uses a caret (^) to show that some text-embedded command has
been used. Carets are displayed regardless of whether or not you are in zoomed-in mode.

Options are set out from the actual text material by a series of dashes followed by the
option description. For all of the descriptions that follow, refer to Fig. D-1.

You may always escape or exit from the options menu by pressing the ESCape key.

D.1 PRINTER CHARACTERISTICS

This section discusses the printer characteristics available from the printer options menu.

Code Meaning		Description
CI	Characters per inch	The print density may be specified from 4 characters per inch to 24 characters per inch. First, select the option code, then press the RETURN key. Enter the selected number of characters per inch, and the RETURN key. Default = 10 per inch Maximum = 24 per inch Minimum = 4 per inch
LI	Lines per inch	Sets the number of lines to be printed per vertical inch. First, select the option code, then press the RETURN key. Enter the number of lines per inch, and press the RETURN key. There are only two options available, 6 or 8 lines per inch. In order to add blank lines, see the SK code on page 264. Default = 6 lines per inch Maximum = 8 lines per inch

261

```
     PW=8.5  LM=0.5   RM=1.0  CI=12  UJ  PL=11.0  TM=0.0  BM=1.0  LI=6  DS
Option:                 UJ: Unjustified     GB: Group Begin        BE: Boldface End
                        CN: Centered        GE: Group End          +B: Superscript Beg
PW: Platen Width        PL: Paper Length    HE: Page Header        +E: Superscript End
LM: Left Margin         TM: Top Margin      FO: Page Footer        -B: Subscript Begin
RM: Right Margin        BM: Bottom Margin   SK: Skip Lines         -E: Subscript End
CI: Chars per Inch      LI: Lines per Inch  PN: Page Number        UB: Underline Begin
P1: Proportional-1      SS: Single Space    PE: Pause Each page    UE: Underline End
P2: Proportional-2      DS: Double Space    PH: Pause Here         PP: Print Page No.
IN: Indent              TS: Triple Space    SM: Set a Marker       EK: Enter Keyboard
JU: Justified           NP: New Page        BB: Boldface Begin
```

Figure D-1 *Options Menu Presentation*

PL Page length   Sets the vertical measurement of the paper you are using. First, select the option code, then press the RETURN key. Enter the selected paper length, and press the RETURN key.
Default = 11″
Maximum = 25.4″

PW Platen width   Sets the distance in inches the print head travels across the paper. First, select the option code, then press the RETURN key. Enter the platen width, and press the RETURN key.
Default = 8.0 inches
Maximum = 13.2 inches

> **Note:** The platen width cannot be greater than what was specified in the Other Activities Menu.

P1 Proportional 1
    and
P2 Proportional 2

In proportional spacing, the amount of space each character takes up varies because of type size and style. For example, a capital M takes up more space on a line than a capital I. Proportionality, then, is based on some minimal horizontal spacing for the smallest character in the set. Each character in the set then takes some multiple of the minimal horizontal spacing. There are two proportional spacing type styles available in the options menu. These are designated P1 and P2. Select the option code, then press the RETURN key.

> **Note:** Each of the different print densities will affect the video display screen for your document. When you select a particular print density, that density will remain in effect until it is changed later in the document.

D.2 PRINTING CONTROLS

This section discusses the printer controls available from the printer options menu.

Code Meaning	Description
EK Enter keyboard.	Stops the printer in the middle of the printing process so that you can enter information directly into a document. This capability is very handy when you want to personalize a letter, memo, or any other document. Select the option code, place the cursor where you want to enter information, then press the RETURN key.
	The word processor portion of AppleWorks will insert a caret at the point where information is entered.
	When printing the document, the printer will stop at the specified spot and wait until you enter the new information and press a carriage return. The printer will then start printing again with the new information inserted into your printed document.
NP New page	This option allows you to format your document by starting new pages anywhere within the text. Select the option code, then press the RETURN key.

Tip: 1. The word processor will not override your inserted page breaks, but it will break pages between your page breaks if text exceeds one page.

2. If you specify a page break within a paragraph, it will be placed at the beginning of the paragraph. To get around this, you must insert a carriage return character in the paragraph.

GB Group begin and GE Group end	Allow you to group information together on one page. First, select the option code, then press the RETURN key at the beginning of the grouped text. Now, escape the printer options menu using the ESCape key. Reposition the cursor to the end of the text group and use the Group End option. Now, everything between these two options will be placed on a single page.
PE Pause each page	You may want to pause after the printing of each page to put in another piece of paper or to review what has been printed. Type PE at the place in the document where you want to pause in the printing, then press the RETURN key.
	Once the printing of a page is completed and the printer stops, you may continue printing by pressing the RETURN key.
	If you want the printer to pause after each and every page, place the pause command at the very beginning of the document.

PH Pause here	Causes the printer to pause at a specific location in a document. Type PH at the place in the document where you want to pause in the printing, then press the RETURN key.
	Once the printing of a page is completed and the printer stops, you may continue printing by pressing the RETURN key.
SK Skip lines	Allows you to skip a number of lines. Type SK, and press the RETURN key. Then enter the number of lines you want to skip, and press the RETURN key. You may skip any number of lines you want, limited only by the fact that you may not skip beyond the start of the next page to be printed.
	Default = 0 lines
	Maximum = 66 lines (one complete page)

D.3 TEXT CONTROLS

This section discusses the text material controls available from the printer options menu.

Code Meaning	Descriptions
LM Left margin	Sets the left margin size in tenths of inches. Type LM, then press the RETURN key. Enter the selected margin size, and press the RETURN key.
	Default = 1″
RM Right margin	Sets the right margin size in tenths of inches. Type RM, then press the RETURN key. Enter the selected margin size, and press the RETURN key.
	Default = 1″
TM Top margin	Sets the top margin size in tenths of inches. Type TM, then press the RETURN key. Enter the selected margin size, and press the RETURN key.
	Default = 0″
	Maximum = 9″
BM Bottom margin	Sets the bottom margin in tenths of inches. Type BM, then press the RETURN key. Enter the selected margin size, and press the RETURN key.
	Default = 2″
	Maximum = 9″
IN Indent	Indents text material for hanging paragraphs and bulleted items. Type IN, then press the RETURN key. Enter the number of characters to indent, and press the RETURN key.
	In a hanging paragraph, the first line of text is at the left margin and all subsequent lines are indented. With this option, text will be automatically indented by the number of characters specified.
	To set a bulleted item or paragraph, type a lowercase o, asterisk or dash sign at the left margin. Then space over, or tab, to where you want text to start. Begin entering text. When the text reaches the second line,

	it will be automatically indented by the number of characters specified.
Text formatting	The following printing options allow you to format text. You may specify that text be justified, unjustified, or centered.
UJ Unjustified	Unjustified means that the left edge is even (each line begins under the line above), the right edge runs ragged.
JU Justified	Justified means that both the left and right edges are even. Spaces are inserted in each line in order to keep lines even.
CN Centered	Centered means text is centered on the page, left and right edges are both ragged.
SS Single space, DS Double space, or TS Triple space	Set the number of blank lines between each line of print. Only one option may be used at a time. Like other options, these will remain in effect until changed. Select the option code, then press the RETURN key.

HE Page header
or
FO Page footer
	Page header and footer options allow you to enter document identification information, page numbering, dates, etc.
	
	    Page headers are printed at the top of a page.
	    Page footers are printed after the last line of text material on the bottom of a page.
	    Page headers and footers may be changed at any time within a document. You may cancel page headers and footers by following the entry with a blank line.

PN Page number	You may override normal page numbering by controlling the numbering of pages with this option. Place the cursor on the page where you want to specify the page number, type PN, and press the RETURN key.
PP Print page number	You can print page numbers in the header or footer of a document. Further, you may annotate the number by typing Page, Page no., Page —, or anything else you want. Place the cursor where you want to position the page number, type pp, and press the RETURN key.
BB Boldface begin and BE Boldface end	The boldface begin and end options let you emphasize (in darker type) a character, word, or phrase within a document. Place the cursor where you want boldfacing to begin, type BB, and press the RETURN key.

> **Tip:** If you boldface a large portion of text, but there is a carriage return typed in the middle of the text, the boldfacing will terminate. Boldfacing *must* be reinstituted after every carriage return.

+B Superscript begin and +E Superscript end	The superscript begin and end options let you place a character, word, or phrase within a document above the normal line of print. Place the cursor where you want the superscript to be set. Superscripting is used in mathematical formulas and manuscript references.

—B Subscript begin
and
—E Subscript end

The subscript begin and end options let you place a character, word, or phrase within a document below the normal line of print. Place the cursor where you want the subscript to be set.

Subscripting is used in mathematical formulas and manuscript references.

UB Underline begin
and
UE Underline end

The underline begin and end options let you emphasize a character, word, or phrase within a document. Select, by typing, the option code followed by a carriage RETURN key. Then place the cursor where you want the underlining to begin.

> **Tip:** If you underline a large portion of text, but there is a carriage return typed in the middle of the text, the underlining terminates. Underlining *must* be reinstituted after every carriage return.

SM Set a marker

Markers range from 1 through 254. By placing markers liberally throughout a document, you have many possible places to move to quickly. Place the cursor where you want to set the marker, type SM, and press the RETURN key.

When you want to find a marker in a document, use the OPEN-APPLE F capability.

Disk Operations

The man does better who runs from disaster than he who is
caught by it.
HOMER, 9TH CENTURY. B.C.

E.0 OVERVIEW

It is very important that you make copies of your working diskettes, data diskettes, program diskettes, and any other diskettes you use.

The ProDOS 1.1.1 program, the FILER, available for the Apple II family of computers, makes copies of diskettes. This appendix discusses how to use the program.

Five diskettes are included in the AppleWorks software package—Apple Presents, volumes 1 and 2, a startup disk, a program disk, and a sample files diskette.

One of the first things you should do is make backup copies of these diskettes and format additional data diskettes to hold files. The startup and program disks are write-protected. This means you are unable to write any information to those diskettes. Therefore, it is recommended that you make copies of at least those two diskettes since they are so important. Copies of these diskettes must be made using the ProDOS FILER program. After you have made the copies, place the originals in a safe place so they will not be destroyed.

ProDOS stands for "Professional Disk Operating System," and was first introduced in 1984; 1.1.1 is a version of that operating system. An operating system is a set of computer programs that controls the overall operation of a computer system; it serves as the executive manager of the information stored in memory and on diskettes. The operating system allows you to store, retrieve, or rearrange information.

E.1 PRODOS

Since AppleWorks was originally recorded using the ProDOS operating system, a very brief explanation of the operating system will be included in this appendix.

The distinction between ProDOS terms and a ProDOS program, such as FILER, will be differentiated by capitalizing the name of ProDOS programs. Further, the pathnames to these programs will contain slash marks as separators or delimiters. This convention is consistent with the requirements of ProDOS.

The term *file* will refer to any collection of data stored on a diskette, regardless of its type. A file may be an Applesoft II BASIC program file, a binary file, a random access file, or any other named and stored collection of information.

Section E.1.1 discusses the relationship between directories and file names, and shows how ProDOS works.

Sections E.1.1.1 through E.1.1.4 explain the minimal composition of a startup diskette and the programs involved.

Sections E.1.2 and E.1.2.1 discuss the logical arrangement of volumes, directories, and files. The rules for directories and volumes are shown, along with a comparison to DOS 3.3. The chapter concludes with a detailed explanation of file names, pathnames, and prefixes.

E.1.1 How ProDOS Works

ProDOS is an operating system that allows you to manage many of the resources available to Apple II computers with at least 64K memory. The system functions primarily as a disk-based set of programs that help you operate your system; however, it also will handle interrupts and perform some memory management. ProDOS will mark files with a date and time, provided you have a clock/calendar card installed, usually in slot 4 of the Apple IIe.

All ProDOS startup diskettes normally have certain files in common. These are:

PRODOS
BASIC.SYSTEM
STARTUP

The PRODOS file contains the ProDOS operating system program. This program performs the communications required between other system programs, Applesoft II BASIC programs, and computer hardware items.

The file BASIC.SYSTEM is a system program that will communicate between the system user and the operating system. A ProDOS system program, such as the BASIC.SYSTEM, FILER, or CONVERT programs supplied when you purchased ProDOS, are assembly language programs. Each program will accept commands from an operator, check commands for validity, and take appropriate action.

The STARTUP program is the first Applesoft II BASIC program that is executed immediately after the operating system has finished booting. In DOS 3.3 you were allowed to define the name of the boot program to be executed. With SOS 1.1 or SOS 1.3 for the Apple III, the required boot program name is HELLO. With ProDOS, the name STARTUP is required.

Memory in Apple II family of computers is divided into 256-byte segments. Each of these segments is considered a page of memory. For each 256-byte segment used, ProDOS will represent that page by setting a bit to 1 in the system bit map memory area.

When ProDOS is initialized, all memory used is marked "used" (set to 1) in the system bit map. As ProDOS runs, it marks each new page used by setting the appropriate bit in the system bit map. When a page is released, that bit in the system bit map is reset (set to 0).

E.1.1.1 A Startup Diskette

ProDOS is able to support and communicate with many different types of disk drives, whether full size, half-height, hard disk, or mini-floppy, and the particular physical slot location of the disk drive.

The diskettes inserted in the physical disk drives are known as *volumes* and are identified by names known as volume names. Volumes and volume names are discussed in Section E.1.2.

Today, almost every Apple II family computer system will have at least one disk drive. That disk drive is known as the system's *startup* or *boot* drive. This drive will normally be joined to the drive 1 connection on the disk controller card that is normally installed in slot 6. For the discussion that follows, it will be assumed that:

1. The system startup drive is connected to slot 6, drive 1, in an Apple IIe and is the built-in drive in an Apple IIc.

2. Your system is configured to accept ProDOS.

The diskettes that cause your system to start up are known as startup diskettes. A startup diskette must contain all of the information needed to bring a program from the diskette into your system's memory and commence executing the program.

Any ProDOS diskette can be made into a startup diskette by placing the correct files on that diskette. At power-up time, a copy of the PRODOS program is automatically transferred from the diskette into memory and executed.

A ProDOS startup diskette has the following characteristics:

It was formatted using the ProDOS FILER program.

It has the PRODOS program in its volume directory.

It has the BASIC.SYSTEM or other XXXX.SYSTEM program in its volume directory.

It has an Applesoft II BASIC program called STARTUP in its volume directory.

When you install the startup diskette into the startup drive (S6,D1) and power up your system, the AUTOSTART ROM chip program executes. This forces the system to boot up from the startup diskette, executing the ProDOS operating system, and preparing your system to perform work.

E.1.1.2 The PRODOS Program

The PRODOS program is just what the name implies. It is a set of machine language routines that provides the interface to any disk drives manufactured by Apple Computer,

Inc., or other compatible disk drives for the Apple II computers. ProDOS is an operating system program that allows you to manage many of the resources available to the Apple II family of computers plus handle interrupts and simple memory management. In addition, ProDOS allows you to interface your own particular routines and additions.

PRODOS has a number of major modules. These are:

System program (receives user commands)
External device routines
Command dispatcher
Machine language interface
Block file manager (disk driver and clock/calendar routines)
Interrupt receiver/dispatcher (interrupts handling routines)

E.1.1.3 The BASIC.SYSTEM Program

This part of the ProDOS operating system contains all of the operating system comands and error routines that are supported by ProDOS. BASIC.SYSTEM allows the user and the operating system to communicate.

In DOS 3.3 the entire operating system is contained in one program. In ProDOS the operating system is divided into two parts. This arrangement allows you to insert, add to, or modify your system's operation. PRODOS contains only the most essential parts of the operating system. BASIC.SYSTEM allows you to communicate with disk drives from within Applesoft II BASIC or Pascal. You may want to install other or different system programs on a diskette. System programs are recognizable in a catalog presentation by the SYS abbreviation in the TYPE column.

When your system boots up, the PRODOS program is loaded into memory and then executed. Then the first system program stored on the diskette is loaded into memory and executed. Therefore, you need not have BASIC.SYSTEM as the next file to be executed. Any file with a name XXXX.SYSTEM may be loaded into memory and executed. The XXXX may be any combination of letters and numbers forming a valid name.

E.1.1.4 The STARTUP Program

The STARTUP program is an Applesoft II BASIC program run by BASIC.SYSTEM when booting is finished. The Apple II family of computers operating in DOS 3.3 allows you to name this program anything you desire, provided it is memory-resident when that diskette was initialized. It may be written in either of the two BASIC languages. ProDOS requires that this program be written in Applesoft II BASIC and be called STARTUP.

E.1.2 Volumes and Files

A file is the basic information storage unit. Any file may contain any set of information such as names, numbers, letters, pictures, Applesoft II BASIC program, lists, machine language program, or graphs.

A file may be defined as a collection of related information stored on some media using a common name. When a file is stored on a ProDOS diskette, it is assigned a name and a file type. After a file is stored, access to the information stored in that file is gained through the use of that file's name. The file's type determines the kind and character of information stored in the file.

When assigning names to a file, there are a few rules that must be followed. In the following paragraphs, the ProDOS file name conventions will be given followed immediately by the DOS 3.3 conventions. In this way you will be able to easily make comparisons and quickly understand the differences.

ProDOS file name:

Composed of up to 15 characters.

The first character must be a capital letter of the alphabet.

All alphabetic characters may be used (A–Z and a–z).

All numeric digits may be used (0–9).

The period character (.) may be used.

Lowercase characters are automatically converted to uppercase.

Names must be unique. This means that no two names are to be exactly the same in the same directory.

Files of the same name must be in different directories or on different diskettes.

DOS 3.3 file name:

Composed of up to 30 characters.

The first character must be a capital letter.

All characters are allowed except a comma (,).

Names must be unique.

Files of the same name must be on different diskettes.

Figure E-1 shows a number of legal and illegal ProDOS file names with comments concerning the illegal file names.

```
Legal File Names     Illegal File Names  Comments
-----------------    ------------------  --------------------
TWO.NAMED.FILES      2.NAMED.FILES       Begins with a number
D2                   .D2                 Begins with a period
A.123.FILE           A 123 FILE          Contains spaces
FUNNY.FACE           FACE,FUNNY          Contains a comma
DISESTABLISH         DISESTABLISHMENT    More than 15 characters
DUMMY.DATA           DUMMY/DATA          Contains a slash character
Funny.file           funny.file          First character not capital
```

Figure E-1 *ProDOS File Name*

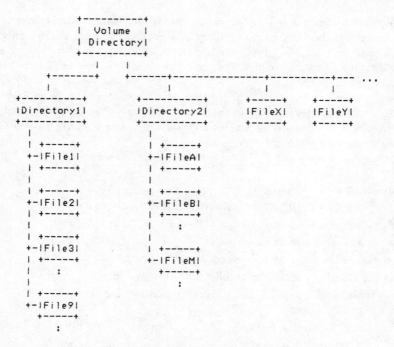

```
                          +----------+
                          |  Volume  |
                          | Directory|
                          +----------+
                              |    |
                         +-------+  +------+----------------+----------+--- ...
                         |              |              |          |
                    +----------+   +----------+    +-----+    +-----+
                    |Directory1|   |Directory2|    |FileX|    |FileY|
                    +----------+   +----------+    +-----+    +-----+
                      |              |
                      | +-----+      | +-----+
                      +-|File1|      +-|FileA|
                      | +-----+      | +-----+
                      |              |
                      | +-----+      | +-----+
                      +-|File2|      +-|FileB|
                      | +-----+      | +-----+
                      |              |    :
                      | +-----+      |
                      +-|File3|      | +-----+
                      | +-----+      +-|FileM|
                      |    :           +-----+
                      |                   :
                      | +-----+
                      +-|File9|
                        +-----+
                           :
```

Figure E-2   *Directory File Examples*

There are many types of files—program files, text files, binary files. The most important type known is the directory file.

E.1.2.1 The Directory

A directory file is like any other file except that it contains only the names, locations, and types of files in that directory. Figure E-2 shows two different directories.

This figure shows that the volume directory presently contains four files. These are two additional directories or subdirectories and two additional files. Each subdirectory contains a number of additional files. The diagram also shows that additional files and directories may be added up to the capacity of the diskette. In fact, ProDOS is able to support a file structure of up to 32 megabytes.

Notice that the directories may contain any number of files of any type. In fact, one or more of the files in a directory may be another directory, known as a subdirectory. ProDOS allows you to have up to and including 64 levels of directories on any one diskette or other storage medium. You will find that trying to handle more than four or five levels of directories is difficult—it becomes somewhat lengthy to program, to remember, and to type in correctly.

By the way, a formatted diskette does not have to contain the operating system. The FILER program is used to place a special directory on a newly formatted diskette, the volume directory. This is the main directory for the entire diskette. The volume directory characteristics are shown in Fig. E-2.

A ProDOS volume directory:

Is on every ProDOS-formatted diskette.

Is named when you format a diskette.

Identifies the entire contents of that diskette.

Is the diskette's name.

May contain up to 51 files.

May not be created using the CREATE command or the FILER command, Make Directory.

Cannot be removed using the DELETE command.

Cannot be protected using the LOCK command.

May only be removed by reformatting or renaming the diskette.

If you want to see the contents of an entire diskette, use the volume directory name with the CAT or CATALOG command.

Some of the files on the volume directory may be directories, containig the names and addresses of other files on the diskette. This can be immediately recognized by the DIR abbreviation in the TYPE column to the right of the file name.

E.1.2.2 The Pathname

ProDOS must know how to find any file that you want to retrieve from a diskette. In order to do this, you must define to ProDOS "the yellow brick road" to follow from the diskette's volume directory to the storage location of the file you want. This road is called the *pathname*. The pathname concept is not supported in DOS 3.3.

The pathname defines to ProDOS how to proceed from the volume directory to the file being retrieved. For example, suppose you want to know the PROFIT information from the subdirectory LEMONADE.STAND in the volume directory MY. The pathname would be:

`/MY/LEMONADE.STAND/PROFIT`

A ProDOS pathname:

Is a series of file names, preceded and separated by slashes.

Has a slash as the first character in the pathname.

Has a volume directory file name as its first entry.

Is less than 65 characters long, including slashes and all subdirectory names and file name.

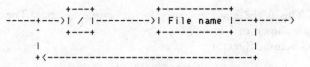

```
             +---+            +-----------+
-----+--->| / |--------->| File name |---+----->
     ^     +---+            +-----------+    |
     |                                       |
     +<--------------------------------------+
```

Figure E-3   *ProDOS Pathname Structure*

These rules are shown in Fig. E-3.

Let us look at a typical set of files that might be stored on a diskette. A file storage structure is shown in Fig. E-4.

From Fig. E-4 you can see how files are organized on a diskette. The volume directory name is MY. This directory contains three files—BANK, HOME, and CREDIT.CARDS. The files BANK and HOME are subdirectories. The BANK subdirectory contains two files named NOTES and CASH. The NOTES file is another subdirectory that contains the files DUE and PAID. The HOME subdirectory also contains two files named STOCKS and BONDS. The pathnames to each of the files on the MY diskette are:

```
/MY/BANK/NOTES/DUE
/MY/BANK/NOTES/PAID
/MY/BANK/CASH
/MY/HOME/STOCK
/MY/HOME/BONDS
/MY/CREDIT.CARDS
```

Another view of the pathnames to the diskette contents is shown below. Notice that the directories and subdirectories are shown with a slash character preceding the name and no slash character is shown for file names. The reason for this is because ProDOS allows you to set a partial pathname known as the prefix (see Section F.1.2.3). With a properly assigned prefix, you need only refer to a file by its name.

```
/MY
  /BANK
    /NOTES
      DUE
      PAID
    CASH
  /HOME
    STOCKS
    BONDS
  CREDIT.CARDS
```

Now you know how to proceed from the volume directory to a file and how a pathname is constructed. It would really be nice if there was a shorthand way to set or save a pathname or partial pathname. Fortunately, there is a way to reduce your typing on the keyboard or reduce the size of your coding requirements. It is called the prefix.

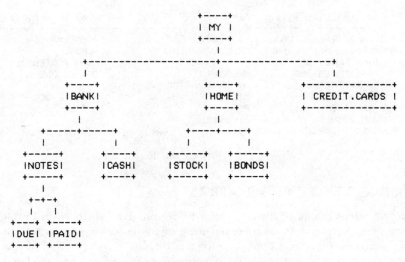

Figure E-4   *Typical Disk File Storage*

E.1.2.3 The Prefix

As you store new files on a diskette in different directories or subdirectories, the pathname required to reach those files could get rather long. As pathnames get longer, typing errors are more likely to occur. ProDOS provides you with a means of having to only type a pathname or partial pathname once. It is called prefix. The prefix capability is not supported by DOS 3.3.

Assigning the prefix variable name to the pathname or to a partial pathname allows you to refer to a particular file name without having to type in the entire pathname. A partial pathname is less that part of the pathname that has been assigned to the prefix.

The best way to understand the prefix concept is through the use of some simple examples. These are shown in Fig. E-5.

Some of the examples in Fig. E-5 show the pathnames that were shown in Fig. E-4. The third column entries in Fig. E-5 are partial pathnames. A full pathname is formed by concatenating the prefix with the partial pathname. If a prefix does not match any portion of a pathname, you should change the prefix name.

It is recommended that you thoroughly understand the pathname and partial pathname concept because you will be using them frequently in your programming and when using AppleWorks. The rules for forming a partial pathname are shown below.

A ProDOS partial pathname is:

A file name, or a series of file names separated by slashes.

The pathname minus the current prefix.

Less than 65 characters long, including pathnames and slashes.

```
ProDOS must find file:     Current PREFIX is:        You should type:
-----------------------------------------------------------  ------
/DISKNAME/REALLY/LEGAL     /DISKNAME/                 REALLY/LEGAL
/DISKNAME/REALLY/LEGAL     /DISKNAME/REALLY/          LEGAL
/MY/BANK/NOTES/DUE         /MY/                       BANK/NOTES/DUE
/MY/BANK/NOTES/DUE         /MY/BANK/                  NOTES/DUE
/MY/BANK/NOTES/DUE         /MY/BANK/NOTES/            DUE
/MY/HOME/STOCK             /MY/                       HOME/STOCK
/MY/HOME/STOCK             /MY/HOME/                  STOCK
/MY/HOME/BONDS             /MY/HOME/                  BONDS
/MY/CREDIT.CARDS           /MY/                       CREDIT.CARDS
```

Figure F-5   Prefixes and Pathnames

E.2 USING THE FILER PROGRAM

This section discusses one of the two major utility programs included in ProDOS. The functions performed by this program are many of the housekeeping, organization, and general system operations. Without this program, the day-to-day operation of your system would be far more ineffective and less productive. For those of you who are familiar with DOS 3.3, there are two programs provided on the System Master diskette that are direct corollaries to these two expanded utilities in ProDOS. Figure E-6 shows these program sets:

The /PRODOS/FILER program performs all of the functions that the FID program performed plus a number of others. The /PRODOS/FILER program allows you to organize the information stored on a diskette. The /PRODOS/FILER will probably be used more than any of the other programs on the user's disk.

In order to use the /PRODOS/FILER program, to boot the ProDOS user's disk, and from the main menu screen select the F, /PRODOS/FILER, option. This will clear the screen, bring the /PRODOS/FILER program into memory, and automatically execute the program.

Once the program is executing, just follow the screen options.

E.2.1 ProDOS Filer Menu

The /PRODOS/FILER program has a number of subprograms that operate either upon a diskette as a whole or upon the individual files stored on a diskette. These programs are normally called utility programs. Figure F-7 shows these main program categories.

In a number of the subprogram screens, default values are shown. In those cases, you

```
ProDOS                         DOS 3.3
-----------                    -------------
FILER                          FID and COPYA
```

Figure E-6   ProDOS Programs

```
*******************************************
*                                         *
*    APPLE'S PRODOS SYSTEM UTILITIES       *
*                                         *
*        FILER  VERSION 1.0.1              *
*                                         *
*   COPYRIGHT APPLE COMPUTER, 1983-84      *
*                                         *
*******************************************

            ? - TUTOR

            F - FILE COMMANDS

            V - VOLUME COMMANDS

            D - CONFIGURATION DEFAULTS

            Q - QUIT

       PLEASE SELECT AN OPTION
```

Figure E-7   *Filer Main Screen*

may select the defaults by simply pressing the RETURN key. If you want to change the default value, simply type your required value.

One of the handy features of the /PRODOS/FILER program is the use of the ESCape key. You can use this key to restart a screen from the beginning, return to a previous screen, or back out of a selection. This allows you to be able to change subprograms and screens easily. It is consistent with AppleWorks.

By the way, if you make a typing error and enter a keystroke that does not correspond to one of the legitimate commands, the /PRODOS/FILER program is very forgiving and allows you to reenter the correct keystroke.

By selecting the ? - TUTOR option, you will be given information about the individual file commands and terminology definitions that may be unfamiliar to you, at least for now.

File commands affect an individual file. Section F.2.3 discusses this subprogram.

Volume commands are those that affect a diskette as a whole unit. Section F.2.4 discusses this subprogram.

The Configuration Defaults option lets you customize defaults to match your particular system. This option is not discussed.

The Quit option allows you to return to the user's disk Main Menu or any other diskette of your choosing.

E.2.2 Tutor

The ProDOS TUTOR screens are for the purpose of giving you information without you having to read a book like this one to remember what is required. The ProDOS TUTOR is entered by typing the ? (Question Mark) key on the keyboard.

As you proceed through this appendix, you will notice that each menu screen has a tutor option. The use of the tutor is very straight forward. Make the selection using the ?, question mark, key and follow the continuation prompting at the bottom line of each screen.

E.2.3 File Commands

This set of subprograms works with individual files stored on a diskette. Figure E-8 gives the File Commands video display screen that is first presented when the F option is selected from the main /PRODOS/FILER menu.

E.2.4 Volume Commands

This set of commands allows you to operate with diskettes as an entire unit. The word "volume" is another term for disk or diskette. In most cases, "volume" will refer to the Apple computer floppy or flexible diskette; however, the term also applies to Apple's hard disk drive ProFile. ProFile is a 5MB mass storage media. The 5MB capacity is like having 35 floppy diskettes available to you simultaneously. ProDOS supports both forms of disk storage. Figure E-9 shows these commands.

The ? - TUTOR option works the same here as described earlier and needs no further explanation.

The F command allows you to format an entire volume. This command's corollary in DOS 3.3 is the INIT command.

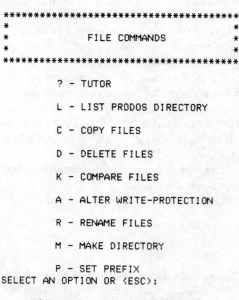

```
****************************************
*                                      *
*            FILE COMMANDS             *
*                                      *
****************************************

            ? - TUTOR

            L - LIST PRODOS DIRECTORY

            C - COPY FILES

            D - DELETE FILES

            K - COMPARE FILES

            A - ALTER WRITE-PROTECTION

            R - RENAME FILES

            M - MAKE DIRECTORY

            P - SET PREFIX
    SELECT AN OPTION OR <ESC>:
```

Figure E-8   *File Commands Screen*

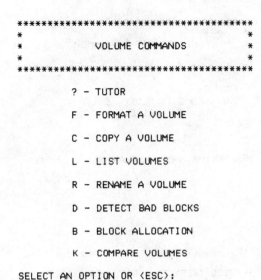

```
*****************************************
*                                       *
*          VOLUME COMMANDS              *
*                                       *
*****************************************
        ? - TUTOR

        F - FORMAT A VOLUME

        C - COPY A VOLUME

        L - LIST VOLUMES

        R - RENAME A VOLUME

        D - DETECT BAD BLOCKS

        B - BLOCK ALLOCATION

        K - COMPARE VOLUMES

 SELECT AN OPTION OR <ESC>:
```

Figure E-9   Volume Commands Screen

The C command allows you to copy one volume to another. The corollary in DOS 3.3 is COPYA.

The L options allows you to list files on a volume. This subprogram has a corollary in the FID program of DOS 3.3.

The R - RENAME option lets you rename a volume. For example you may want to change /BLANK15 to /GL.MAY.84 for "General Ledger—May 1984." This option is not discussed.

The D - DETECT BAD BLOCKS option detects bad blocks that might be present on a diskette. This option is not discussed.

The B - BLOCK ALLOCATION option gives you the allocated blocks as used presently on a diskette. This option is not discussed.

The K - COMPARE VOLUMES option allows you to compare volumes. This option is not discussed.

E.2.4.1 Format a Volume

This screen allows you to prepare a volume to accept programs, file, or data. All diskettes *must* be formatted before you can store data on the diskette. Every computer manufacturer uses a slightly different diskette recording scheme, so they provide either system or utility software that explains their recording scheme. Figure E-10 shows you the screen for formatting a volume.

The surface of the recording system is divided into sections called blocks. A block of data is 512 bytes long. In DOS 3.3 terminology, this would be two sectors since a sector

```
**********************************
*                                *
*         FORMAT A VOLUME        *
*                                *
**********************************

--FORMAT--
  THE VOLUME IN SLOT:  6
               DRIVE:  1




NEW VOLUME NAME: (/BLANK00          )
```

```
--PRESS <RET> TO ACCEPT:<ESC> TP EXIT--
```

Figure E-10   *FORMAT A VOLUME Display Screen*

holds 256 bytes of information. There are also 35 tracks of 8 blocks each, where each track is marked for recording data.

Notice that you can accept the default volume name assigned by the /PRODOS/FILER or one of your choice. If you accept the default, volumes will be named as follows:

/BLANKxx

In this case, the xx represent numbers that start with 00 and increment by one each time you accept a default value. The range of numbers are from 00 through 99. Then the number sequence will recycle from the beginning.

Further, you may format a volume using any legitimate slot-drive combination, including a ProFile hard disk, if you have one. Remember that the ESCape key may always be used to restart a screen or to escape that selection.

When you enter a slot-drive combination or a volume name of your own, all you have to do is type over the default values or name presented on the screen.

You will probably have some diskettes that you previously formatted, but now want to reformat to store new information. When ProDOS determines that the diskette already has information stored on it, you will be asked to verify that you wish to destroy all previous information. Do not answer the question lightly, because once you respond by telling the format program to destroy previous information, there is no retreating. The stored information is gone.

After a diskette is successfully formatted, you will see the message:

`FORMAT COMPLETE`

Remove the formatted diskette from the disk drive and label it with the volume name, contents, and current date.

Note: If you are going to format a mass-storage disk like the ProFile, you will get the message:

WARNING: YOU ARE ABOUT TO FORMAT A LARGE DISK

If you made a mistake, use the ESCape key to terminate the selection. If it is what you want, type RETURN key.

E.2.4.2 Copy a Volume

It is always a good idea to make copies of your diskettes. Even though the data stored on a diskette is very stable and highly reliable, disasters can happen. So, take out "volume insurance" and make backup copies of your diskettes.

In the previous section, it was stated that you must format a diskette before you are able to store data on that diskette. Now you will be given the exception to the rule. When you copy one volume to another, the Copy A Volume option will first reformat the destination diskette before copying the contents of the source diskette. If there is anything at all on the destination diskette you want to keep, move those files so they won't be lost.

When making a copy of a volume, you may maintain the same name or change the name on the new volume. Figure E-11 shows you the screen for copying a volume.

The source (original) diskette in the above example is placed in slot, 6, drive 1. The destination (new or copy) diskette is placed in slot 6, drive 2.

By the way, if you have a single drive system, place your source volume in drive 1 and be prepared to do a lot of diskette swapping. Fortunately, the copy program will place messages on the video screen telling you which diskette is to be placed in the disk drive.

When all of the copying has been completed, you will be given the message:

`COPY COMPLETE`

E.3 USING THE CONVERT PROGRAM

Because of the formatting differences between DOS 3.3 and ProDOS, you will have to convert all DOS 3.3 diskettes to ProDOS. The CONVERT program has been included in ProDOS for the purpose of converting DOS 3.3 programs and files to the new ProDOS environment. This program performs a similar function to the MUFFIN program provided when the transition was made from DOS 3.2.1 to DOS 3.3.

```
********************************************
*                                          *
*              COPY A VOLUME               *
*                                          *
********************************************

--COPY--
  THE VOLUME IN SLOT:  6
               DRIVE:  1

    TO VOLUME IN SLOT:  6
               DRIVE: ( )

  NEW VOLUME NAME:




    --PRESS <RET> TO ACCEPT:<ESC> TP EXIT--
```

Figure E-11 COPY A VOLUME *Display Screen*

There are a few cautions, however. The CONVERT program will not transfer DOS 3.3 or ProDOS random access files. You will have to find some other way to transfer these files.

E.3.1 ProDOS Convert Menu

The Main Menu gives you the ability to choose any of the capabilities of the CONVERT program. If you do not understand how to use the program, select the Tutor option by typing a question mark on the keyboard.

It is recommended that you set the date first if there is no date showing. This will give you the created date on your ProDOS diskette when you transfer files.

E.3.2 Reverse Transfer Direction

This option allows you to change the direction of the transfer. When you select this option, the screen will only change in the direction line. This direction display actually wraps around in this area.

E.3.3 Change DOS 3.3 Slot and Drive

This option lets you adjust the slot-drive combination to suit your particular system. When selecting this option, you may enter new information, enter partial information, or accept defaults by pressing the RETURN key.

```
                  CONVERT Menu
Direction: DOS 3.3 S6,D2 ---> ProDOS
Date: 30-JAN-84
Prefix: /PRODOS/


-------------------------------------------


    R - Reverse Direction of Transfer

    C - Change DOS 3.3 Slot and Drive

  , D - Set ProDOS Date

    P - Set ProDOS Prefix

    T - Transfer (or List) Files



-------------------------------------------


Enter Command: ?    ? - Tutor, Q - Quit
```

Figure E-12   CONVERT Main Menu

Note: When transferring files from ProFile to DOS 3.3, change the slot-drive combination from the ProFile S5,D1 to DOS S6,D1 or D2.

F.3.4 Set ProDOS Prefix

This option allows you to change the ProDOS prefix for the purpose of converting programs and files from many different diskettes. Make sure that you have entered the correct prefix before attempting to transfer any files.

F.3.5 Set ProDOS Date

Since there is a place for the modification and creation date when you place files on a diskette, you need to have a way to date-stamp your files.

F.3.6 Transfer or List Files

This option is probably the one that you will use most. This option allows you to list the files on the DOS 3.3 diskette, and then move files to the ProDOS diskette.

ASCII Character Codes

I know sage, wormwood, and hyssop, but I can't smell
character unless it stinks.
EDWARD DAHLBERG, 1965

```
 DEC = ASCII decimal code
 HEX = ASCII hexadecimal code
CHAR = ASCII character name
 n/a = not applicable
CTRL = CONTROL
```

```
Apple II+, Apple IIe, and Apple IIc
DEC  HEX  CHAR WHAT TO TYPE              Meaning
---  ---  ---- ------------             --------------
  0   00  NULL CTRL-@                    Null character
  1   01  SOH  CTRL-A                    Start of heading
  2   02  STX  CTRL-B                    Start of text
  3   03  ETX  CTRL-C                    End of text
  4   04  EOT  CTRL-D                    End of transmission
  5   05  ENQ  CTRL-E                    Enquiry
  6   06  ACK  CTRL-F                    Acknowledge
  7   07  BEL  CTRL-G                    Bell
  8   08  BS   CTRL-H or <--             Back space
  9   09  HT   CTRL-I                    Horizontal tab
 10   0A  LF   CTRL-J                    Linefeed
 11   0B  VT   CTRL-K                    Vertical tab
 12   0C  FF   CTRL-L                    Formfeed
 13   0D  CR   CTRL-M or RETURN          Carriage return
 14   0E  SO   CTRL-N                    Shift out
 15   0F  SI   CTRL-O                    Shift in
 16   10  DLE  CTRL-P                    Data link escape
 17   11  DC1  CTRL-P                    Device control 1
 18   12  DC2  CTRL-R                    Device control 2
 19   13  DC3  CTRL-S                    Device control 3
 20   14  DC4  CTRL-T                    Device control 4
 21   15  NAK  CTRL-U or -->             Negative acknowledgement
 22   16  SYN  CTRL-V                    Synchronous idle
 23   17  ETB  CTRL-W                    End of transmission block
 24   18  CAN  CTRL-X                    Cancel
 25   19  EM   CTRL-Y                    End of medium
 26   1A  SUB  CTRL-Z                    Substitute
 27   1B  ESC  CTRL-[ ESCAPE or ESC      Escape
 28   1C  FS   CTRL-\                    File separator
 29   1D  GS   CTRL-] SHIFT-M Apple II+  Group separator
 30   1E  RS   CTRL-^                    Record separator
 31   1F  US   CTRL-_ n/a Apple II+      Unit separator
```

```
Apple II+, Apple IIe, and Apple IIc
DEC   HEX   CHAR  WHAT TO TYPE
---   ---   ----  ------------
32    20          SPACE
33    21    !     !
34    22    "     "
35    23    #     #
36    24    $     $
37    25    %     %
38    26    &     &
39    27    '     '
40    28    (     (
41    29    )     )
42    2A    *     *
43    2B    +     +
44    2C    ,     ,
45    2D    -     -
46    2E    .     .
47    2F    /     /
48    30    0     0
49    31    1     1
50    32    2     2
51    33    3     3
52    34    4     4
53    35    5     5
54    36    6     6
55    37    7     7
56    38    8     8
57    39    9     9
58    3A    :     ;
59    3B    ;     ;
60    3C    <     <
61    3D    =     =
62    3E    >     >
63    3F    ?     ?
```

```
Apple II+, Apple IIe, and Apple IIc
DEC   HEX   CHAR  WHAT TO TYPE
---   ---   ----  -------------
 64    40    @     @
 65    41    A     A
 66    42    B     B
 67    43    C     C
 68    44    D     D
 69    45    E     E
 70    46    F     F
 71    47    G     G
 72    48    H     H
 73    49    I     I
 74    4A    J     J
 75    4B    K     K
 76    4C    L     L
 77    4D    M     M
 78    4E    N     N
 79    4F    O     O
 80    50    P     P
 81    51    Q     Q
 82    52    R     R
 83    53    S     S
 84    54    T     T
 85    55    U     U
 86    56    V     V
 87    57    W     W
 88    58    X     X
 89    59    Y     Y
 90    5A    Z     Z
 91    5B    [     [ Apple IIe and IIc only
 92    5C    \     \ Apple IIe and IIc only
 93    5D    ]     ] Apple IIe, Apple IIc, and Shift M Apple II+
 94    5E    ^     ^
 95    5F    _     _ Apple IIe, Apple IIc, and n/a Apple II+
```

```
Apple IIe and Apple IIc
DEC   HEX   CHAR WHAT TO TYPE
---   ---   ---- ------------
 96    60    `       `
 97    61    a       a
 98    62    b       b
 99    63    c       c
100    64    d       d
101    65    e       e
102    66    f       f
103    67    g       g
104    68    h       h
105    69    i       i
106    6A    j       j
107    6B    k       k
108    6C    l       l
109    6D    m       m
110    6E    n       n
111    6F    o       o
112    70    p       p
113    71    q       q
114    72    r       r
115    73    s       s
116    74    t       t
117    75    u       u
118    76    v       v
119    77    w       w
120    78    x       x
121    79    y       y
122    7A    z       z
123    7B    {       {
124    7C    |       |
125    7D    }       }
126    7E    ~       ~
127    7F   DEL     DEL
```

Questions and Answers

He who asks questions cannot avoid the answers.
CAMEROON PROVERB

This appendix answers a number of common questions that may not have been fully answered or covered in the main part of this book.

Q: When I am typing text, do I need to press the RETURN key when I reach the end of a line?

A: No. The word processor is different from a typewriter in that you do not have to press a RETURN key when you reach the end of a line. You do need to press the RETURN key when you want to start a new paragraph or skip a line. Where the line ends depends on the margin settings and the justification format.

Q: When entering printer option codes, does it matter whether I type the option code in upper or lower case?

A: No. The option codes may be entered in either upper- or lowercase letters.

Q: Do I have to specify the disk slot and drive number when I save and load files?

A: No. When storing or loading files from a diskette, the storage location is specified from one of the Other Activities menu options. Once you have specified the standard storage location, AppleWorks will remember that specification.

Q: Can I print a file without first loading it into the Desktop?

A: No. A file must first be loaded into memory on the Desktop before it can be printed.

Q: If I accidentally delete a file, is there any way I can get it back?

A: No. The only way is to have a backup file stored on another diskette or on the same diskette with another name. It is recommended that you take out "accident insurance" and have backup copies of all of your files.

Q: Can I save my own set of printer options so that I do not have to recreate them each time?

A: Yes. Create a file with all of your frequently used printer options already entered. Load that file into the Desktop, change the file name, and you are ready with a new document.

Q: What is a string?

A: A string is a sequence of characters treated as a unit in a program.

Q: What do I do when I get a "disk full" message?

A: The best solution is to change your data disk and then save the file on the disk with enough storage room on it to hold the file.

Q: What happens when I am told that the Desktop is full?

A: AppleWorks requires that you get rid of the largest file on the Desktop. First, save the file and then remove it from the Desktop. After that is done, it is recommended that you save and remove other files from your Desktop so that you have room to add to other files.

Q: What is a text value?

A: That is a value in the spreadsheet that is actually a numeric value. For example the year 1984 might be a text label for a column or row.

Q: When I move a template from the spreadsheet to the word processor, do the formulas also move?

A: No. Only the values for cells are moved.

Q: Can I move text labels in a template by using cell pointers?

A: No. Some spreadsheet programs do allow you to do this, but AppleWorks does not allow moving of text labels with pointers.

Q: Do I lose a file on the Desktop when I use the Help screen?

A: No. The Help screen does not disturb the files on the Desktop. The Help screen can be accessed by pressing OPEN-APPLE ?.

Q: Does the word processor have a split-screen capability?

A: No. Only the spreadsheet has a split-screen capability.

Q: How do I see the formulas entered into an individual cell in the spreadsheet?

A: First, place the cursor on the cell and look at the command line which contains the complete formula in that cell. Second, use OPEN-APPLE Z to have all cells presented with formulas. A column width may need to be expanded in order to see complete formulas throughout the column.

Q: How can I square the contents of a column category in the data base?

A: First, create a calculated category. Then use the category value to create the square of the category in the calculated column.

Q: Sometimes I press the wrong OPEN-APPLE command. How do I recover from that?

A: The best way to terminate the wrong command execution is to use the ESCape key a sufficient number of times to return to the Main Menu. Then select a file from the Desktop and continue processing.

Q: Sometimes AppleWorks locks up and I cannot continue. What do I do?

A: There may be many reasons for this. The only way to recover is to completely restart your system from the beginning. Use CONTROL OPEN-APPLE RESET to reboot it. This procedure, of course, loses all files in memory.

Q: Does the word processor allow for right-justification of text material?

A: No. You can left-justify, center, or fill-justify text. The only way to right-justify is to enter the text and then move the line(s) to the right margin by using the either the space bar.

Q: What should I do if I can't get my printer to print all of the options available in AppleWorks?

A: If you are using an ImageWriter, the best thing to do is to check to make sure your printer, serial interface card, and cables are correctly connected and set up. Make sure you have entered options correctly. If you are not using ImageWriter, check your printer manual to determine if the machine will support the options of AppleWorks. If it does, make sure you have entered the printer keys correctly.

Printer Problems

The printing press is either the greatest blessing or the greatest
curse of modern times, one sometimes forgets which.
J. M. BARRIE, 1896

H.1 APPLEWORKS AND PRINTING

AppleWorks can print to other devices than just printers. It can print to the Clipboard, to floppy disks, or to a ProFile hard disk. Each part of the AppleWorks integrated program has its own method of printing. To print from one of the AppleWorks application programs you must be in that section of AppleWorks. That means you cannot print the spreadsheet from the word processor. You can print the screen at any time with the OPEN-APPLE H command.

- The data base, the word processor, and the spreadsheet can print to the printer.
- All three parts of AppleWorks can print to a text (ASCII) file on a formatted disk.
- The data base and the spreadsheet print formatted reports to the Clipboard.
- The data base and the spreadsheet print DIF files.
- The data base prints formatted reports on the screen.
- You can always print the video display with OPEN-APPLE H.

The following diagrams show how the print command works with the three parts of AppleWorks.

H.2 ADDING AND DELETING A PRINTER

AppleWorks allows you to define three printers for your screen. These can be ASCII files to the disk, two different printers in different slots (1,2,4,5,7), or printers defined for the same slot.

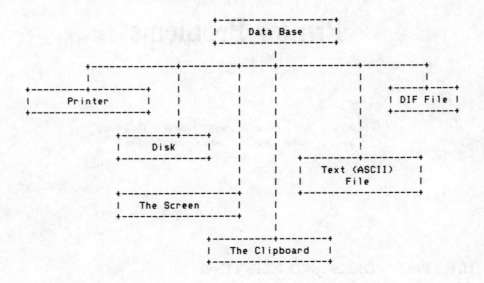

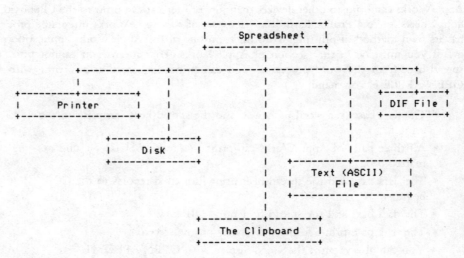

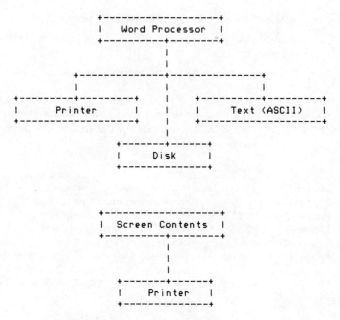

Figure H-1   *The Print Command*

To add a printer to your Printer Information screen follow the outline in the box below.

1. Choose Other Activities from the Main Menu screen.
2. Choose "Specify Information" about your printer(s).
3. Choose Add or Delete a printer. A maximum of three are allowed.
4. If you choose to delete a printer, you will be asked to specify the one to delete. Select the number that identifies that printer and press the RETURN key.
5. Select a printer from the list on the screen, if your printer is listed. If not, select number 11 to set up a custom printer.
6. You will be asked to type a name for the printer. Your name can be any word you choose but limited to 15 characters.

To define the generic specifications of your printer, consider the following:

1. Does your printer require a line feed after each return?
2. Does your printer accept top-of-form commands?

3. Do you want the printer to stop after each page?

4. The width of your printer platen (80 columns is 8.0 in.) with a print size of 10 characters per inch.

5. List of printer commands for underlining, boldface, superscript, and subscript.

The following table lists some printer specification codes. If your printer is on the list of supported printers, AppleWorks will set up the commands for you. If your printer is not on the list, skip the next section.

Code	Display	Effect
Escape X	_____	Starts underlining of text.
Escape Y		Stops underlining of text.
Escape !	BOLD	Starts boldface printing of text.
Escape "	BOLD	Stops boldface printing of text.
Escape T20		Line feeds 20/144 inches.
Escape F	Superscript	Combined with 20/144 line feed advances paper for superscript.
Escape R	Subscript	Combined with 20/144 line feed backs up paper for superscript.

H.3 PRINTING THE DISPLAY

The video display screen can be printed from any part of AppleWorks, including the command screens. To print the display, press OPEN-APPLE H. The entire screen will be printed just as it appears. This is very helpful when working with tables or references from one area of a document that need to be included in another area.

H.4 CHANGING THE DISPLAY PRINTER

The display printer is the printer selected when you press OPEN-APPLE H.
To change the printer location:

1. Choose Other Activities from the Main Menu screen.

2. Choose Specify Information.

3. Type 1 and press the RETURN key.

4. Choose your printer on the Printer Information screen. Use number or arrow keys to make your selection, then press the RETURN key.

5. Use the ESCape key to return to the Main Menu.

H.5 PRINTING TO THE CLIPBOARD

After a data base or spreadsheet report has been formatted, it can be printed to the Clipboard so that it can be included in a word processor document. To print to the Clipboard, you must use OPEN-APPLE P from either the spreadsheet, the data base, or the word processor.

After determining the portion of the data base or spreadsheet you want printed to the Clipboard, select "print." Your report will now be on the Clipboard for use in the word processor.

H.6 PRINTING TO A TEXT ASCII FILE

You can print all three parts of AppleWorks to a text ASCII file on a disk to be used by other programs. Text files do not contain special printing codes and options. They are formatted just as if they were printed to the printer.

- Word Processor documents printed to a text file contain the same RETURNs as in the word processor.
- Data base text files printed contain RETURNs after each entry.
- Spreadsheet reports printed to a text file have RETURNSs after each cell. Text files printed from the spreadsheet can be used as a source for the data base.
- You must save your files as AppleWorks files either before or after printing to a text file.

To print a text ASCII file, use the OPEN-APPLE P command from the spreadsheet, the data base, or the word processor.

H.7 PRINTING TO THE DISK

Sometimes you may want to print to the disk instead of the printer. Be sure to save the file with a unique name before printing it to the disk. Once a file has been printed to the disk, AppleWorks can no longer use it as a word processor file. You can still load it into AppleWorks but all of the print commands and special codes will have been lost.

One of the benefits of printing to a disk is that it allows you to send text to another computer. If your communication software is in DOS 3.3, you must first convert the file to DOS 3.3 using the ProDOS CONVERT program on your ProDOS User's Disk.

To print to a disk, use the OPEN-APPLE P command from the spreadsheet, the data base, or the word processor.

H.8 PRINTING A SPREADSHEET REPORT

Once you have formatted a working spreadsheet template, set up the printer options.

To print a report:

1. Make sure you are in Review/Add/Change screen.
2. Place the cursor where the printing is to start.

3. Press OPEN-APPLE P.

4. You have several options for the amount of the report you want to print. These are "All," "Specific Rows," "Specific Columns," or "Block." Select an option. "All" refers to the entire template that has information in it, but not the blank cells of the template. If you choose "Rows," "Column," or "Block," move the cursor to highlight the area that is to be printed, then press the RETURN key.

5. If you choose to print a spreadsheet template to the printer that is wider than your printer platen, you need to either change the characters per inch setting or print the report in sections.

6. You can print to the printer, disk, Clipboard, DIF file, or to a text ASCII file. Select the printing location.

7. If your report has a header, AppleWorks asks you to type the report date and press the RETURN key, or to accept the default report date by pressing the RETURN key. The default date is the last date that you typed.

8. If you choose to print to a printer, AppleWorks will ask how many copies to print. You can select up to nine copies. If more copies are needed, print the report again. Press the RETURN key to begin the printing of your report.

9. If you choose to print to a text ASCII file or a DIF file, select the defined device to use when printing to a disk. AppleWorks asks for a pathname and/or file name for the report. Type the pathname and/or file name in the form, /BLANK00/MYFILE. Then press the RETURN key to begin printing.

10. During the printing of the report to the printer, you can press the ESCape key to return to Review/Add/Change, or press the space bar once to halt printing, then press it again to continue printing. Remember, if your printer has a buffer built in, printing will not stop until the buffer has dumped its contents.

H.9 PRINTING A DATA BASE REPORT

After you have formatted a data base report, you can print it to the printer, text ASCII file, disk, DIF file, screen, or Clipboard.

To print a data base report:

1. Make sure you are in the Report Format display.

2. Press OPEN-APPLE P.

3. Choose the device where you want the report printed.

4. If your report has a header, AppleWorks asks you to either type a new date for the report and press the RETURN key, or to accept the default date by pressing the RETURN key. The default date is the last date that you typed.

5. If you choose to print to a printer, AppleWorks will ask you how many copies to print. You can print up to nine copies. If more copies are needed, print the report again. To begin printing, press the RETURN key.

6. If you choose to print to a text ASCII file, DIF file, or to a disk, you will be asked for a pathname and/or file name for your report. Type the pathname and/or file name in the form, /BLANK00/MYFILE. To begin printing, press the RETURN key.

7. During the printing of the report to the printer, you can press the ESCape key to return to Report Format screen, or press the space bar once to halt printing, then press the space bar again to continue printing. If your printer has a buffer built in, printing will not stop until the buffer has dumped its contents.

H.10 PRINTING A WORD PROCESSOR DOCUMENT

This section explains how to print a word processor document. It also discusses special printing options that allow you to pause during printing or after each page so you can insert paper into your printer.

To print a word processor document:

1. Press OPEN-APPLE P from the Review/Add/Change screen to begin the printer set up.

2. Several options are given for printing. These are "Beginning," "This Page," and "From the Cursor."

3. If you want to print all of the document, choose "Beginning." This prints all of the document including page headers and footers. Press the RETURN key to begin printing.

4. If you want to print from the beginning of a specific page and don't know the page number, press the ESCape key to go back to Review/Add/Change. Once in Review/Add/Change, press OPEN-APPLE K for page breaks to be calculated. AppleWorks will tell you how many pages you have and show you the page breaks. Move the cursor just below a page break line. Press OPEN-APPLE P to start the printer options again, select the page number, and press the RETURN key.

5. If you want to print from the cursor position, move the cursor in front of the text you want to print. Press OPEN-APPLE P to start the printer options, select "From the Cursor," and press the RETURN key.

6. Select the printer for the document, and press the RETURN key. AppleWorks will ask you how many copies you want. You can select up to nine copies. If you need more than nine, print the document again. Enter the number of copies to print and then press the RETURN key.

7. If you want to print on single sheets of paper, you need to print single pages at a time. If you are going to use several pages of single-sheet paper, it's best to set up a printer on the print screen that stops at the end of each page.

8. If you need to set up single-page printing, select the Other Activities option. Select "Specify Information" about your printer. On the Printer Information screen, select the printer you want to set up as the single-page printer. AppleWorks shows you the Change a Printer screen. From this screen select number 3, which tells the printer to stop after a page.

9. If you need to insert special information, you must stop the printer at certain positions in the document. To stop the printer, move the cursor to the left of the position in the document where text is to be inserted and press OPEN-APPLE O. Select EK from the printer options. The printer will stop at that position in the document and let you insert text. Once you have completed the insertion, press the RETURN key to continue printing.

10. During the printing of the report, press the ESCape key to return to Review/Add/Change or press the space bar once to halt printing. Press the space bar again to continue printing. If your printer has a buffer built in, printing will not stop until the buffer has dumped its contents.

H.11 PRINTING TO A DIF FILE

AppleWorks can write the DIF format from either the spreadsheet or the data base, so you can save files that could be used in other programs. AppleWorks can also read DIF files created by AppleWorks or other spreadsheet or data base programs.

To print a DIF file from the spreadsheet:

1. You must be in the Review/Add/Change screen of the spreadsheet program.

2. Use the OPEN-APPLE P command to print the report from the spreadsheet.

3. You can choose printing "All," "Rows," "Columns," or "Block." Select "Row" or "Column" only when printing a DIF file from the spreadsheet. If you choose "All" or "Block" you could hang your system and loose the entire file.

4. Once you have the Print screen you will be asked where you want to print the report. Select "To a DIF file." You will then be asked whether it should be in row or column order. Most often you will be printing DIF files in column order, since this is normally the correct order for loading information into the data base or spreadsheet.

5. You will now be asked to enter a pathname and/or file name. This is entered in the form, /BLANK00/MYDIF.File. Press the RETURN key to begin writing your DIF file to disk.

To print a DIF file from the data base, you must be in the Report Format screen. From here you can select to print your report to a DIF file.

1. Use the OPEN-APPLE P command to print the report from the data base.

2. Once you have the Print screen, you will be asked where you want to print the report. Select "To a DIF file."

3. You will now be asked to enter a pathname and/or a file name. This is entered in the form, /BLANK00/MYDIF. Press the RETURN key to begin writing your DIF file to disk.

H.12 SERIAL PRINTER SETTINGS

If you are using a serial interface card with your printer you will need to set the baud rate, data format, and parity before you can use your printer with AppleWorks. There are several other switches that may need to be changed to obtain the special enhancements from your printer.

There are three places that need to set the standard serial interface settings: on the serial interface card, on the serial printer, and in AppleWorks. You should set your serial interface card switches first then record this information for setting the switches for your printer and AppleWorks.

If you are using the Apple IIe, the Apple Super Serial card, and the Apple ImageWriter with AppleWorks, you only need to set the serial card and the ImageWriter printer switches. AppleWorks has already been set.

The first thing that needs to be positioned on the Super Serial card is the jumper block. There are two positions for the jumper block on the Apple Super Serial card—the modem and the terminal position.

> **Caution:** Make sure the power switch is turned *off* on your printer and *on* on your computer.

If you are using the Apple Super Serial card with your printer, you will need to set the jumper block in the correct position for the printer. The Super Serial card normally comes with the jumper block set in the modem position, so the block will need to be turned to terminal. To turn it around, you will need to lift the jumper block and align the arrow pointer to the terminal position. It may be necessary to lift the block with an IC

```
+----------------------------------------------------------------+
|  SWITCH 1          on  = open       SWITCH 2                    |
|  POSITION          off = close      POSITION                   |
+----------------------------------------------------------------+
|  1   2   3   4   5   6   7       1   2   3   4   5   6   7  |
+----------------------------------------------------------------+
|  off off off on  off off off    on  off off on  on  off off |
+----------------------------------------------------------------+
```

Figure H-2   *Serial Interface Switch Settings*

```
+----------------------------------------------------------------+
|  SWITCH 1          on  = open       SWITCH 2                    |
|  POSITION          off = close      POSITION                   |
+----------------------------------------------------------------+
|  1   2   3   4   5   6   7   8       1   2   3   4  |
+----------------------------------------------------------------+
|  on  on  on  on  off off on  on     off off on  on  |
+----------------------------------------------------------------+
```

Figure H-3   *Printer Switch Settings*

puller or some other type of tool. Make sure you have not bent or misaligned any of the pins on the jumper block when reinstalling it into its IC socket. Use the procedure given in the ImageWriter manual.

After repositioning the jumper block, you will need to set the interface card switches to their correct position. There are two switch blocks on the Super Serial card that need to be set. They are labeled as SW1 (switch number one) and SW2 (switch number two). There are two positions for each switch in the switch blocks, either *open* or *close* (also referred to as *on* and *off*). Switches are read in the depressed position, not in the raised position. Use the end of a pencil or pen to depress these switches. Once they are set To the correct position, record their settings for use in setting the printer switches. Figure H-2 shows the correct switch settings for the Apple Super Serial card and the Apple Image-Writer.

To set standard printer instructions, you may need to change some switch settings inside of the printer cabinet. These switches control the baud rate, data format, parity, and other enhancements. Each printer has its own list for setting switches. Look up these settings in your printer manual. Figure H-3 shows the settings for switch 1 and switch 2 of the Apple ImageWriter. Once these switches have been set, you can begin using AppleWorks with your printer.

To set serial interfaces from inside AppleWorks, you will need to be in the Printer Code Display screen.

1. From the Printer Code display, select number 5. AppleWorks gives you a display called Serial Interfaces. You will set the baud rate, data format, and parity for your printer.

2. Select number 1 to set the baud rate for your printer. AppleWorks will give you a list of baud rates from which to choose. Enter your selection and

press the RETURN key. AppleWorks returns you to the Serial Interface display.

3. From the Serial Interface display, enter the information for data format and parity just as you did for the baud rate. AppleWorks gives you a list from which to choose. After entering your selections, press the RETURN key. AppleWorks returns you to the Serial Interface display screen.

Once you have entered this information, you can use the enhancements of your printer with AppleWorks. If you have trouble with the printer and AppleWorks, you may need to call your computer dealer for help in setting these switches.

H.13 STARTUP DISK MODIFICATION

If you are having problems using one of the printers listed on the Add a Printer screen, you should contact your Apple computer dealer for help. Your dealer should have a disk that can modify your AppleWorks Startup disk for your printer.

Glossary

"A definition is the enclosing of a wilderness of ideas within a wall of words."
SAMUEL BUTLER, 1902

Access time—The time required to locate and read or write data on a direct access storage device, such as the disk drive.

Address—1. A numeric location of data, usually in memory. This is normally expressed as a hexadecimal number.
2. A diskette address, normally expressed in terms of the track and sector numbers.

Apple IIc—A compact personal computer in the Apple II family, manufactured and sold by Apple Computer, Inc.

Apple IIe—A personal computer in the Apple II family, manufactured and sold by Apple Computer, Inc.

Applesoft II BASIC—An extended version of the BASIC programming language used with the Apple II Plus, Apple IIe, and Apple IIc computers. An interpretive language for creating and executing programs.

AppleWriter 1.0—A powerful text processor for the Apple II and Apple II Plus computers.

AppleWriter II—A word processor for the Apple II, Apple II Plus, and Apple IIe computers.

Application program—A program that uses the computer for some specific purpose or task, such as word processing or financial modeling.

Argument—The value on which a function operates.

ASCII—An abbreviation for the American Standard Code for Information Interchange. It is the code with which the Apple computers represent the characters you type at the keyboard.

Auxiliary slot—The special expansion slot inside the Apple IIe used for the Apple 80-Column Text Card or Extended 80-Column Text Card.

Back up—To make an exact duplicate of a file, diskette, etc.

BASIC—Beginners All-Purpose Symbolic Instruction Code. A common, high-level programming language. It was developed by Kurtz and Kemeny at Dartmouth College in 1963 and has become one of the most popular microcomputer languages.

Binary—1. The representation of numbers in terms of powers of two.
      2. A term used to describe the base 2 number system in which the digits 1 and 0 are used.

Binary file—1. A file whose data is to be interpreted in its binary form.
      2. A file of the BIN type.

Bit—A single binary digit in the binary number system. This is the smallest possible unit of information consisting of a simple two-way choice.

Block—512 bytes of data. This is the unit of storage used by ProDOS.

BLOCKS—When you use the CAT or CATALOG command, the column on the screen labeled BLOCKS lists the number of blocks of disk space occupied by the file in that directory.

Boot—The process of getting a computer system powered up and running.

Boot disk—A disk that contains all of the information needed to get the computer system running when power is turned on.

BPS—Bits Per Second. A common measure of the rate of flow of information between digital systems.

Branch—This refers to a departure from the normal sequential order of processing.

Buffer—1. An area in memory that stores data temporarily.
      2. A memory area that holds information until it can be processed.

Bug—An error in hardware or software. An error in a program that causes the program not to work as intended.

Byte—A group of consecutive bits (usually 8) forming a unit of storage in the computer and representing one alphanumeric character. This is the smallest unit of information in memory that may be addressed.

Caret—1. A printing character on the keyboard (^).
      2. The keyboard symbol used to represent special nonprinting word processor text-embedded commands.

CAT—This command causes a list of the names and characteristics of all files in a directory to be displayed in the 40-column format.

CATALOG—1. A list of all files stored on a diskette.
      2. This command causes a list of the names and characteristics of all files in a directory to be displayed in the 80-column format. See CAT.

Category—One kind of information in a data base file.

Cell—The individual element space that marks the intersection of two coordinates in a spreadsheet template.

Cell indicator—The sign that shows a cell's contents in a spreadsheet template.

Cell layout—The specification that tells how the information in a cell or group of cells is to be displayed.

Character—A letter, digit, punctuation mark, or other symbol used in printing or displaying information. Normally thought of as being one of the ASCII set of characters.

Character set—The entire set of characters that can be printed by a device such as a printer.

Clipboard—The area in a computer's random access memory (RAM) used for the cut-and-paste operations in AppleWorks.

Command—1. The portion of an instruction that specifies the operation to be performed.
2. A communication from the user to a computer system directing it to perform some immediate action.

Computer—An electronic device for performing predefined computations at high speed and with great accuracy.

Controller card—A peripheral card that connects a device such as a printer or disk drive to a computer and controls the operation of the device.

Coordinates—The row and column intersections that comprise a spreadsheet template addressing scheme.

Cursor—The blinking character displayed on the Desktop screen that indicates your current position in a document. This is where the next character typed or entered will be placed.

Cut and paste—The transfer of information from one file to another.

Data—A general term that is used to denote any or all information, facts, numbers, letters, or symbols which can be processed or produced by a computer.

Data base—The portion of AppleWorks that organizes, stores, retrieves, and modifies information in lists.

Debug—To locate and correct an error or the cause of a problem.

Default—A value, action, or setting that is automatically used by AppleWorks when no other explicit information has been given.

Delimiters—1. Characters that limit the size, range, or limits of some physical or logical element of a computer system.
2. Characters that separate elements in names, such as pathnames.

Desktop—The area of the Apple computer's random access memory (RAM) reserved for AppleWorks files that are currently active.

Desktop index—The list of files on the Desktop. This is accessed by typing the OPEN-APPLE Q keystroke combination.

Destination—1. The copy-to cells in the spreadsheet program of AppleWorks.
2. The receiving diskette when copying files or volumes.

Device—1. A physical apparatus for performing a particular task or achieving a particular purpose.
2. A hardware component of a computer system.

DIF files—Data Interchange Format. Files created by VisiCalc and many other programs that allow for easy data interchange.

Directory file—A file that contains the names and locations of other files stored on a diskette.

Disk—A magnetic storage peripheral device.

Disk drive—A peripheral device that reads and writes information on the surface of a magnetic diskette.

Diskette—An information storage medium consisting of a flat circular magnetic surface on which information is magnetically recorded.

Disk II drive—A model of disk drive made and sold by Apple Computer, Inc.

Disk operating system—A computer program that allows the computer to control peripheral devices and communicate with one or more disk drives.

Display—1. Information displayed visually, especially on the video screen.
2. To exhibit information visually.
3. A visual device.

Document—A collection of information in the form of text, created and used by the word processor portion of AppleWorks.

DOS—Acronym for Disk Operating System. See *Disk operating system.*

Edit—To change or modify. For example, to insert, remove, replace, or move text in a document.

Element—1. A member of a set or collection.
2. One of the set of variables making up an expression or formula.
3. A cell in the spreadsheet.

Embedded—Contained within a document.

Entry—1. An individual piece of information in a data base category.
2. The information in a cell in a spreadsheet.

Entry line—The line where you type or edit information that goes in a spreadsheet cell.

ESCape character—1. An ASCII character.
2. The character used in AppleWorks to exit from the current processing.
3. The character used in the FILER to exit from the current processing.

Field—In a data base file, a string of characters.

File—A collection of information stored as a named unit on a peripheral storage medium, such as a diskette.

File name—The name that identifies a file.

Fixed decimal format—The cell format that causes spreadsheet numbers to be displayed with a fixed number of decimal places.

Flexible disk—A diskette made of a flexible plastic coated with a magnetic material, usually a ferrous oxide. The usual sizes are 7½ " and 5¼ ".

Floppy disk—See *Flexible disk*.

Font—A complete set of type in one size and style of characters.

Format—1. A predetermined arrangement of data.
2. The form in which information is organized or presented.
3. To prepare a blank diskette to receive information by dividing its surface into tracks and sectors.
4. The general shape and appearance of the printer's output.

Formula—A mathematical representation combining pointers and functions that define a desired calculation.

Function—1. A representation that stands for a calculation. In AppleWorks it starts with a @.
2. An instruction in a programming language that converts data from one form to another.

Group total—A subtotal for a like set of numbers in a data base report.

Hard copy—Information printed on paper.

Hardware—In computer technology, the physical components.

Header—See *Report header*.

Insert cursor—The underline blinking cursor that allows you to insert text into any document.

Interface card—A peripheral card that implements a particular interface allowing communication between the computer and a peripheral device, such as a printer or modem.

K—A symbol equivalent to the number 1024. Commonly used to indicate one thousand.

Keyboard—1. The set of keys built into the Apple IIe or Apple IIc computer, similar to a typewriter keyboard.
2. Used for typing information into a computer.

Keystroke—The act of pressing a single key or combination of keys on a keyboard.

Label—Information in a spreadsheet worksheet or template that identifies numeric information.

Label format—The specification that tells how labels are displayed in the spreadsheet worksheet or template cells.

Label-style report—The data base report style that prints record entries vertically down the page.

Line indicator—The indication at the bottom of the word processor screen display specifying the cursor line position.

Main menu—The list of AppleWorks main selection options from which you make a single choice.

Memory—1. One of the basic components of a computer.
2. The main storage unit of the computer system.

Menu—1. A table of items from which selections are made.
2. A list of choices presented by a program on the Desktop video screen from which you make a selection.

Modem—MOdulator-DEModulator. A peripheral communications device.

Nibble—Unit of storage containing half of a byte (4 bits).

Numeric—A data type that is numeric in nature. Refers to numbers.

OPEN-APPLE command—1. A key on the keyboard of an Apple IIe and Apple IIc.
2. Combinations of keystrokes that call for a particular AppleWorks feature.

Operating system—A machine language program that manages a multiplicity of functions in a computer system, including peripherals.

Option—An item in the syntax of a ProDOS command that determines a single aspect of the computer's action.

Other activities menu—The secondary list of AppleWorks options.

Output—1. Data that results from computer processing.
2. Any of the devices involved in printing or storing the results of computer processing.

Overstrike cursor—The rectangular blinking cursor that lets you replace, type over, the character under the cursor.

Page—1. A screenful of information.
2. A group of 256 bytes of memory.

Pathname—The series of file names AppleWorks must follow to find a file. They are preceded and separated by slashes that indicate the entire path from the volume directory name to the file that AppleWorks is going to use.

Peripheral—Auxiliary equipment used in the computer system that is external to the computer itself.

Pitch—The number of characters per inch printed along a horizontal line.

Platen width—1. The horizontal width size of the platen on a printer.
2. The distance the printhead on your printer is allowed to travel from left to right.

Pointer—1. A type of spreadsheet value. May begin with a + or − sign and points to the contents of another cell.
2. An address or number of a block of data.

Prefix—A setable pathname that indicates a directory file.

Printer options—Specifications used for printing AppleWorks documents.

PR#—This command sends output to the slot specified.

ProDOS—The name of the Professional Disk Operating System. The operating system for AppleWorks and the Apple IIe.

/PRODOS—The volume name of the disk that contains the ProDOS program.

ProDOS command—Any one of the 28 commands recognized by ProDOS.

ProFile—A rigid disk storage medium manufactured by Apple Computer, Inc., used for the mass storage of information.

Prompt—A message appearing on a display terminal that requests the user to enter information.

Protection—Prohibiting specific kinds of changes to a spreadsheet template or worksheet cell(s).

Quit—The Main Menu selection option that allows you to exit AppleWorks.

RAM—Abbreviation for Random Access Memory.

Random access memory—Memory in which the contents of individual locations can be read from or written to in an arbitrary or random order. The contents of memory are lost when the computer is turned off.

Record—All the information about an item in a data base file. A data base file may contain many records.

Record layout—The way data base records are displayed.

Report format—The specifications that define the layout of a data base report. A maximum of eight are allowed per data base file.

Report header—The title and date information.

Ruler—The vertical, invisible sectioning of a file that allows you to move quickly through the file by using the OPEN-APPLE 1 through OPEN-APPLE 9 keystroke combinations.

Save—To transfer information from random access memory to a peripheral storage medium.

Scroll—To change all or part of the contents of the Desktop video screen by shifting information out at one end of the Desktop video screen to make room for new information at the opposite end of the screen. This is usually done by using the arrow keys.

Sector—The smallest addressable unit on a diskette track that may be changed.

Software—Programs and program instructions. For example, AppleWorks.

Source—1. The copy-from cells in the spreadsheet.
2. The location of copy-from information.

Spreadsheet—The portion of AppleWorks that creates and modifies numeric information in a worksheet or template form.

Start up—1. The AppleWorks diskette that is used to start the AppleWorks program from a cold start.
2. If power is already on, warm start, pressing simultaneously the CONTROL-OPEN-APPLE-RESET keystroke combination.

Strike over—1. To replace information in a document under the cursor using the overstrike cursor.
2. To over-type text.

Subdirectory—A file that contains the names and locations of other files on the disk and that is not the volume directory.

TAB—1. An ASCII character.
2. A key on the keyboard.

Table-style reports—The data base report style that prints record entries horizontally across the page, in rows and columns.

Template—A grid of rows and columns in which text, numbers, and formulas can be stored, allowing complex calculations to be defined in a simple, easily understood way. This is usually a completed spreadsheet. See *Worksheet*.

Text file—A file or document containing information expressed in ASCII form.

User—The person operating or controlling a computer system.

Value—The numerical information in the spreadsheet, including numbers, pointers, formulas, and functions.

Video—1. A medium for transmitting information in the form of images to be displayed on the screen of a cathode ray tube.
2. Information organized or transmitted in video form.

Volume—A source or destination of information, such as a diskette.

Window—That portion of a collection of information that is visible on the video screen.

Word processor—1. A computer program that processes the entry of words from a keyboard.
2. The portion of AppleWorks that creates and modifies information in letters, memos, reports, manuscripts, or any written document.

Worksheet—1. An incomplete spreadsheet template.
2. A grid of rows and columns in which text, numbers, and formulas can be stored, allowing complex calculations to be defined in a simple, easily understood way. See *Template.*

Wraparound—The automatic continuation of text from the end of one line to the beginning of the next.

Write—To transfer information from the computer to a destination external to the computer, such as the disk drive storage media, printer, or modem.

Write-protect—1. To prevent new information from being written onto a diskette.
2. To protect the information on a diskette by covering the write-enable notch with a write-protect tab.

Zoom in—1. To present data base records in the single-record layout form.
2. To present the word processor documents with the embedded printer options displayed.

Zoom out—1. Opposite of zoom in. To present data base records in the multiple-record layout.
2. To present the word processor documents without the embedded printer options displayed.

Index